Battle

Walking Gallipoli

Battleground Series

Battleground

Walking Gallipoli

Stephen Chambers

Series Editor
Nigel Cave

Pen & Sword
MILITARY

First published in Great Britain in 2019 by
Pen & Sword Military
an imprint of
Pen & Sword Books Ltd, 47 Church Street
Barnsley, South Yorkshire, S70 2AS

Copyright © Stephen Chambers, 2019

ISBN 978 147382 564 2

The right of Stephen Chambers to be identified as Author
of this work has been asserted by him in accordance with the
Copyright, Designs and Patents Act 1988.

A CIP catalogue record for this book is
available from the British Library.

Typeset in Times New Roman by Chic Graphics

Printed and bound in England by
CPI Group (UK) Ltd, Croydon CR0 4YY

Pen & Sword Books Ltd incorporates the imprints of
Pen & Sword Archaeology, Atlas, Aviation, Battleground, Discovery,
Family History, History, Maritime, Military, Naval, Politics,
Railways, Select, Social History, Transport, True Crime,
Claymore Press, Frontline Books, Leo Cooper, Praetorian Press,
Remember When, Seaforth Publishing and Wharncliffe.

For a complete list of Pen & Sword titles please contact
PEN & SWORD BOOKS LIMITED
47 Church Street, Barnsley, South Yorkshire, S70 2AS, England
E-mail: enquiries@pen-and-sword.co.uk
Website: www.pen-and-sword.co.uk

Contents

Acknowledgements

Without the help of many individuals and organisations this walking guide would not have been possible. The Gallipoli campaign can only truly be understood by treading the ground that the men, from both sides of the trenches, fought, bled and died; thanks, therefore, go to: Clive Harris, Rory Stephens and Peter Hart who have walked Gallipoli with me, inspiring me in different ways to bring the battlefield alive; in Turkey, to those who live and breathe the Gallipoli battles (Çanakkale Savaşı, as it is known locally): Haluk Oral, Kenan Çelik, Şahin Aldoğan, Gürsel Akıngüç, Mustafa Onur Yurdal, Bill Sellars and Eric Goossens, and some of the best battlefield guides on the Peninsula – Adem Biçer, Bariş Yeşildağ and Bulent Yilmaz Korkmaz to name but a few; of course, and by no means least, to Nigel Cave, Series Editor, whose guidance along the way has kept me on the straight and narrow.

From individuals to organisations, museums, libraries, websites and the like, the list of those who have helped is almost endless. I am very

'Boys Come Over Here' poster.

grateful to: the staff at The National Archives, the Imperial War Museum, the Australian War Memorial and a huge list of friends from The Gallipoli Association and Great War Forum, both rich hives of valuable campaign information. I cannot fail to mention the unrelenting work of the Commonwealth War Graves Commission, caring for the British and Dominion war dead in Gallipoli and elsewhere around the world.

Sadly, the veterans have long since faded away; but they are not forgotten. Their stories continue to be told and are used here to illustrate the human aspects of war. Contemporary material in the form of war diaries, divisional and regimental histories have been referenced. The published diary of Sir Ian Hamilton and Aspinall-Oglander's Official History are both a 'must' read, although both stand in the shadow of the Australian official historian, Charles Bean, whose detailed account of Anzac is second to none, even if some of his judgements and criticisms have been tempered by the years. I have made use, as appropriate, of some personal accounts in the form of letters and diaries as well as a large assortment of maps and photographs. I acknowledge the authors of all of these people, for without this material there would be no story to tell. With historical documents it is always difficult to trace all the copyright holders, so for any who have not been contacted, please

Ottoman Turkish recruitment poster.

accept my apologies, and feel free to contact me if you feel it necessary. To all these people and others I have forgotten to mention, please accept both my sincere apologies and my thanks.

No research and writing would have been made possible without the support and love of my family, so by no means last to Joanne, Lewis and Jessica for their patience and understanding.

Stephen Chambers
England and Gallipoli, 2019

Series Editor's Introduction:
Walking Gallipoli

Almost twenty years ago I went (with my father) on our first tour of Gallipoli, organised by Len Sellers, who devoted much of his time to researching and publishing on the Royal Naval Division, which played such a significant part in the Gallipoli Campaign. Amongst our small group was Stephen Chambers, making a second trip to the peninsula; and likewise completely taken with what we saw in that memorable five or six days there.

Eighteen months later found me back again, accompanied by Stephen, this time for a tour of two weeks. I came better prepared to follow the campaign on the ground, having to play catch up to Stephen, who had already read extensively about it. To me Gallipoli up to that time had been a distraction – as also the other fronts away from France and Flanders – and I felt that I had enough on my plate without getting sucked into a deeper study of the other theatres of the war. That view was changed by that first visit and reinforced by its sequel, which enabled us to enjoy a very leisurely, at our own pace, schedule as we explored that beautiful landscape, much as it was when the invasion and the subsequent battles dominated the newspaper headlines of ninety odd years earlier.

From that second visit came the determination to extend the *Battleground Europe* series to Gallipoli – an ideal campaign in ideal country for it. Access to much that was significant is accessible to the public, even if the terrain itself often provides major challenges. There are numerous vantage points over key parts of the battlefield. The cemeteries of the CWGC, as on the Western Front, provide valuable reference points, which have been complemented by the number of Turkish memorials that have been added over the years, most especially in the last twenty years or so. There is better mapping available – on our joint visit in 2001 we were reduced to using Cold War era Soviet maps to get any detail.

Since then, of course, there have been several *Battleground* books on the Campaign (all bar one by Stephen) so that this all-encompassing touring guide comes almost at the end of the planned series, with only *Krithia* to follow. This means that it has the advantage of all the work that has been done by him before, along with the fact that he has now been leading regular Gallipoli walking and vehicle tours for many years.

This brings a wealth of practical experience of visiting the sites as well as the accrued knowledge of researching the various stages of the Campaign.

Gallipoli retains for most of the year an other-worldly feel, a place that has an atmosphere of tranquillity and possesses notable beauty, yet it is shaded with a feeling of sadness. Of course this is true of any of the major battlefields of the world, especially those where the tragedy of young, lost lives are told by lines of headstones and heartfelt epitaphs in cemeteries scattered across the landscape. Yet the atmosphere of Gallipoli is its own, unrepeatable elsewhere; when combined with even the sketchiest knowledge of the events of 1915 it becomes all the more painful. We can enjoy the dramatically diverse landscape – which was to prove such a challenge to the allied invaders. Each sector of the battlefield is topographically individual – from the flat maritime plain of Suvla bordered a high ridge on the left and the heights to the east, to the narrow beach area of Anzac and the hills and precipices towering above it, to Helles, with its beaches that develop into a plain reaching up to the lower hills. A visit to this battlefield informs us so much about the evolution of the campaign and what happened on the ground; it is almost indispensible in order to arrive at a coherent understanding of the Dardanelles Expedition.

This book will provide a visitor with limited time (ideally not too limited: three days would be a minimum to get the full benefit of this book), who might only get to visit a part of the battlefield, sufficient information as to what happened in its various constituent parts and how best to follow it on the ground. The outline of events is accompanied by well chosen personal accounts that breathe life into bald facts and the movement of battalions, necessary details as these are. Each time I get one of Stephen's books to edit I make a promise to myself that I should get back for another visit – and this one has been no exception to that rule.

Nigel Cave
Stresa

List of Maps

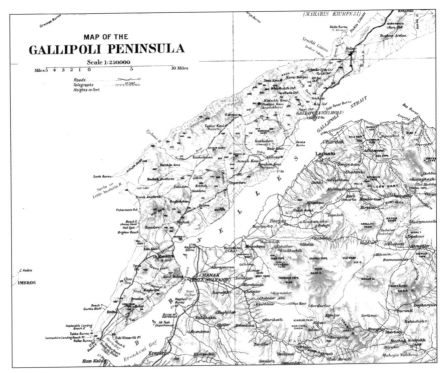

Introduction

Gallipoli today.

Gallipoli is an exquisitely beautiful and tranquil place, with its turquoise waters, stretches of sandy beaches, wild flower covered meadows and pine forested hills, such a contrast to what occurred here over a hundred years ago. Those visiting this battlefield often comment on its eerie atmosphere of sorrow and solitude, something that has certainly been experienced by me. Alan Moorehead, in 1956, wrote in his *Gallipoli* that,

> 'The cemeteries at Gallipoli are unlike those of any other battlefield in Europe ... In winter moss and grass cover the ground, and in summer a thick carpet of pine needles deadens the footfall. There is no sound except for the wind in the trees and the calls of the migrating birds who have found these places the safest sanctuary on the peninsula ... Often for months at a time nothing of any consequence happens, lizards scuttle about the tombstones in the sunshine and time goes by in an endless dream.'

The biggest change since the time Moorehead wrote this has been the massive increase in visitors. Its history and the landscape's outstanding beauty make it a popular location for battlefield visitors from all over the world, not only for Australians, New Zealanders and British, but also for Turks. In Turkey, the Gallipoli (Çanakkale) battlefield is one of the most visited places because of its association with Atatürk and the birth of modern day Turkey and because it was the greatest Ottoman victory of the Great War. Annually over two million Turks make their pilgrimage to the ground where modern Turkey was born. There are two major dates when the Peninsula becomes busy; 18 March and 25 April. In March the Turks visit in large numbers, as this date in 1915 was when their forces were victorious over the Anglo-French fleet in their attempt to force the Dardanelles. 25 April is Anzac Day, a national holiday in the calendar of every Australian and New Zealander, who descend on the area in large numbers (though often neglect Helles and Suvla). However, away from these periods, the weekends or if you venture away from the main tourist areas, you will see very few visitors and little to disturb the serene and beautiful landscape of this land.

Outside of the major commemorative dates, the best times to visit Gallipoli is spring or autumn. In late spring (May) the weather is moderate and the days are long. You can experience the unique natural spring environment on the peninsula, with magnificent wild flowers, mild and fresh temperatures, local life and smaller crowds, and competitively priced hotels and services. In early autumn (September), after the stifling hot summer, the weather becomes milder again, but the days are shorter. The battlefield in autumn is no longer lush with greenery, but would have turned a scorched sandy-brown colour after the long hot summer, reminiscent of the 1915 campaign photographs. A further bonus is that most of the crops will have been harvested. Whilst the autumn is a very good season to travel to Turkey because of the mild and comfortable temperatures, it is, however, the high season for Turkey's popular destinations, so book hotels early.

The war comes to Gallipoli
Within a few months of the opening of hostilities on the Western Front in August 1914 there was deadlock and with no obvious way to break it. Casualties had been enormous – just over two million men by January 1915, unprecedented numbers; there were no longer any illusions about a speedy end to hostilities.

It was clear that this conflict was different; armies had not been able to alter their tactics in response to this industrial scale war that, at this stage, made the defensive significantly stronger than the offensive. Destruction was on a massive scale, in human cost and the increasing devastation of the war zone area. With political and popular pressure growing, the British looked for an alternative strategy for 1915, making use of naval superiority. Opening a new front was discussed, but where: an amphibious landing on German's Baltic coast, an offensive through the Balkans or maybe an attack against Turkey? Attention turned to Turkey at the beginning of 1915; Russia was threatened by the Ottoman Army on the Caucasus Front and she appealed to her allies for support. The British, with French support, decided that this could best be achieved by mounting a naval expedition to the Dardanelles.

The objective of this strategic vision was, by capturing Constantinople (now Istanbul), to force German's ally Turkey and its vast Empire (which included the territories of modern Turkey, Syria, Jordan, Israel/Palestine, Lebanon, Iraq, Iran, Kuwait, Yemen and the western coastline of Arabia), out of the war. This knockout blow would open a warm water supply route to Russia from the Aegean, through the Dardanelles and into the Black Sea. Russian troops on the Caucasus Front could be released to reinforce her forces facing Germany and Austria-Hungary. It was also hoped that by opening a new front it could influence the neutral Balkan states and Greece to enter the war on the Entente side. A combined effort would then assist the Entente powers in removing the Turks and its Ottoman empire, seen as the 'sick man of Europe', as a threat. They were seen as an easy target, due to over a century of decline and weakened by political instability, military defeat and civil strife.

The campaign would be a risk with a far from certain outcome. If successful it was hoped to shorten the war; but if it failed, the consequences were beyond calculation. Would the war be lengthened by not concentrating efforts on the Western Front against the main power, Germany? Would the neutral states join the Central Powers? Would the Suez Canal and Mesopotamian oilfields fall to the Turks? Would a defeat weaken Britain's influence in the east, in particular India, threatening the

The Empire Needs Men!

jewel in the British Empire? Although a valid gamble in the minds of the War Council, the campaign's poor planning and execution shattered any glimmer of hope in a catalogue of mismanaged sea and land battles.

The Gallipoli campaign can be described in four stages: the initial efforts of the Anglo-French navy to force the Dardanelles; the landing of the Mediterranean Expeditionary Force (MEF) in April 1915; the land offensives between May and August; and the final evacuation of the MEF in January 1916. The objective of *Walking Gallipoli* is to take the reader through the campaign stages by outlining events and walking the ground.

Chapter 1

Forcing the Dardanelles

No part of the Dardanelles, from its Aegean entrance to its junction with the Sea of Marmara, was free of defence. From the days of Xerxes, Alexander the Great and the Roman Empire, this stretch of strategic waterway had been fought over. By 1915, the combined defences of the Dardanelles comprised not only forts with large calibre guns, but minefields, shore-based torpedo tubes, mobile howitzers and field guns, the main concentration of which was at the Narrows. Breaking this natural bottleneck was the key to opening the Dardanelles.

Both Britain and Germany had been energetically wooing the Turkish Government during 1914; if Turkey and its Ottoman empire could not be kept neutral, its presence as an ally, however shaky its military capacity, was essential to the interests of both in the east. The German military mission in Turkey, under the leadership of General Liman von Sanders, was charged with modernising the Ottoman Army. Similarly, a British naval mission in Constantinople, under Vice Admiral Arthur Limpus, had the task of reorganising the Ottoman Navy. Two new generation dreadnoughts, *Sultan Osman I* and *Reshadieh*, were under construction at this time in British shipyards. They had been largely financed by nationwide street collections and special taxes in Turkey.

The prelude to war with Turkey.
Just before Britain declared war on Germany on 4 August 1914, Winston Churchill, First Lord of the Admiralty, temporarily requisitioned both Ottoman ships, renamed them HMS *Agincourt* and HMS *Erin*, and added them to the British Grand Fleet in the North Sea. Although it was a logical decision taken in order to protect British waters, its insensitivity outraged the Turks and both political and public opinion swung towards Germany. This was dreadful timing for the British on the eve of war. It did not take long for Germany to exploit this.

Winston Churchill, First Lord of the Admiralty.

1

Already running the Mediterranean gauntlet were the German battlecruiser *Goeben* and the light cruiser *Breslau,* under the command of Rear-Admiral Wilhelm Souchon. Through guile and British incompetence, Souchon successfully evaded the Anglo-French Mediterranean fleet in August, embarrassing the British. Having arrived off the entrance to the Dardanelles, the Turks allowed the Germans safe passage through them and on to Constantinople, where they were promptly transferred over to the Ottoman Navy. Now the Turks had two practically new ships that showed that Britannia did not rule the waves.

In direct contravention of international law, German General Weber Pasha swiftly closed the Dardanelles and began making desperate efforts to encourage the Turks to strengthen the Dardanelles' defences. For Britain this was a particular blow, as the loss of the Black Sea link with Russia was compounded by the Ottoman threat to British imperial possessions and influence in Egypt, southern Arabia and the Persian Gulf. Turkey then put into effect plans to attack Russia in the Caucasus, in order to regain her former territory, and to attack British interests in Egypt (the Suez Canal) and the Persian coast. The threat to Suez could severely impede Britain's communications with India, whilst an attack on British assets on the Persian coast would threaten oil supplies on which the newest British warships depended. Britain had little choice but to respond.

The triumphant Souchon was quickly appointed head of the Ottoman Navy. Britain was not blind to what was happening, and protested that the ships should be impounded and the German crews sent home. Turkey nevertheless maintained her 'armed' neutrality, and still would not commit to war. However, this inertia did not last for long. Under the direction of Enver Pasha, the Turkish Minister of War, the *Goeben* and *Breslau* (renamed *Yavuz Sultan Selim* and *Midilli*) were dispatched with their German crews and a rag tag fleet of Ottoman cruisers, destroyers and torpedo boats to raid the Russian Black Sea ports. On 29 October they began bombarding these ports, which clearly showed where Turkey's allegiances lay. Britain and France sent an ultimatum to Turkey that night and then severed diplomatic relations. On 2 November Russia declared war on Turkey.

Enver Pasha, Ottoman Minister of War.

Although Britain was not yet officially at war with Turkey, on 3

November, in a rapid response to Souchon's unprovoked attack on the Black Sea ports, Churchill ordered the navy to bombard the outer forts that guarded the mouth of the Dardanelles. This was to be a demonstration only and, to reduce risk to the Anglo-French fleet, it would be conducted at long range. As Vice Admiral Sir Edmond Slade, a former Director of Naval Intelligence, remarked at the time, 'a little target practice from fifteen to twelve thousand yards might be useful'. HMS *Indomitable* and *Indefatigable* duly bombarded the forts at Sedd-el-Bahr on the European side, whilst the French ships *Suffren* and *Verite*, targeted the forts at Kum Kale on the Asiatic side. After ten minutes of negligible return fire, a lucky shot detonated the magazine at Sedd-el-Bahr, killed eighty-six Turkish defenders and destroying large parts of the fort.

For this early British 'success' there was much criticism within the Admiralty. Vice Admiral Sackville Carden was accused of 'lunacy', 'irresponsibility' and for making an 'unforgivable error' of judgement, giving the game away. Although partly true, this was a bit of an over-reaction, as for three months the Germans and Turks had been improving the defences. Additionally, where else were Britain and France going to attack, if not at the Dardanelles? That aside, any surprise the Entente may have had was now gone. Worse still, in defiance of the received 'ships versus forts' wisdom, it gave the navy confidence that their guns could destroy forts and force the Dardanelles by ships alone. There had been a centuries-old Admiralty debate on whether ships alone could reduce forts. There was a saying: 'A ship's a fool to fight a fort'. Thus, tactics were changed when fighting land batteries. John Ericsson (maritime engineer and inventor) stated: 'A single shot can sink a ship, but a hundred salvos cannot silence a fort'.

On 5 November 1914 Britain and France declared war on Turkey.

Strategic considerations.

Apart from blockading the entrance to the Dardanelles and engaging in limited submarine activity with varying results, the area ceased to be a focus for the British. However, on 2 January 1915, Russia asked Britain and France for a diversionary attack to help release the pressure on the Caucasus Front. Even though Russia had decisively defeated a Turkish attack there, the strain on Russia's military machine was evident. It was Britain's aim to see Russia focus on Germany, not Turkey. It was this request that brought the Dardanelles back to the attention of the War Council. Kitchener immediately latched onto the idea of a tactical naval attack in the Dardanelles, as long as no troops were involved. France supported the idea and offered a naval squadron to help.

Sir Edward Grey, the British Foreign Secretary, stated:

'The attack on the Dardanelles was agreed on the express condition that it should be a naval operation only; it was under no circumstances to involve the use of troops... If it did not succeed, it was to be treated as a demonstration and abandoned.'

It was under these conditions that Lord Kitchener, Secretary of State for War, agreed to the operation. The Admiralty was suitably stocked with munitions (more than could be said for the army at this stage) and, if this battle could be won by ship alone, a cheap and easy victory would be welcomed. Kitchener had spoken and nobody, not even the British Cabinet, questioned him. The elderly First Sea Lord, Admiral Sir John "Jacky" Fisher, impressed by the young Churchill and intimidated by Kitchener, openly agreed to this naval operation. Only older ships were allocated to the Dardanelles; thus Fisher could retain the main fleet to counter the German threat to the United Kingdom across the North Sea.

First Sea Lord, Admiral 'Jacky' Fisher.

The plan was to send the fleet up through the Dardanelles and into the Sea of Marmara from where it would create havoc, paralysing all Turkish movements in the area. The fleet would then proceed to Constantinople, the country's capital. It was hoped that the sight of this great armada would be enough to force the belligerent Turks to capitulate and then transfer their allegiances to the Triple Entente, the alliance linking Russia, France and Britain. If not, the navy would start to destroy the city and await the white flag to be hoisted.

Strategically the plan made sense, although it did have its flaws, based as it was on false assumptions. Political and military leaders in London believed that the Turks lacked the ability and determination to put up much of a fight: a naval bombardment alone could destroy the Dardanelles defences and once the fleet had arrived off Constantinople a *coup d'état* would occur. Putting that aside, no thought was given to sustaining an operation even if the Ottoman army did withdraw its forces from Thrace. Military land support to keep the Dardanelles open for re-supply would be needed but it was not planned. Cooperation with Russia would be necessary, so that control of the Bosporus could be affected. Putting all this aside in the short term, these were risks that Britain and

France were willing to take to knock Turkey out of the war and re-establish the warm-water route to Russia, along which she exported half of her goods, including nine tenths of her grain. With the Russian bear re-focussed on Germany, it was hoped that further German resources would be moved to the east, thus allowing the deadlock to be broken on the Western Front. Doubtless, it was felt, this show of might would influence Greece, Bulgaria and possibly Romania to join a Balkan coalition against the Central Powers. If it all went wrong, however, the effect would be dire.

Tactical considerations.

Who was to command the Eastern Mediterranean fleet? When the British Naval Mission in Constantinople was wound up in September 1914, consideration was given to appointing Admiral Limpus, with his vast knowledge of Ottoman defence matters. However, he was consigned to supervise the dockyard at Malta. Almost incredibly, it was thought that to appoint him to command operations against his old friend, Turkey, would not be 'sporting'. Instead Vice Admiral Sackville Carden was chosen.

Vice Admiral Sackville Carden.

Demonstrations apart, Fisher and Churchill had in mind a major naval attack. Carden was asked if he thought the scheme was practical by using naval gunfire against the forts. He thought it was so long as he had sufficient ships and time. He should have known better; since the days of Lord Nelson all knew that ships and forts do not mix. To give the operation the best chance of success it was necessary to occupy both sides of the Narrows, and everyone at the Admiralty realised this. In 1906, the Committee of Imperial Defence had written a feasibility study on this very operation, that showed that a combined operation, the military working with the navy, was vital to success. This, however, appears to have been conveniently forgotten. In 1911, even Churchill declared that forcing the straits by ships alone would fail. Theory aside, in 1807 Rear-Admiral Sir John Duckworth's fleet experienced untold problems with the forts when forcing this same waterway; this would be nothing compared with what faced the Eastern Mediterranean Fleet in 1915. The defences of the Dardanelles were now more than just a few old guns.

In London, Fisher was now having second thoughts and was concerned how quickly the operation had gathered pace. *Damn the Dardanelles! They will be our grave.* The more concerned he was, the more uncooperative he became, eventually falling out with Churchill and resigning. Carden's support for it remained resolute and, because of this, the War Council allowed the operation to continue. If it failed, it would be treated as a demonstration only.

Carden's plan was to destroy the outer forts, prematurely awakened on 3 November 1914, and then: reduce all defences, permanent and semi-permanent, up to and including the forts at the Narrows; sweep the minefields from the entrance of the Straits as far as the Narrows and silence the forts above the Narrows and proceed into the Sea of Marama.

This would be achieved by long-range bombardment, direct and indirect, followed by a bombardment at closer range with secondary armament. There was a likelihood of mines, especially floaters, which would be dealt with by rifle fire or by being netted and towed away. Moored mines would be cleared by minesweepers.

The Naval Operation
Phase 1: Reducing the Defences.
Using twelve capital ships, four French and eight British, a long-range bombardment began at 10 a.m. on 19 February 1915 against three forts guarding the entrance of the Dardanelles: Sedd-el-Bahr, Kum Kale and Orkanieh. The shelling was from seven miles away, which kept the fleet out of range of the forts' guns. The guns of the fleet were powerful enough; its fire could blow away huge chunks of earth and stone but was not so good at destroying the guns that were positioned behind. There were also concerns with accuracy and indeed only a small proportion of

February 1915 assault on the Dardanelles.

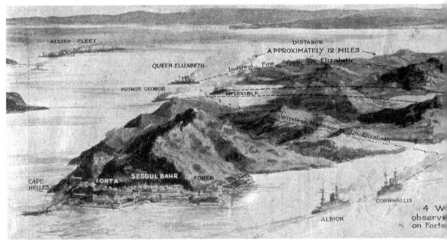

the armour piercing and high explosive shells actually hit their targets. This was hardly surprising as the targets were barely visible at such a long range. Many shells missed and sank into the soft earth, whilst the damage of those that did hit was difficult to assess at that range. The fleet closed in to survey the damage and even though all three forts were in ruins the Turks still fired back. With failing light and facing an enlivened defence, Carden withdrew the fleet for the day.

Bad weather then frustrated the operation. It was not until 25 February that the bombardment could be recommenced. This time the ships of the fleet, under the command of Rear-Admiral John de Robeck, were brought in closer to target the batteries between Kum Kale and Kephez. The Turks almost immediately struck back, hitting HMS *Agamemnon* several times, killing three men. Although the damage was superficial, it did highlight how vulnerable these battleships were when anchored or near to the shore. HMS *Queen Elizabeth* came forward and for an hour focused its fire on Sedd-el-Bahr, eventually putting its guns out of action by direct hits. But to gain a direct hit took skill and a little luck, and it was not going to be any easier with the other forts.

For the first time at Gallipoli, boots were then put on the ground. Small parties of sailors and marines landed the following day to survey the destruction and to destroy any remaining guns, mountings, munitions and searchlights in the Kum Kale, Orkanieh and Sedd-el-Bahr forts. These raids were initially successful, a Victoria Cross was won by Lieutenant-Commander Eric Robinson, and the parties withdrew without casualties. However, when this was repeated on 4 March the marines and sailors were met with resistance, and fighting took place in the Kum Kale and Orkanieh forts. This mission failed, with seventeen killed and twenty-four wounded. The raid on Sedd-el-Bahr faired a little better, but a premature withdrawal also had to be called when resistance strengthened.

Although hampered by the weather the plan was progressing, with at

An illustration of the naval attack on the Dardanelles.

least three of the outer forts put out of action. Carden optimistically reported that he hoped to be in Constantinople in two weeks. This encouraging news of an impending victory was supplemented when a German wireless message was intercepted indicating that the Turkish forts were running low on ammunition, which subsequently proved to be inaccurate. The outer forts may have been put out of action, but the inner forts, most of which were out of view, still needed suppressing – not to mention the howitzer and torpedo tube positions. A howitzer was ideal for destroying the smaller minesweepers and whilst they posed no threat to the larger capital ships, the torpedoes and mines certainly did. Without this capability being removed, the fleet could not progress.

Phase 2: Minesweeping.
Whilst the forts were being bombarded, the minesweepers, mostly requisitioned North Sea trawlers with civilian crews, were directed up the Dardanelles to sweep for mines. The trawlers worked in pairs, dragging a steel cable below the surface across the minefield. Early efforts had been unsuccessful, largely due to these little boats having difficulty in reaching the minefields, which were some five miles up the Straits. Against the strong currents and Turkish fire, they were not given an easy time. Despite some superficial armour to protect the crew, the boats were vulnerable to howitzer fire and the field guns concealed along the shoreline. One trawler was reported as being hit eighty-four times!

During the first week in March, Commodore Roger Keyes, Carden's Chief of Staff, concentrated efforts on sweeping the mines by night. The

Turkish defences were still good; and on most nights the minesweepers were spotted by the searchlights, followed seconds later by intense fire. It was paramount that the Turks kept the minefields secure at any cost. Throughout this period, no mines were destroyed; and more often than not Turkish fire kept the minesweepers away. Despite the best efforts by the British and French, little headway was being made.

Churchill was getting impatient with the lack of progress since operations started, and urged Carden on. Kitchener now appreciated the need to send troops to the Dardanelles; on 12 March Lieutenant General Sir Ian Hamilton was appointed as the commander of this new Mediterranean Expeditionary Force. He would arrive on the eve of the main all-naval assault, scheduled for 18 March. Before this, however, there would be another setback. Admiral Carden, suffering a nervous breakdown, announced that he could not continue. Although Rear-Admiral Rosslyn Wemyss succeeded Carden, he willingly allowed Acting Vice-Admiral John de Robeck to continue the operation as commander of the fleet.

The plan was to attack with ten battleships, six British, four French. The first line would comprise the most modern, their task to bombard the forts, to be followed by four French ships firing at shorter range. The third line would be more aged British ships, which would press home the attack. The minesweepers would again be the key to the operation. Clearing the minefields caused huge problems for the specially converted fishing trawlers, and their volunteer civilian crews. Bolstered by Royal Navy crewmen, these small vessels were not designed for speed, and could only achieve about six knots. With up to a four-knot current running against them, they were practically sitting ducks and easy prey to the howitzers. On 13 March, they attempted to clear a path under the cover

Shells landing near HMS *Amethyst.*

of darkness, but they were spotted by searchlights and, despite the protection of the cruiser HMS *Amethyst*, had to be withdrawn under heavy fire, losing two of their number. Four further trawlers and two picket boats were damaged. *Amethyst* was also damaged and suffered the loss of twenty-seven sailors killed and forty-three wounded. Sweeping continued each night with varying success until 18 March but, despite the brave and almost suicidal efforts of these men, the three-week effort only accounted for twelve mines destroyed. Without a path through the minefields, the operation was doomed to fail.

Phase 3: Silencing the Forts.

The 18 March attempt to force the narrows was an unmitigated disaster. The Anglo-French fleet's intentions were made clear in the bright sunlight, which enabled all those ashore to view this great armada, as clear as the Naval Review at Spithead in July 1914. Leading the first wave in HMS *Queen Elizabeth*, de Robeck steamed up to the Kephez minefield and began a long range bombardment of the Narrows forts at Chanak and Kilid Bahr. Eight miles away, the Narrows forts could not reply, but the coast and mobile-based artillery could, hitting all of the ships in this first line (*Queen Elizabeth, Agamemnon, Lord Nelson* and *Inflexible),* along with their flank protection (*Prince George* and *Triumph*). The damage was superficial but, nevertheless, during this initial ninety minutes of action it showed that the Turks were still full of fight.

Just after midday de Robeck signalled forward his second wave, which comprised Admiral Émile Guépratte's French squadron (*Bouvet, Charlemagne, Gaulois* and *Suffren*), supported by HMS *Majestic* and *Swiftsure*. This line began well and laid down such a bombardment that the forts almost fell silent. One Turkish account suggested that by 2 p.m. 'all telephone wires were cut, all communications with the forts were interrupted, some of the guns had been knocked out … in consequence the artillery fire of the defence had slackened considerably'. The third wave was then signalled forward, comprising HMS *Albion, Irresistible, Ocean* and *Vengeance*; but now matters started to go wrong for de Robeck.

The first casualty was *Gaulois;* hit by a shell quite badly below the waterline, it was ordered to withdraw completely. During the retirement of the remainder of this wave, led by *Suffren,* an unknown danger was waiting towards the Asiatic shore. During the night of 7/8 March a new string of twenty-six mines was secretly laid parallel to the shore of Erenköy Bay by the minelayer *Nusret*. The location was chosen wisely, as it was here that the battleships were manoeuvring. This one single action would become the turning point of the whole naval campaign.

Following *Suffren,* the *Bouvet* began to move into this danger zone when suddenly there was a loud explosion. Both surprise and panic followed. When the water spray had cleared, all witnessed the *Bouvet* sinking in less than two minutes, taking to the bottom ninety-five per cent of her 704 crew. As the third wave then turned, disaster struck again. This

German illustration of the Turkish forts returning fire.

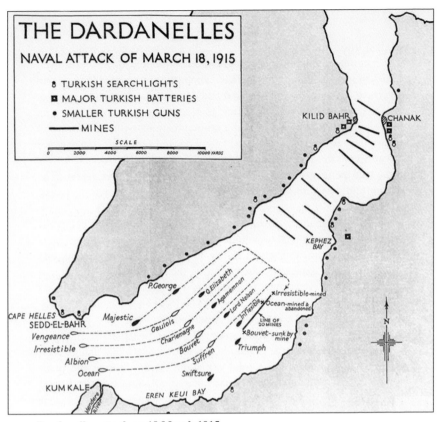

THE DARDANELLES

NAVAL ATTACK OF MARCH 18, 1915

8 TURKISH SEARCHLIGHTS
◧ MAJOR TURKISH BATTERIES
• SMALLER TURKISH GUNS
—— MINES

SCALE

0   2000   4000   6000   8000   10000 YARDS

KILID BAHR   CHANAK

KEPHEZ
BAY

CAPE HELLES
SEDD-EL-BAHR
Vengeance
Irresistible
Albion
Ocean
KUM KALE

Majestic

P.George

Gaulois

Charlemagne

Bouvet

Suffren

Swiftsure

EREN KEUI BAY

Q.Elizabeth

Agamemnon

Lord Nelson

Inflexible

xIrresistible-mined
Ocean-mined &
abandoned

LINE OF
20 MINES

xBouvet-sunk by
mine

Triumph

N

Dardanelles attack on 18 March 1915.

time the British ship *Irresistible* hit a mine close to the *Bouvet's* watery grave. The Turkish gunners, with a renewed lease of life, began to target the crippled *Irresistible*, which had to be abandoned, the crew being taken off by a nearby destroyer. De Robeck was now seriously concerned, believing that the Turks were floating mines down the Dardanelles. He suspended the attack. Keyes, in HMS *Wear*, was ordered to tow in *Irresistible* supported by *Ocean* and *Swiftsure*. There was another sudden explosion. *Ocean* had hit a mine and moments later a shell hit her steering gear disabling the ship. The crew from *Ocean* had to be evacuated. Leaving the empty hulks of *Ocean* and *Irresistible* to their fates, *Wear* and *Swiftsure* withdrew. As darkness fell, Keyes returned to sink *Irresistible* and rescue *Ocean* if he could, but was too late, as both had sunk.

Keyes, a passionate believer in offensive action, was keen to continue the attack the following day, despite the loss of three battleships and the *Gaulois, Suffren* and *Inflexible* out of action. He was convinced that the

Turks had expended vast quantities of ammunition to the extent that some of the main forts were down to their last rounds. Whilst this was true and the Turks had lost about fifteen per cent of their heavy guns, this was against the loss of a third of the fleet. With the current rate of loss of capital ships, the attack could not be sustained for more than another day. Both Wemyss and de Robeck had no other option than to cancel the attack.

The Land Campaign

Witnesses to the failed 18 March operation were General Sir Ian Hamilton and Lieutenant General Sir William Birdwood (commanding ANZAC). Their presence undoubtedly influenced Wemyss and de Robeck. It was now clear that the battleships could not force the Straits until the minefields had been cleared; but the minefields could not be cleared until the defending guns had been destroyed. These guns could not be destroyed until the army was ashore. No longer would the Aegean be the preserve of the Admiralty.

It was a predicament with one clear answer. On 22 March, de Robeck told Churchill that for the fleet to be successful it needed the army to take the forts on the Aegean side from the rear. Kitchener was also of the same opinion now, although he wanted an early conclusion to the operation. He could not afford for it to turn into a long-winded campaign and a further drain on military resources that he knew were best placed on the Western Front.

HMS *Irresistible* after being abandoned on 18 March 1915.

The fleet stepped back from the limelight. All hopes now rested with the army to execute what would be the largest amphibious operation the world had known. However, there would be no victory on the cheap. For the Turks, the failure of the naval attack was a massive boost to their morale; they had defeated the mighty Royal Navy, in what would be its most significant failure of the Great War.

During the following month Hamilton drew up plans for the capture of the Dardanelles by landing on the Gallipoli Peninsula. However, since the halt to the naval action on 18 March the Turks, in a hurried effort, had been improving the defences for a predicted landing. Roads were constructed, boats gathered to transport troops and equipment across the narrows, beaches were wired and mined. All around the beaches and coastal ridges trenches had been dug and field artillery positioned.

The landings were by no means viewed as straightforward. The Official History states that 'a serious difficulty connected with an opposed landing on the coast of a little-known country is the impossibility of affecting any adequate reconnaissance of the ground over which the first battle must be fought'. Contrary to the belief that it was a 'little-known country', adequate reconnaissance was carried out. The intelligence gathered was a mixture of sea observation, aerial reconnaissance and a selection of reasonably accurate maps of the region. Enemy depositions and defences were fairly accurate known, but this was not going to be the main obstacle.

The Ottoman Fifth Army, under the command of General Otto Liman von Sanders, comprised two corps totalling six divisions and a cavalry brigade, about 100,000 men. Liman von Sanders deployed two divisions (3rd and 11th) at Besika Bay on the Asiatic coast, two divisions (5th and 7th) and a cavalry brigade at Bulair to the north of the peninsula, and the 9th and 19th divisions along the Aegean coast and Cape Helles. Sanders' defence strategy was based on mobility instead of a rigid defence and allocated a minimum number of troops to guard the coastline whilst the bulk of the forces were held inland, ready to counter a landing wherever it was made.

The Mediterranean Expeditionary Force (MEF) was a combined force of some 75,000 British, French, Australian and New Zealand troops. Hamilton was a very capable and intelligent soldier; he was even acknowledged by the German General Staff, which noted that he was the single most experienced soldier alive in the world at that time. Despite Hamilton's reputation and the respect in which he was held, the challenge he faced was of epic proportions. His task was to execute an opposed amphibious landing, with little more than five weeks to prepare, 3,500 miles away from home – the biggest such operation in the history of warfare.

To facilitate the landing of as many troops as possible in a single day, and to confuse the enemy as to the main effort, Hamilton decided to split his force into two main attacks. His plan was to land the 29th Division of 17,600 men (Major General Sir Aylmer Hunter-Weston), the last formed regular division of the British army not yet sent to the Western Front, across five beaches around the tip of Cape Helles. The day one objective for this force would be the capture of the vital high ground of Achi Baba, which overlooked the beaches.

Landing ten miles to the north would be Lieutenant General Sir William Birdwood's Australian and New Zealand Army Corps (ANZAC), which consisted of two divisions (30,638 men). This newly created and untried force had the task of severing the Turkish line of communications by affecting a landing north of Gaba Tepe. Once a bridgehead had been secured by the capture of Sari Bair and Gaba Tepe, the Anzacs would advance towards Maidos, effectively cutting off Turkish reinforcements to the south of the peninsula and thus allowing the best chance of success for Hunter-Weston's forces in the south. The ultimate objective for the MEF was the Kilid Bahr plateau, the vital high ground that overlooked the forts at the Narrows. Quite simply, the objective was to capture Kilid Bahr, destroy the forts from behind and allow the navy through the Dardanelles.

Vice Admiral John de Robeck and General Sir Ian Hamilton.

As strategic secrecy had failed, not helped by the British calling the landing force the 'Constantinople Expeditionary Force' and, in any case, the operational intent was difficult to mask – clearly the naval actions were to break through the Dardanelles, Hamilton's only option was a surprise landing that could be exploited quickly. To support both landings a diversionary feint attack would be affected on the Asiatic shore by a French division at Kum Kale, whilst the remainder of *Corps Expéditionnaire d'Orient* (16,700 men), under the command of General Albert d'Amade, would appear in their transports off Besika Bay. Similarly, at Bulair, in the Gulf of Saros, the Royal Naval Division

The British 42nd Division marching off to war.

(10,000 men) would carry out a demonstration in order to hold the main Turkish reserves in this area. This complex plan was designed by Hamilton to confuse Liman von Sanders as to the real landing, and thus limit his reaction time. If successful, von Sanders would be kept guessing as to where the main landing was taking place, thus allowing Hamilton time to establish his forces ashore rapidly. The landing force was mainly assembled in Mudros Harbour on the island of Lemnos, with smaller bases at Tenedos, Imbros and Skyros. The date chosen for the landings was 23 April 1915; due to bad weather it was postponed for forty-eight hours. It was not until Sunday, 25 April, over a month after the failed naval attack, that the land campaign could start.

Tour 1

The Dardanelles

This half-day tour is designed to give you a flavour of these actions, which can be completed on foot, or by vehicle. If you choose to include Achi Baba, allow a full day as this includes nearly forty additional kilometres of driving.

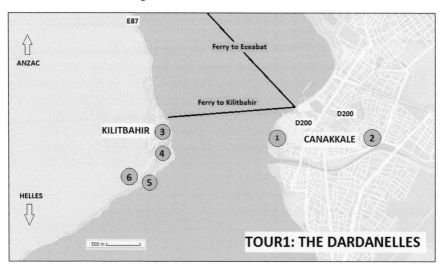

Any battlefield tour of Gallipoli is not complete without visiting the key defences of the Dardanelles (*Çanakkale Boğazi*). The area today is littered with wrecks from the campaign; within the Dardanelles rests the *Bouvet*, HMS *Irresistible*, HMS *Ocean* and at least two submarines. Along Gallipoli's Aegean coastline are the wrecks of HMS *Goliath*, HMS *Majestic* and HMS *Triumph*. With permission some of these can be dived for the more adventurous or visited on the surface by boat. Check out the local scuba diving clubs for more information. Others need not get wet, as the naval campaign is as much about the shore based efforts of the Turkish defenders as it was about the might of the Anglo-French Navy attempting to force their way through the Narrows.

Çimenlik Castle and Naval Military Museum.

The tour begins at **Çimenlik Castle** and **Naval Military Museum (1) (40°08'47.4"N 26°23'56.9"E)** in Çanakkale. This fort used to go by the name of Kale-i Sultaniye, and it is this structure where Çanakkale takes its name (Çanak is the old town's name and Kale is Turkish for castle). Çimenlik was constructed by Sultan Mehmet II between 1452-1463 to help control the straits at their narrowest point. Çanakkale expanded as a port and by 1914 had a population of some 16,000. The majority of houses at the time were wooden, so many were badly damaged or destroyed by shelling during the First World War. Few original buildings, made of wood or stone, now survive in the city.

Çimenlik Castle and its grounds now houses the Çanakkale Naval Military Museum and the floating replica of the *Nusret*, the famed minelayer. Entry into the outer grounds is free, but there is a small charge for the castle and to go aboard the *Nusret*. There is a lot to see; field guns, mines, shore-based torpedo tubes and even the remains of a German submarine, UB-46, which was sunk in the Black Sea in 1916. Within the walls of the castle is evidence of the campaign, namely the remains of a 15-inch shell from HMS *Queen Elizabeth* that had bedded itself within the thick stones walls. It is also worth visiting the Gallipoli campaign museum, housed inside the Keep. Opening times vary, depending on season, so please check before visiting. Although the *Nusret* is moored on the shoreline for most of the year, note that she is seaworthy and does on occasions leave to attend other events.

The story of the *Nusret* is well told. You will learn about the night of 7/8 March when its commander, Captain Hakki Bey, who only days previously had suffered a heart attack, took his ship out to Erenköy Bay,

Ottoman minelayer, the _Nusret_.

Mines on the _Nusret_.

south of the main minefields at Kephez Point. He laid a fresh line of mines parallel to the shore in an area observed to be used by the Entente battleships to manoeuvre. On 18 March, when the warships tried to turn in Erenköy Bay, four of them hit these mines; three ships, _Bouvet_, HMS _Irresistible_ and HMS _Ocean_ were sunk and a third ship, HMS _Inflexible_, was badly damaged. This little ship could be said to have changed the course of history as naval efforts to pass the Dardanelles were abandoned the following day.

Leave the Naval Museum and walk to the **British Chanak Consular Cemetery (2) (40°08'45.0"N 26°24'55.2"E).** The cemetery, which is close to the town stadium, is about two kilometres east of the Naval Museum and feribot terminal, and is known locally as the English Cemetery (İngiliz Mezarlığı). It is located on Şevket Bey Sk. towards Setboyu Cd. The cemetery is enclosed by a stone wall and its gates are kept locked by the CWGC (see Advice to Visitors regarding access).

The cemetery contains graves from 1860 to 1965, including several from 1918 to 1920 when the British were stationed at Chanak during the period of occupation. The last British officer to die at Gallipoli is buried here: Lieutenant Frederick Wolley Dod, pre-war a well-known Canadian lepidopterist and entomologist. He died of enteric fever in July 1919 while serving with the force occupying the Dardanelles after the war. There are also several graves belonging to the Australian Light Horse and Canterbury Mounted Rifles who died as a result of the influenza pandemic that broke out in 1918/1919. The cemetery contains thirty-eight British and Dominion burials of the First World War and one from the Second. The Commission also cares for seven war graves of other nationalities and a number of non-war graves in the cemetery.

Graves of interest include Lieutenant Commander Theodore Brodie (who had a twin brother, Commander Charles Brodie of HM Submarine *B6*, who also served in the Dardanelles in 1915 and survived the war). Theodore Brodie was killed on 17 April 1915 when HM Submarine *E15* ran aground whilst attempting to break through the Dardanelles on passage into the Sea of Marmara. *E15* dived too deep and was caught in a strong current and ran aground near Kephez Point, directly under the guns of the Dardanos Battery. Brodie was killed in the conning tower by shrapnel and six of his crew were killed by chlorine gas, released when seawater came in contact with the batteries during a second shell strike. The remaining twenty-five men of Brodie's crew were captured and were interned as prisoners of war. Those who were killed were buried on the beach near where the submarine sank, to be moved to this cemetery after the war. *E15* still lies off Kephez Point today. Those identified are Brodie, Able Seaman Frederick Cornish and Engine Room Artificer Ernest Hindman.

The first allied servicemen to be captured were the French crew of the submarine *Saphir*; on 15 January 1915 it accidentally grounded whilst also attempting to force the Dardanelles. It is believed that she managed to pass ten lines of mines and then either hit a mine or was hit by a shore battery before grounding. Her crew scuttled the boat, leaving fourteen who were killed or drowned, the remaining thirteen captured. During the night of 25 April Australian submarine *AE2* became the first Entente submarine successfully to pass through the Dardanelles. She spent four days marauding the Sea of Marmara until her luck ran out when she was spotted by a torpedo boat, damaged and scuttled. All of *AE2*'s crew, including her captain, Lieutenant Commander Henry Stoker, became prisoners of the Turks. Of the 512 Entente officers and men captured at Gallipoli, 142 of these men are known to have died whilst in captivity. Buried here are the graves of two such prisoners of war: Private Edward Clifton, 9/Lancashire Fusiliers (LF) and Private Edward Bailey, 6/Loyals. Both died of their wounds whilst being transferred to Constantinople.

There are several non-military graves of interest that are linked to the

Submarine E15 after capture.

campaign. Basil Wood Bourne was a veteran of the campaign who had served at Gallipoli as a corporal in 3 Australian Field Artillery Brigade and ended the war with a commission. Bourne was on a pilgrimage as part of the 50th anniversary of the landing and died from a heart attack whilst stepping off the tour bus near Anzac Cove. Major Edgar Banner, founder of The Gallipoli Association, was a witness and recounted the full story in *The Gallipolian* (Christmas 1969).

'Later on, when we had time to adjust ourselves to the situation, it was agreed that this was a fine way to go out. Up to that moment

Grave of Lt-Commander Theodore Brodie.

Grave of an Anzac, Basil Bourne.

a long and happy life with no worries; now, attaining a half-century wish and being at last once again where he had spent an eventful and exciting time in his younger days. To us of course it was a tragedy, but for the Anzac, an octogenarian who knew that his circulation was such that he might expire at any moment, what more would he have asked? ... We were accompanied by a most helpful representative of the War Graves Commission ... because of this he was able to expedite the proceedings by arranging for burial that day at the Christian cemetery in Çanakkale. At sunset that day the whole of our party of veterans, one hundred strong, medals worn, marched with the Anzac for the last time.'

There are also two New Zealand nurses buried here; Rosalind Webb and Jean Walker. They were on their way to visit Anzac, in particular the grave of Major David Grant, Rosalind's grandfather, who was killed on Baby 700 on 25 April (see chapter 3). On 11 November 1965, Armistice Day, near Lapseki, their car was involved in a traffic accident and both women were killed. What is unusual about Bourne, Webb and Walker are their CWGC style headstones. Although not unique, it is poignant that they are marked in a similar way to those to whom they had come to pay their respects.

Return to the *feribot* port for the crossing to Kilitbahir (Kilid Bahr) or Eceabat (Maidos). Crossing the Dardanelles, note the Dur Yolcu Memorial. It portrays a large image of a Turkish soldier, a flame and an inscription from a famous poem by Necmettin Halil Onam: *Stop traveller. This earth you tread unaware is where an era ended.* The second verse, not shown here, continues, *Kneel down and lend an ear. This quiet mound is where the heart of a nation beats.* The poem is similar in sentiment to Rupert Brooke's 'The Soldier'.

If you take the Eceabat ferry it is approximately four kilometres to Kilitbahir, which can be reached by car, taxi or public minibus (*dolmuş*). From the ferry wharf in Ecebat, turn left and follow the road along the Dardanelles coast until you reach the village of Kilitbahir.

The most impressive feature of **Kilitbahir (3) (40°08'52.2"N 26°22'47.3"E)** is the recently restored clover-shaped castle (Kilitbahir Kalesi). Kilitbahir means 'lock of the sea'. As with Çimenlik Castle on the opposite side of the Narrows, Kilitbahir Castle was also constructed by Fatih Sultan Mehmet II in 1462-63. Together they control the straits at their narrowest point, just 1.25 kilometres across. Because of its antiquity no guns were actually placed in the castle in 1914 and thus it did not come under fire from the Allied fleet.

Stop, Traveller!

Leave Kilitbahir Castle and follow the road south (*Yalı Caddesi*) for 250 metres to the **Namazgâh Battery (4) (40°08'41.4"N 26°22'46.0"E)** (*Namazgâh* means prayer site), which dates from the late nineteenth century. Left derelict since the campaign, the fort was restored in 2007 and now houses a small museum that tells the story of the naval battle. This large battery was within the most heavily fortified area of the Dardanelles and was headquarters of 2/Heavy Artillery. This unit was equipped with sixteen artillery pieces, two of which were long-range, the rest short range bar two anti-aircraft guns. Namazgâh first came into action on 5 March during the preliminary bombardments and came under

Kilitbahir Castle.

heavy shellfire on 18 March, which temporarily silenced the battery; it returned into action soon after.

Leave the battery and continue south along the coast road for 300 metres to the large bronze statue of **Corporal Seyit (5) (40°08'27.1"N 26°22'31.3"E),** one of the best-known wartime Turkish heroes. Seyit, a timber cutter, was from the village of Edremit-Havrant, where he was renowned for his great strength, apparently capable of walking around with a large log under each arm. Legend is told that on 18 March a gun in Mecidiye Fort was hit that destroyed the shell loading mechanism of the gun. Seyit, stripped to the waist, carried in his arms, or possibly on the small of his back, a 213 kilogram shell for this gun. He repeated this feat not once, but three times, firing the gun alone at the Entente fleet. The last shell supposedly hit and sank HMS *Ocean*. Although evidence points to the warship being sunk by a mine that had been laid by the *Nusret*, the myth of Seyit sinking the ship continues and even grows. After the battle Seyit was asked to recreate this superhuman feat for the press but was unable to do so. Without the adrenalin of the battle he was photographed later holding a wooden training shell. Seyit survived the war and died in the 1930s. The statue is a fine tribute to the Turkish gunners who stood firm against the bombardments of February and March 1915.

On the opposite side of the road, by the entrance to the fort, is the **Mecidiye Fort, Cemetery and Memorial (6) (40°08'28.4"N 26°22'29.4"E).**

Corporal Seyit Gun in Mecidiye Fort.

Sixteen Turkish artillerymen who died during the naval bombardments of Mecidiye Battery are buried here. The battery, armed with two 28 cm and four 24 cm guns, was never fully silenced during the naval attacks, although earth thrown up by the shell explosions jammed the gun mechanisms and, more significantly, casualties caused spells in which gun fire was interrupted. The commander of the battery, Captain Hilmi Bey, who was killed during the attack, is buried in Istanbul's Edirnekapı Cemetery.

From this memorial, continue on foot up the slope to Mecidiye Fort, the site where Seyit performed his feat. Two days before this famous action American Ambassador Morgenthau visited the fort:

Statue of Corporal Seyit.

'When I was there, however, the place was quiet, for no fighting was going on that day. For my particular benefit the officers put one of their gun crews through a drill, so that I could obtain a perfect picture of the behaviour of the Turks in action. In their mind's eye these artillerists now saw the English ships advancing within range, all their guns pointed to destroy the enemies of the Prophet. The bugleman blew his horn and the whole company rushed to their appointed places. Some were bringing shells, others were opening the breeches, others were taking the ranges, others were straining at pulleys, and others were putting the charges into place. Everything was eagerness and activity; evidently the Germans had been excellent instructors, but there was more to it than German military precision, for the men's faces lighted up with all that fanaticism which supplies the morale of Turkish soldiers. These gunners momentarily imagined that they were shooting once more at the infidel English, and above the exercise shouts I could hear the singsong chant of the leader, intoning the prayer with which the Moslem has rushed to battle for thirteen centuries.'

From Mecidiye to the mouth of the Dardanelles to the south is about twenty kilometres; the Entente fleet reached within five kilometres of this point, still 250 kilometres short of Constantinople. It was south of

Kephez Point, marked by the white tower on the Anatolian side of the Dardanelles, in Erenköy Bay that the mighty Anglo-French Fleet met its match when they struck the mines laid by *Nusret*. This is the resting place of *Bouvet* and where HMS *Ocean* and HMS *Irresistible* were left to drift and, finally, sink. The white tower also marks the spot of the Dardanos Battery, another fort that helped defend the Dardanelles against the Anglo-French fleet. Despite being heavily bombarded, the fort was never put out of action, proving the Admiralty adage that 'a ship's a fool to fight a fort'. A single shell can sink a ship, but a hundred salvos cannot (necessarily) silence a fort.

Optional Tour – Overview

Achi Baba

From this location, you can either return to Kilitbahir/Eceabat or continue along the coast road to explore the Helles battlefield. To visit Helles, follow the road for approximately seven kilometres, passing the hamlet of Havuzlar, before turning inland. The road will wind through valleys where the Turks housed war cemeteries, supply depots, hospitals and base camps for soldiers fighting on their southern Helles front. After a further seven kilometres, passing the village of Behramlı, you will approach the outskirts of Alçitepe (Krithia). Just before entering the village there is a road to the left that skirts the back of the village. Take this road and follow it for 800 metres, where it forks. Take the left-hand road, signposted for the Alçitepe Baki Terasi (Alçitepe Viewing Terrace). Follow the road as it climbs to the east for two kilometres, till you come to the viewing terrace on your left.

Walk up the steps to the top of the platform. You are standing on the seaward slopes of Alçitepe, which the British called **Achi Baba (40°05'48.9"N 26°15'12.5"E)**. This was the first day objective of General Hunter-Weston's 29th Division, which landed on 25 April 1915. Hamilton needed to seize this key piece of terrain before his forces could continue an advance up the peninsula and take the vital ground of Kilid Bahr, where he would link up with the Anzacs.

Achi Baba Panorama.

If you look out to the coast you will see the mouth of the Dardanelles and the four pillar Çanakkale Martyrs Memorial on the headland of Eski Hissarlik, to the east of Cape Helles. This position is also the location of De Tott's Battery and S Beach. If you look to the right you will see the lighthouse at the end of the Cape and the Helles Memorial. On the left of the Helles Memorial is V Beach; to the right is W Beach, the two main British landing beaches. Looking to the right is the Aegean, and hidden from view are X and Y beaches. The intention of the landing was to capture the little village of Krithia. You can see the mosque in the middle of it in the bowl to your right. At the same time the first day objective was to capture this hill where you are standing. To your north is the Kilid Bahr plateau, an even more formidable natural fortress that overlooks the Narrows. This was General Hamilton's ultimate objective for the land campaign. Once captured, and the Narrows defences neutralised, the fleet could proceed to Constantinople. Neither Kilid Bahr. Achi Baba or the village of Krithia were ever captured.

End of optional tour.

Either return, or continue to chapter 3 to tour the Helles battlefield.

Chapter 2

Anzac

The objective of the Anzac landing was the capture of Gaba Tepe and the Sari Bair range that extended north-east from the sea. It consisted of three long and tortuous ridges that contained numerous gullies and depressions. The head of this was crowned by three rounded hills of near identical height, Chunuk Bair, Hill Q and Hill 971 (Kocaçimentepe), which commanded views of the surrounding area, including the Narrows. For the landing, these objectives were referred to as 'First', 'Second' and 'Third' ridges. These obstacles had to be taken before the army could cross the plain of Maidos, a wide depression that extends from Gaba Tepe to Kelia Liman, and reach the Narrows beyond, a distance of approximately eight kilometres. The place chosen for the covering force was just over a kilometre of sandy beach about two kilometres north of Gaba Tepe, and immediately south of what became Anzac Cove.

The landing on 25 April 1915 was made in conjunction with the British at Helles and the French at Kum Kale. Lieutenant General William Birdwood's ANZAC's would be landed at Z Beach, between Gaba Tepe and Ari Burnu. The Corps consisted of the Australian 1st Division (command by Major General William Bridges) and the New Zealand and Australian Division (commanded by Major General Alexander Godley); the total strength was 30,638 men, all of whom were volunteers who enlisted in 1914 specifically to assist Britain in the war.

The plan was fairly straight forward – or was on paper. A covering force consisting of 3 (Australian) Brigade, from the 1st Australian Division, would land its 4,000 men, under the command of Colonel Ewen Sinclair-MacLagan, to secure a forward screen. To maximise surprise, they would land before dawn and then push forward as quickly as possible to set up covering positions along the Third Ridge, from Battleship Hill to Gaba Tepe, before daybreak. The covering forces left flank was to be secured by the immediate landing of 2 (Australian) Brigade, which would land moments after the initial wave. Their objective was to extend the line northwards, capturing Sari Bair to the high point of Kocaçimentepe. Next to land would be 1 (Australian) Brigade, which was to be held in reserve near the beach.

THE THREE ANZAC RIDGES

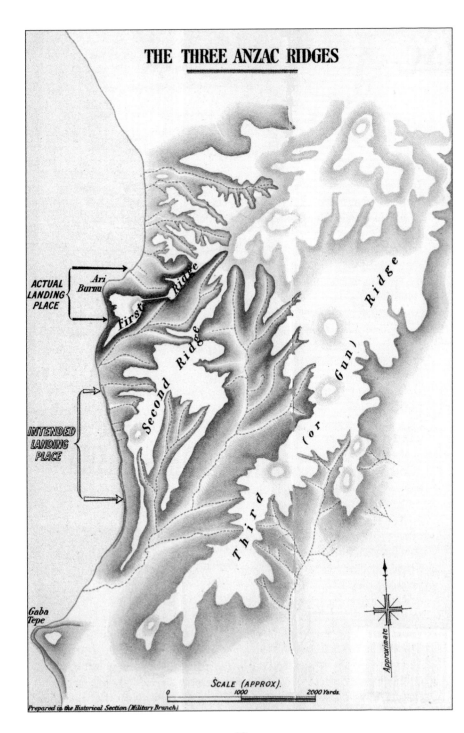

ACTUAL
LANDING
PLACE

Ari
Burnu

First Ridge

Second Ridge

Third (or Gun) Ridge

INTENDED
LANDING
PLACE

Gaba
Tepe

Approximate

SCALE (APPROX).
0   1000   2000 Yards.

Prepared in the Historical Section (Military Branch)

If the landing were successful at this stage this reserve brigade, together with the New Zealand and Australian Division, would leapfrog through the newly captured positions and capture Mal Tepe, a rise about ten kilometres from the landing. With the heights denied to the Turks, the Anzacs could threaten the northern flank of the Kilid Bahr Plateau, engage the Turkish reserves in the area and cut off those retreating from Helles. They would then wait for the main British advance from Helles to join them.

Because Gaba Tepe was known to be heavily defended by four 15-cm guns, the intended landing was to be placed to the north, where likely resistance was understood to be lighter. The landing site chosen was to be within a five kilometre stretch of coastline between Gaba Tepe in the south and Fisherman's Hut in the north. Intelligence at the time reported only a few unconnected trenches and a series of gun emplacements, many appearing vacated. With a company in reserve near Gaba Tepe, the 2/27 Regiment was thinly spread, having deployed its remaining three companies over eight kilometres of coastline. The concern to the British command was not these defenders but the large number of troops known to be concentrated in the area, estimated to comprise two divisions, approximately 20,000 men. The divisions were part of General Esad Pasha III Corps; the Ottoman 19th Division, which was based near Boghali, and the Ottoman 9th Division, headquartered on the Kilid Bahr Plateau itself.

The Landing
With a mix of battleships and destroyers, it was the Royal Navy's task to take the covering force (men from 9/AIF, 10/AIF, 11/AIF and 12/AIF) to about three kilometres offshore, from where steam pinnaces would make the next phase of the journey inshore. To land the covering force, twelve pinnaces, each towing four rowing boats, would be used. In order for the landing to be made on a broad front, each tow needed to keep a set lateral distance from each other; however, in the darkness and with few bearings this proved near impossible. This in effect caused the pinnaces to bunch closer together and, with erratic steering, some boats crossed the lines of others, mixing the battalion landing order. About 4.00 a.m., when the faint silhouette of the shore and Ari Burnu headland could be made out, it was realised that the boats were just over a kilometre north of their intended landing place. Facing them were rugged, steep gorse covered cliffs and ridges, some ninety metres high, not the lowland hills that were expected. Too late to change course, as light was approaching, each boat was set adrift to row the last fifty metres to the shore. As the first boats approached Ari Burnu a bright signalling light was seen. The splash of

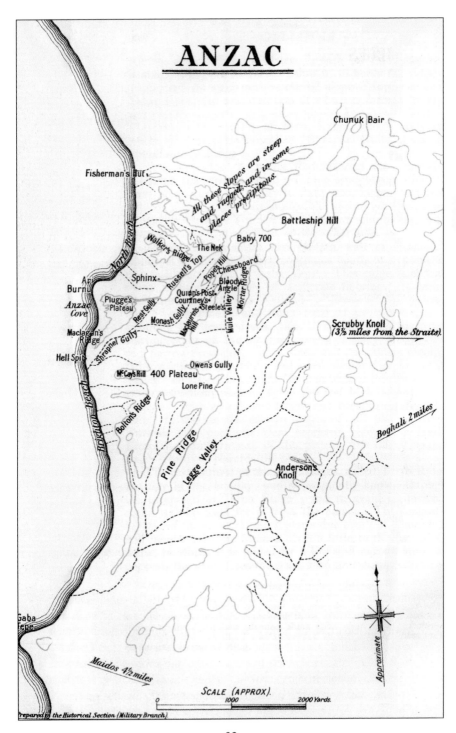

ANZAC

Chunuk Bair

Fisherman's Hut

All these slopes are steep and rugged, and in some places precipitous.

Battleship Hill

Walker's Ridge
The Nek
Baby 700
Russell's Top
Sphinx
Pope's Hill
Chessboard
Ari Burnu
Bloody Angle
Plugge's Plateau
Quinn's Post
Courtney's
Anzac Cove
Rest Gully
Steele's
Maclagan's Ridge
Monash Gully
Mule Valley
Mortar Ridge
Hell Spit
Shrapnel Gully

Scrubby Knoll
(3½ miles from the Straits).

McCay's Hill 400 Plateau
Owen's Gully
Lone Pine

Bolton's Ridge

Pine Ridge

Legge Valley

Boghali 2 miles

Anderson's Knoll

North Beach
Brighton Beach

Gaba Tepe

Approximate

Maidos 4½ miles

SCALE (APPROX).
0   1000   2000 Yards.

Prepared by the Historical Section (Military Branch).

Coming ashore at Anzac, 25 April 1915.

oars continued until the silence was broken a few metres from the shore, when the first shots rang out: the Anzacs' baptism of fire had begun.

The first boats to hit the beach, shortly before 4.30 a.m., were those of 9/AIF, which had reached the shore before any firing began. Three tows on the left that carried 11/AIF landed 180 metres north of Ari Burnu and were in good order. The remaining nine tows arrived mixed up and clustered together around the head of Ari Burnu and a small cove, later known as Anzac Cove. When the first shots rang out, the remaining boats quickly made for the shore regardless of position. It was probably fortunate that they landed where they did as any nearer to Gaba Tepe, where the defences were known to be stronger, would have caused higher casualties.

Both sides were taken by surprise; the Turks were not expecting a landing here, and the Australians were not expecting the sheer and scrub covered cliff faces and ravines that now faced them. Aspinall-Oglander in the official history explains that

'Even in the time of peace the precipitous ridges and tortuous ravines which formed the first Australian and New Zealand battlefield are an arduous climb for an active and unarmed man, while the steep, scrub-covered gullies are so confusing that it is easy to lose one's way. To preserve the cohesion of an attack across such country, immediately after an opposed landing in the dark, and without previous reconnaissance, would be an impossible task for the best-trained troops in the world.'

Anzac Cove during the morning of 25 April 1915.

Confronted by this unfamiliar landscape that offered the defenders all the advantages, there was immediate confusion as the officers tried to work out their location. The importance of pushing forward had been drilled into them, so quickly the keen and eager men, after dropping their packs and fixing bayonets, scrambled up the scrub and thorny holly-oak covered slopes to the summit of First Ridge, later named Plugge's Plateau.

The few defenders that had survived the bitter hand-to-hand struggle on Plugge's Plateau retired down the southern side of the hill into the valley below, taking up fresh positions in the thick scrub or up on Second Ridge.

The Turks knew the terrain very well. The official history indicates that the Turk was not the only opposition:

> '...the delaying power of well-armed and well concealed marksmen, favoured by a perfect knowledge of the ground, is undoubtedly very great. Nevertheless, there can be little doubt that the extreme difficulties of the country played an even greater part than the opposition of the enemy in frustrating the Australian plan.'

After Plugge's had been secured, the Australians pushed on to capture 400 Plateau, on Second Ridge. The plateau was a wide scrub covered

The firing line on Second Ridge.

heart-shaped area of relatively flat ground that had two 'lobes': the northern became known as Johnston's Jolly, the southern as Lone Pine. The Australian advance was so quick that they had overrun a Turkish mountain gun battery in The Cup, a hollow to the eastern end of Lone Pine. From the southern end of Anzac Cove, around Hell Spit, the

Turkish field gun in action.

remaining wave of the covering force was landed in good order. With Second Ridge captured, small groups of men began to probe towards Third Ridge and the fortifications of Gaba Tepe, where they had orders to silence the guns. Neither of these objectives were ever reached.

The main body lands.

Although the landing had been going well, Sinclair-MacLagan soon became aware that his brigade was in disarray, fragmented in small groups all over the scrub covered hills and ravines. The Australians still enjoyed the element of surprise; however, although advanced parties had penetrated well over a kilometre inland, they were few in number and unsupported. Concerned by the situation and knowing the counter-attack could come at any time, Sinclair-MacLagan halted the advance and ordered his men to entrench along Second Ridge. This would be easier to defend and, as it was closer to the beach, it would be nearer to the reserves and supplies. Making the decision not to entrench on Third Ridge, his final objective, which was undefended at this time, he gifted this key terrain to the Turks and denied the Australians this dominant position overlooking the Maidos Plain and Turkish lines of communications. This error in judgement was arguably the undoing of the Anzac plan, and the main contributor to all the problems caused by the limited beachhead that the Anzacs had to endure during the next four months.

Along Second Ridge Sinclair-MacLagan set up 'posts' (later named after their commanders: Steele's – after Major T. Steel, 14/AIF; Courtney's – after Lieutenant Colonel R. Courtney, 14/AIF; Quinn's – after Major H. Quinn 15/AIF; and Pope's – after Lieutenant Colonel H. Pope, 16/AIF), positions that were to be fiercely contested throughout the campaign. Whilst the ridge was being entrenched detachments were sent to hold forward positions on the edge of 400 Plateau. As soon as the Australians halted their advance and began to dig in, the heavily outnumbered and thinly spread 200 defenders from 2/27 Regiment had achieved their mission. All they needed to do now was wait for the remainder of the regiment to reach them, after which the counter-attack could begin.

By 5.30 a.m. the leading elements of Colonel James McCay 2 Brigade began to land and, using a broader front as per the original intention, the brigade came ashore with few casualties. Sinclair-MacLagan immediately ordered them to the right of the line, instead of sending them to protect the left, northern, flank. MacLagan convinced McCay that the original plan could not be carried out and that he must divert his entire brigade to guard the right flank. He was fearful that this southern area was at immediate risk from counter-attack, and without his men this flank would almost certainly break. McCay was recorded to say, *it is a bit stiff to disobey orders first thing,* but reluctantly accepted MacLagan's revised orders and change of plan. This decision was undoubtedly influenced by pre-landing intelligence that positioned Turkish camps close to the area. By taking this action MacLagan was not ignoring the importance of Baby 700 and the vital ground of the Sari Bair ridge, which he understood to be relatively safe and uncontested. He knew that Baby 700 was a natural junction of the second and third ridges and the gateway to Chunuk Bair and Hill 971. It also commanded views of Monash Gully[1], the Anzac line of communication from the beach to Second Ridge. However, with 2

---

1. Monash Gully was named after Colonel (later General Sir John) Monash, at the time commanding officer of 4 Australian Infantry Brigade. Monash Gully was a continuation of Shrapnel Valley.

Men from 2 (Australian) Brigade landing.

Brigade now protecting the vulnerable right flank, this left him with little strength on the left to secure Baby 700 and beyond. The northern flank and the heights would remain open to counter-attack until 1 Brigade and the New Zealanders could be landed.

The treacherous terrain, in particular the dense scrub, was an obstacle that affected movement, observation and communication, making defence or any coordinated advance difficult for the Anzacs. It was impossible to distinguish friend from foe, and invited intense firing as soon as anyone tried to stand up. Shelling had steadily increased since early morning and by midday the troops were under almost constant shrapnel fire, for which there was no reply. As the Official History says:

'… to lie out in the thick scrub under this shrapnel fire, separated from and out of sight of their comrades, unsupported by friendly artillery, ignorant of the situation, and imagining that they were the sole survivors of their units, was a severe strain to young troops in their first day of battle.'

At this stage of the battle Turkish artillery fire could not be suppressed due to the unavailability of Anzac field artillery and the ineffectiveness of naval gunnery support. Except for a 10-pounder Indian mountain battery, no further guns were ordered ashore until the perimeter had been stabilised. Even when another Indian mountain battery and an Anzac 18-pounder battery were permitted ashore in the late afternoon, siting them effectively was severely hampered by the terrain. The heavy weight of naval fire was of little use due to the flat trajectory of their guns, which made it difficult to target and hit positions inland. As observation improved the navy's fire became more effective, although there were still problems locating the Turkish artillery or even distinguishing enemy troops amongst the thick scrub. Royal Naval Air Service aircraft helped with the observation, but the Turkish guns ceased fire whenever a plane was near, so that spotting the camouflaged artillery positions proved extremely difficult.

Major General Bridges, commanding the 1st Australian Division, came ashore to witness the confusion the landing was now in. He had three Australian brigades and two New Zealand battalions committed to the battle. Still at sea aboard their transports was Colonel John Monash's 4 Brigade and the remaining half of the New Zealand Infantry Brigade. Their immediate landing was requested but following the original timetable was proving difficult. Wounded were being evacuated in the boats allocated for landing troops, and the return journey was taking longer as artillery fire had forced the shipping to withdraw further out to sea to avoid being hit. Reinforcements were desperately needed ashore to exploit the earlier successes, but they were stranded upon their transports. When they eventually did land in the afternoon it was too late.

General Bridges, 1st Australian Division.

Counter-attacks

The Turks had been cautious in their initial response to the Anzac landing as it was uncertain whether this was a feint or their main thrust. Colonel Mustafa Kemal, commanding the 19th Division, was at his headquarters in Boghali early that morning when he heard firing from the direction of Ari Burnu. He received a report about 6.30 a.m. from Colonel Halil Sami, commanding the 9th Division, confirming the landing. Sami had already ordered Lieutenant Colonel Şefik Aker to march the remaining two battalions of 27 Regiment, with an artillery battery and machine gun company, from nearby Maidos to Third Ridge. It was just after 7.00 a.m. that the forward elements arrived and began to deploy along its length. Reinforcing the survivors of Major Ismet's

Colonel Mustafa Kemal, 19th Division.

2/27 Regiment, which had done so well in delaying the Australian advance since 4.30 a.m., they quickly prepared to make the first counter-attack of the day. As predicted, this was to fall on Sinclair-MacLagan's right flank. The battle for the Second Ridge had begun.

Meanwhile Mustafa Kemal had personally led 57 Regiment onto the heights around Chunuk Bair, soon to be followed by 72 and 77 Regiment. The whole 19th Division added the needed numbers to support 27 Regiment in the counter-attack. At this time von Sanders remained cautious, believing that Bulair was still at risk, and kept two divisions for its defence. For Kemal the Anzac movement towards Sari Bair was enough to convince him that this was the main threat and he realised that he needed to get there before his enemy. The forward element of 57 Regiment had reached the summit of Chunuk Bair just before 10.00 a.m., where they reinforced a small party of exhausted survivors from 2/27 Regiment. With the race to the heights won, Kemal now planned to attack.

The day's chaotic fighting centred on two key features, 400 Plateau and Baby 700. On 400 Plateau the thick scrub meant that men lying prone were invisible, which made it difficult to maintain contact with adjacent units. When standing up to move the men were visible to the Turks, thereby provoking a hail of small arms fire and shrapnel. Lacking any coherent organisation, small groups of men would advance, either following the original orders to reach Third Ridge or MacLagan's new orders to reinforce the newly established firing line. Many of the men went forward in search of the 'firing line', but this was in vain as none had been established. What existed were small groups of men that had become detached, lost, pinned-down and further reduced by casualties. Many of the actions that day went unrecorded as small isolated groups of men were wiped out, lost forever in the small gullies and thick scrub-covered spurs of the area.

By 4.00 p.m. the Australians on the forward slopes of the plateau had been steadily pushed back. The Cup had been lost, along with the three artillery pieces that had been captured earlier that morning. 27 Regiment were soon pushing hard against Johnston's Jolly, Lone Pine and Bolton's Ridge; by nightfall the forward Australian positions on Pine Ridge had already been overrun. The defensive line was not ready for the relentless counter-attacks thrown at it, which had taken the Anzacs by surprise. On the heights men in forward positions on Battleship Hill fell back on to Baby 700, where a new struggle had begun. The hill changed hands five times during the course of the battle, eventually falling to the Turks after Kemal's relentless attack and overwhelming numbers had crushed the thin lines of Anzac defenders. The survivors now fell back to the saddle of land between Baby 700 and Russell's Top, called The Nek.

The brunt of the early fighting fell upon 27 and 57 Regiments, who by dusk were exhausted. 77 (Arab) Regiment came into the line to the south, whilst 72 (Arab) Regiment entered to the north, thus committing the whole of 19th Division to the battle. The day's events had shattered both sides, neither being in any condition to conduct offensive operations. The Anzac beachhead was not large; it was barely three kilometres in length, with a depth of no more than 700 metres. Weakened through mounting casualties, especially amongst the officers, the Anzacs were scattered, tired and confused, often without officers but holding on as best they could. Soon stragglers as well as wounded began drifting back from the line and were found wandering through or taking shelter in the gullies or making their way to the already congested beach. The non-wounded who were collecting were organised into carrying parties to take ammunition and water to the front, whilst the wounded were cared for as best as was possible. Morale was taking a distinct downturn, not helped by the unchallenged enemy artillery.

The situation was dire for the Anzacs, and there were doubts amongst the high command that they could stand the strain of another day. Those that held the line were in a poor condition and reinforcements were few or still out at sea, as was most of the artillery. Medical facilities were atrocious and there were too few personnel and transports to adequately cope with the wounded. The Turks, who had been quick to counter-attack, had recaptured the vital high ground and, encircling the Anzacs, had shut the door to any further advance. The two Anzac divisional commanders, Major Generals Bridges and Godley, reviewed the situation and, with the threat of a major counter-attack in the morning, they concluded that evacuation was the best course of action. If they were to get off Anzac the decision had to be made immediately. The situation was presented to Birdwood, who in turn signalled Hamilton with the following message:

Lieutenant General Sir William Birdwood, GOC Anzac Corps.

'Both my divisional generals and my brigadiers have represented to me that they fear their men are thoroughly demoralised by shrapnel fire to which they have been subjected all day after exhaustion and gallant work in morning. Numbers have dribbled back from the firing line and cannot be collected in this difficult country. Even the New Zealand Brigade, which has only recently been engaged, lost heavily and is to some extent demoralised. If troops are subjected to shellfire again tomorrow morning there is likely to be a fiasco, as I have no fresh troops with which to replace those in firing line. I know my representation is most serious, but if we are to re-embark it must be at once.'

Hamilton and his staff reviewed the situation; they concluded that, although Anzac may have been on the verge of collapse, the risk of re-embarking two divisions whilst in contact with the enemy, even if they had the boats available, was too great. Hamilton had started to pen a reply when information arrived that the Australian Submarine HMAS *AE2*[2], under the commander of Lieutenant Commander Henry Stoker, had broken through the Dardanelles defences, sunk an enemy ship off Chanak and was now in the Sea of Marama. This news could not have come at a better time, thus adding weight to Hamilton's resolute and definite order to Birdwood:

Submarine *AE2*.

'Your news is indeed serious. But there is nothing for it but to dig yourselves right in and stick it out. It would take at least two days to re-embark you, as Admiral Thursby will explain to you. Meanwhile, the Australian submarine has got up through the Narrows and has torpedoed a gunboat at Chunuk. Hunter-Weston, despite his heavy losses, will be advancing tomorrow which should divert pressure from you. Make a personal appeal to your men and Godley's to make a supreme effort to hold their ground.

Ian Hamilton

'P.S. You have got through the difficult business; now you only have to dig, dig, dig, until you are safe.'

---

2. *AE2* went on to harass Ottoman shipping in the Sea of Marmara until 30 April 1915, when she was damaged by a torpedo boat and scuttled to avoid capture. The crew were all taken prisoner.

Under the cover of darkness, both sides began to improve their defences, the day ending with uncertainty of what the next day would bring. Dawn on 26 April came and there was no counter-attack. The Ottoman 19th Division, who had been hard pushed at Anzac, was in no position to attack again without reinforcements. Both the 5th and 7th Divisions were still with von Sanders at Bulair, where the RND had successfully delivered their ruse; fooled or not, von Sanders was not going to release them until he was clear that the Anzac landing was not a feint. It did not take him long and by nightfall reinforcements began moving south.

On 27 April, now reinforced by two fresh regiments (33 and 62 Regiment), Kemal wasted no time and made a daylight attack against the Anzac perimeter. This attack faltered against the combined firepower of the Anzac defenders and under the weight of Royal Navy's 12 and 15 inch shells that smashed the attackers' massed ranks. Exhausted from the continuous fighting since the landing, Hamilton reinforced the Anzacs with four battalions from the RND: Chatham, Deal and Portsmouth Battalions, Royal Marine Light Infantry, and Nelson Battalion. Comprising mainly war recruits, these fresh-faced men were thrown into the defensive line along the Second Ridge where one of them, Lance Corporal Walter Parker RMLI, would win Anzac's first Victoria Cross.

Holding the line.
On 2 May it was the turn of the Anzacs to attack and test their enemy's resolve. A joint New Zealand and Australian attack, supported by the RND, was launched to improve the local tactical positions, aiming to remove the Turks from the Chessboard and Baby 700. The attack, which began at dusk after a short, fifteen-minute, bombardment, began badly, with few battalions having had time to prepare. Both 13/AIF and 16/AIF managed to get to the top of the ridge at the end of Monash Valley, but upon reaching the crest were met by heavy machine gun fire. The Otago Battalion, which arrived ninety minutes late, advanced from Pope's Hill into the dark and joined up as best they could with the Australians; however none managed to reach the Chessboard. During first light misfortune continued as friendly artillery fell onto the Australian positions. Reinforcing the survivors of the first attack, Chatham and Portsmouth Battalions advanced; but in the daylight they soon fell victim to a Turkish machine gun in German Officer's Trench. Firing into the rear and flank of the RND, this gun made the exposed slopes impossible to hold. The survivors were forced to withdraw back to their starting lines. Thereafter the slope in front of the Chessboard became known as Dead Man's Ridge.

By 3 May it was apparent that both sides were at a stalemate. A

'Western Front' style of trench warfare was being established, with neither side having the resources to break the deadlock. Wrapped inside a natural amphitheatre of ridges, topped by trench systems sometimes no more than ten metres apart, nearly 20,000 men lived, burrowed into the cliffs in dugouts, sheltered in the ravines under tarpaulin sheets or behind the sandbag walls of trenches. Here they worked, slept, ate, played, fought and died. Nowhere was safe at Anzac, and generals as well as privates were just at risk. On 14 May General Birdwood was wounded, albeit lightly, but was able to return to duty. The following day Major General Bridges was wounded, shot by a sniper whilst crossing an exposed section of Monash Valley. His wound proved fatal. He died on 18 May aboard a hospital ship; his body was repatriated and he now lies in the grounds of Duntroon Military College.

Anzac Cove.

Both sides settled into trench life and, whilst there was no major battle between 3 May and 6 August, this is not to mean that it remained quiet. Brigadier General Monash described the incessant noise of Anzac in a letter home.

'The bullet which passes well overhead, especially if fired from a long range, has a sharp sudden crack like a whip, and really feels as if it is very close. Our own rifle fire, listened to from behind

43

the firing-line, sounds like a low rumble or growl. Our machine guns are exactly like the rattle of a kettledrum. The enemy's rifle and machine gun fire, on the other hand, sounds as if it were directly overhead, in a medley of sharp cracks like the explosions of packets of crackers just overhead, even though the fire is actually coming from the front, a half-mile away. The enemy's shrapnel sounds like a gust of wind in a wintry gale, swishing through the air and ending in a loud bang and a cloud of smoke, when the shell bursts. Unless one gets in the way of the actual fragments of the shell itself, the Turkish shrapnel does very little harm. Our own artillery is the noisiest of all, both the discharge of the guns and the bursting of the shells being ear-splitting, with a reverberating echo that lasts 20 or 30 seconds. We have been amusing ourselves by trying to discover the longest period of absolute quiet. We have been fighting now continuously for 22 days, all day and all night, and most of us think that absolutely the longest period during which there was absolutely no sound of gun or rifle fire, throughout the whole of that time, was 10 seconds. One man says he was able on one occasion to count 14, but nobody believes him!'

War Letters of General Monash, pp 35-36.

On 16 May, the Turks, reinforced by the 2nd Division, prepared for another attack. This time it would be a night attack, in the hope that the dark would not only mask their troop build-up but would also provide some protection from enemy fire, in particular that from the Royal Navy, which had proven so devastating during their previous daylight assaults. Unfortunately for the Turks, they had given away their intent. During the previous afternoon large-scale troop movements had been spotted by a Royal Naval Air Service reconnaissance flight, so the whole Anzac sector was on alert. When the Turks began to bombard the lines at 5.00 p.m. the afternoon before, it was a sure sign that an attack would follow. At 3.30 a.m., on 19 May, the night attack began, falling mainly on the centre of the line along Second Ridge. The Anzacs crowded their fire trenches almost shoulder to shoulder as they fired ten-rounds rapid into the on-coming Turks.

'From flank to flank the darkness was stabbed with licking flashes of cordite and the stutter of machine guns joined into the harsh discord of the rifle fire and the hard smack of field guns. Shells screamed overhead, and when they burst with a crash the upper darkness was pierced as with fiery breath and with a high pitched, droning whine the shrapnel pellets came to earth. The air was filled with dust and acrid fumes.'

Corporal Thomas McNamara, 11/AIF.

The sheer weight of numbers briefly achieved success at Courtney's Post, where the Turks managed to break into the front line. There was a second Victoria Cross awarded at Anzac as a result of this attack; this time it went to an Australian, Lance Corporal Albert Jacka, 14/AIF, who single-handily recaptured the trench. By 5.00 a.m. the Turkish assault had clearly failed, although the attacks continued until midday, resulting in a total cost of some 10,000 casualties. The Anzacs suffered about 628 casualties and fired an astonishing 950,000 rifle and machine gun rounds and 1,900 shells.

Lance Corporal Albert Jacka, VC.

With No Man's Land now strewn thick with bodies, the Turks called for an official armistice. After negotiations, Hamilton and von Sanders agreed that an armistice would take place on 24 May to facilitate the removal and burial of the dead. For the first time firing stopped at Anzac. Delimiting parties, holding up Red Cross and Red Crescent flags, met their opposite numbers between the trench lines whilst stretcher bearer parties collected the dead. Lieutenant Colonel Percy Fenwick, a New Zealand medical officer, described the awful scene.

'The Turkish dead lay so thick that it was almost impossible to pass without treading on their bodies. The stench was awful. The Turkish doctor gave me some pieces of wool on which he poured some scent and asked me to put them into my nostrils. I was glad to do so. The awful destructive power of high explosives was very evident. Huge holes, surrounded with circles of corpses blown to pieces, were scattered about the area over which we walked. Everywhere lay the dead - swollen, black and hideous - and over all a nauseating stench that made one feel desperately sick.'

Reminiscences of Anzac, p. 39.

With the truce over, the summer months at Gallipoli were to bring little respite. The beaches were narrow, cramped and continually swept by shell fire. Landings were only possible when the wind was blowing in a certain direction. Owing to the appearance of enemy submarines, all capital ships

THE
SYDNEY **MAIL**
Wednesday, October 6, 1915.

The Armistice Turks burying their dead. (*The Sydney Mail,* Oct 6, 1915)

THIS unique photograph—one of the most remarkable—to whtwo that have come from the Dardanelles—was taken by a New South Wales soldier (Private Mack, of Coodookla) with a small pocket camera. The photograph was made by the "Sydney Mail" which has secured the exclusive right of reproduction. The picture was taken during the armistice on May 24, when, after several days' furious fighting, the Turks (who had sustained the casualties), were given permission to bury their dead. The soldiers in the photograph are all Turks—some of them are digging graves, while dead comrades lie all around them. The armistice was very honourably observed, and during the interval Turks and Australians freely fraternised. *Right of reproduction reserved.*

THE ARMISTICE: TURKS BURYING THEIR DEAD ON THE SLOPES OF SARI BAIR.

and transports had to be sent to Mudros for safety, which meant that all men, stores, guns, etc., had to be brought thirty kilometres to the shore. The oppressive heat during the day wearied the men and sapped their energy. Water was scarce and much of what they had was shipped from Egypt and then stored in purpose made troughs, tin containers, wooden barrels, earthenware jars, basically anything that could be requisitioned that could store water. Wells were sunk but, with few exceptions, the water thus extracted was far from sufficient to sustain a force of this size. Worst of all were the flies. Great swarms covered the battlefield and bred off corpses and excrement into their millions. When eating it became impossible not to consume anything without a mouthful of flies. Not surprisingly, dysentery became rife and casualties from sickness grew to an extent that more soldiers were being evacuated sick than those with wounds from enemy action. With over a thousand men a week being evacuated and three quarters of the army weakened by this disease, the men of MEF who landed in April were shadows of their former selves. Many found it hard to stagger, let alone walk or run; any new drafts they received did not last long until they became sick as well. Even Hamilton went down with dysentery. It was these weary troops who were needed to launch a major assault once again.

The August Offensive
After the bloody fighting at Helles, during June and July the Turkish commanders were unsure if Hamilton would keep on attacking there, slowly biting away at the Turkish lines, or launch a new offensive elsewhere. The disadvantage with Helles was that it was surrounded on three sides by the sea, which restricted the ability to manoeuvre. At Anzac, where nothing had really been happening since May, opportunities were revisited. It was critical that wherever Hamilton chose to strike he needed to make a success of it. The situation at Gallipoli at this stage was one of stalemate, with heavy casualties and with little progress made since the disappointing results of the initial landings. Anzac remained little more than a narrow beachhead and all efforts to break out of Helles met with failure. On the Western Front the situation was little better; the Second Artois Offensive in the spring had largely failed, despite casualties of 130,000, and dwindling stock of munitions became a new worry for the Allied powers. Gallipoli was once again back on the War Office agenda of options and, with the availability of reinforcements, a plan outlined back in May by Birdwood was adopted.

The plan, which went through several iterations, was not revolutionary in objective but was imaginative in the series of complex stages to reach that goal. This bold and daring plan was essentially a flanking manoeuvre that consisted of a major night break out to the north of Anzac and a left hook sweeping move to the east to facilitate the dawn capture of Sari Bair. This action would cut off the bulk of the Ottoman army's land and sea communications with Constantinople and Asia. After the heights had been secured, there would be a follow-on advance to push the Turks off Second Ridge and to capture Baby 700, Battleship Hill, 400 Plateau and Third Ridge. The primary objective was to capture Sari Bair, whilst the proposed Suvla landing was limited to securing an immediate support base for the offensive. Any advance across the Peninsula would be secondary to this operation. The weakness of the plan, however, was its over complexity and reliance on the completion of each step, critical to the success of the overall offensive. Any delay posed a threat; as the whole idea relied upon a rapid advance and use of initiative, things that

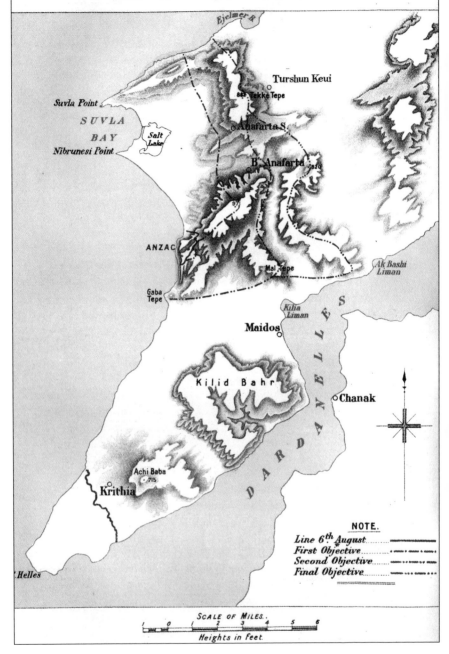

OBJECTIVES
for the August Offensive

Ejelmer R.

Turshun Keui

883 Tekke Tepe

Suvla Point

S U V L A
BAY
Nibrunesi Point

Salt Lake

Anafarta S.

B. Anafarta

97

ANZAC

Mal Tepe

Gaba Tepe

Kilia Liman

Ak Bashi Liman

Maidos

Kilid Bahr

Chanak

D A R D A N E L L E S

Achi Baba
· 715

Krithia

Helles

NOTE.
Line 6ᵗʰ August .... ——————
First Objective .... —·—·—·—
Second Objective .... —··—··—
Final Objective .... —···—···—

SCALE OF MILES.
1 0 1 2 3 4 5 6

Heights in feet.

48

had been lacking so often in the execution of the campaign so far, it did not bode well for success.

The offensive began during the morning of 6 August with several diversionary actions designed to mask the true intentions of the plan. These ranged from a British naval bombardment at Sigacik Koyu near Smyrna (Izmir), to a detachment of some 300 Greek volunteers landing near Enez, north of the Gulf of Saros. The main diversions were local, comprising a feint attack at The Vineyard, Helles, which was planned to draw Turkish attention and reserves to the south, and a similar attack that would take place against Lone Pine at Anzac.

Lone Pine

Commanded by Major General 'Hooky' Walker, the Australian 1st Division's attack at Lone Pine was designed primarily as diversionary but, if successful, the plan allowed for further exploitation by driving a wedge into the enemy's main position. This attack was aimed at focussing Turkish attention to the local areas, thus giving the best chance of success to the breakout. Whilst the British attack at Helles failed, the outcome at Lone Pine would be very different. Ambitious and risky, yes – all previous attacks of this nature had failed and with enormous casualties. However, this scheme had the advantage of careful planning and cunning, which in previous efforts had been conspicuously missing. The attack was scheduled for the late afternoon of 6 August and would be launched by 1 (Australian) Brigade, reinforced by 7/AIF and 12/AIF.

Both positions to be attacked were defended by Colonel Rüştü, 16th Division, who had deployed 125 Regiment on Johnston's Jolly and 47 Regiment on Lone Pine. If the attack on Lone Pine proved successful, an attack on the front line trenches on Johnston's Jolly would then take place. Lone Pine was a formidable fortification, positioned opposite the Australian salient known as The Pimple; less than a hundred metres of open, exposed ground separated the lines. The enemy trenches, protected by barbed wire, were built up by a mix of sandbags and mud bricks, and in places were roofed over with heavy pine logs and earth. The pine log defence is of note as this was to take the Australians by surprise, as it was a feature that had not been correctly identified in earlier aerial reconnaissances.

The frontage to be attacked by Brigadier General Nevill Smyth VC's 1 (Australian) Brigade was just under 200 metres in length and consisted of flat scrubby ground. To reduce the time the attacking forces would be exposed to Turkish fire, the Australians had secretly dug shallow tunnels (in effect Russian saps) under No Man's Land, with designed exits to be opened up just prior to the attack. One such gallery was dug within

Artist's impression of the storming of Lone Pine.

twenty-five metres of the enemy's front line trench. As was often the case with Russian saps, the tunnels were to have another purpose; they could rapidly be converted into communication trenches to allow reinforcements, ammunition and other supplies to reach the captured positions and to allow the wounded to be cleared.

The men would be lightly equipped, with rifle, bayonet, an iron ration (bully beef and biscuits), a full water bottle, two empty sandbags, a gas hood, and 200 rounds of ammunition in their webbing equipment and spare cotton bandolier. Each man was instructed to sew on an artillery distinction white calico patch to their back and one on each arm to help identify the units during the advance.

The attack began at 4.30 p.m. with an hour's bombardment of the area by twenty-eight field guns and howitzers, supported by the Royal Navy. Even though the thick logs that covered the Turkish trenches were good protection from shrapnel, when the high explosive shells began to fall they had the effect of splintering the wood, with devastating effect on the occupants. Major Tevfik Bey, 47 Regiment's commander, adopted the habit of moving his men back during bombardments into the narrow communication trenches and saps for protection. At 5.30 p.m. the bombardment lifted off Lone Pine to continue shelling the rear areas, the signal for the infantry to go over the top.

'At 5.30 we charged with fixed bayonets. I can tell you we got a warm time for a while. The moment we left our trench they opened fire on us with machine guns, rifles and shrapnel from their big guns. Our boys were cut down like grass; but that did not stop us. We charged straight on till we got to the first line of trenches. We very soon took possession of that, killing every Turk that was in it. In about ten minutes we were over every trench we could see. It was a splendid sight to see the boys standing on the edge of the trench, shooting down at the Turks. In less than no time we had them lying two or three deep in the bottom. All the time we were doing this their artillery was pounding away at us with shrapnel. It was when we jumped down into the trenches we had the real fun. We either shot, bayoneted, or knocked them on the heads with the butts of our rifles, whichever suited the purpose best. We scored a great victory, capturing every trench they had, and very few of their men got away.'

Private Harry Clegg, 3/AIF.

Due to the rapid Australian advance there were remarkably few casualties crossing No Man's Land. What followed caused more of a surprise; an anxious moment was spent getting into the front line trench that was covered in pine logs, all of which appeared untouched by the bombardment. Men, frustrated, fired through the loopholes and narrow gaps, whilst others sought ways into the trench system by finding large enough gaps or forward saps via which they could slip into the trench's dark interior. Others had to advance over the front line, where they found uncovered communication trenches to the rear, from where they could enter and then fight along the maze from the rear of the front line. Inside there was semi-darkness as a bitter struggle developed along the labyrinth of trenches and tunnels. By 5.50 p.m. the core of Lone Pine had been reached and minutes later the whole position was reported as captured. The scenes were horrific.

Part of the Australian success must be ascribed to the lack of resistance from the defenders, who had been thinned out in their front line trenches during the bombardment, leaving only a few sentries.

Artist's impression of bombing at Lone Pine.

This undoubtedly helped the first wave to establish positions in the trenches as their advance was largely unopposed. When Tevfik realised that they were under a major attack, it was too late. Despite being caught off guard, the Turks vigorously counter attacked, and during the next forty-eight hours, supported by 15 Regiment, both sides duelled in one of the most severe bomb and bayonet battles ever to be witnessed. The Turks, who lost both their battalion commanders killed (Major Tevfik Bey, 47 Regiment and Major Ibrahim Sukru, 15 Regiment), were desperate to regain their old positions; but the Australians were not going to relinquish them without a fight.

The *Official History* noted:

'Throughout these days of incessant fighting the spirit of the Australian troops was beyond praise, and so great, and almost embarrassing, was the anxiety of the rank and file to take their share in this historic action that at one period the unique precaution had to be taken of posting piquets in the communication trenches leading to Lone Pine to prevent unauthorised men from going into the fight. Reserve troops would wait in long queues for a chance of pushing their way forward, and sums of five pounds and upwards were freely offered, and offered in vain, by employed men in rear to take the place of friends going up to the front line.'

By the morning of 8 August, the worst of the fighting at Lone Pine had ended, although the Turks would continue their attacks for a couple of days. Both sides were completely exhausted from the three days and four nights of constant bayonet and bomb fighting. Birdwood wrote, *God forbid that I should ever see again such a sight as that which met my eyes when I went up there: Turks and Australians piled four and five deep on one another.* Turkish casualties had been heavy: 7,164 men were either killed, wounded, missing or made prisoner. Australian losses amounted to 2,277. It is of interest to note that the majority of the casualties suffered at Lone Pine, an area little bigger than six tennis courts, was not by shellfire but from close hand-to-hand fighting with rifle, bayonet and bombs.

Seven Victoria Crosses were awarded to the Australians for gallantry at Lone Pine, the highest number given to Australians for any single action: Captain A.J. Shout and Private L. Keysor, 1/AIF; Private J. Hamilton, 3/AIF; and Lieutenant W.J. Symons, Lieutenant F.H. Tubb, Corporal A.S. Burton and Corporal W. Dunstan, 7/AIF.

The legend of Lone Pine is remembered as a glorious but costly success of Australian arms; however, it had one unfortunate by-product that would have tragic consequences later. The Lone Pine attack

Australians in the Lone Pine trenches.

Southern Trench in Lone Pine, 8 August 1915.

convinced the Turks that their southern flank was the focus of the main assault and because of this they rushed the best part of four regiments, the 10th, 11th, 24th and 64th, into the area. It was these very same reserves that were sent so quickly to the northern flank when they realised that the New Zealand attack on Sari Bair was occurring. The success of the Australian attack at Lone Pine was therefore a significant factor in diminishing the chances of the allies in securing Sari Bair.

The Nek

Further along Second Ridge the other attacks did not go so well. The midnight attack on German Officers' Trench by 6/AIF failed, as did the Australian Light Horse attack that morning at Turkish Quinn's and The Chessboard. All three positions were part of a semi-circle of Turkish defences that mutually supported each other. Not capturing these positions would have a devastating effect on a later attack that would take place at The Nek. Few events invoke the utter despair, futility and courage of war as the tragic charge of the Australian Light Horse at The Nek on 7 August, an event that has been immortalized in Peter Weir's 1981 Oscar-winning film *Gallipoli*.

The Nek, a narrow bridge of land that stretched between Russell's Top and Baby 700, was a vitally important position in the Anzac sector. It was a perfect bottleneck that was consequently easy to defend. Several well sited machine guns and concentrated rows of trenches that stretched up onto the slopes of Baby 700 made this position all but impregnable. The attack's objective was The Nek to Baby 700, planned to support the New Zealanders assault on Chunuk Bair, an objective that was supposed to be captured during the night of 6/7 August. It was hoped that whilst the Australians were attacking the New Zealanders would already be descending down from these

Artist's impression of the Australian Light Horse charging.

height above Baby 700, catching the Turks in a pincer movement.

The Australian 3 Light Horse Brigade, commanded by Brigadier General Frederic Hughes, were chosen to assault The Nek. The brigade comprised the 8th, 9th and 10th Light Horse Regiments, who had landed at Gallipoli in May 1915 as dismounted infantry, leaving their horses in Egypt. Supporting the assault were two British battalions; 8/Cheshires and 8/RWF, along with 71/Field Company, Royal Engineers. The attack was set for 4.30 a.m. on 7 August, and would follow a bombardment. The frontage of the attack was eighty metres wide, restricting each of the four waves to 150 men each, two waves per regiment. Each of these waves would advance two minutes apart to the first line of enemy trenches, which were only twenty-seven metres away.

Unfortunately, it was clear on the morning of the assault that the preconditions for the attack had not been met; the New Zealanders were held up, so Chunuk Bair had not been captured, and Turkish machine guns that flanked The Nek at a position named German Officer's Trench had also not been captured during that night. Despite this, the senior Anzac command ordered that the attack was to proceed; this time the Light Horsemen would support the New Zealanders' attack on Chunuk Bair and not the other way around as originally intended. This change of situation did not bode well for the Australians.

Not only this, but the bombardment appeared to end seven minutes early, at 4.23 a.m. The reason, it later transpired, was a mistake in the synchronising of watches between the artillery and the officers of 3 Light Horse Brigade. The effect of this resulted in the Turks having ample time to man their trenches, knowing an assault was coming. In addition, the neighbouring assaults by 1 and 2 Light Horse Brigades on Turkish Quinn's and the Chessboard had failed by the time 3 Light Horse Brigade must have realised their 'timing' mistake. Thus, when the first wave of 150 men went over the top, the Turks were not only fully prepared to receive the assault, they were also virtually unmolested in their defence.

Realising their likely fate, Lieutenant Colonel Alexander White, commanding 8/LHR, insisted on leading the first wave of 150 men personally. These men, from Victoria, were immediately met by a murderous hail of rifle and machine gun fire. Within thirty seconds, the colonel and most of his men were casualties. It was clearly evident that any continuation of the attack would be futile in these conditions. Supporting attacks by the other light horse brigades had already been aborted, and the supporting assault by the 8/RWF, to the right flank of Colonel White's men, was also suspended. It was clear that the whole attack had failed; however there was no one left in authority to cancel the second wave of Victorians, who two minutes later 'hopped the bags' and, scrambling over the dead and wounded of their fallen comrades, went to the same fate. None of the men shirked their duty. Few made it even halfway.

Charge of the 3rd Light Horse Brigade at the Nek, 7 August 1915.

Attempting to prevent another wave charging into certain death was Lieutenant Colonel Noel Brazier, commander of the 10/LHR. He claimed that *the whole thing was nothing but bloody murder*. Unfortunately, due to marker flags having been seen in the Turkish trenches, Brazier could not persuade the stubborn Brigade Major, Colonel John Antill, who had taken over command of the Brigade, to stop the attack. After a furious row with Antill, who ordered Brazier to *Push on!*, he reluctantly left, but not before he said, *Thanks, but don't forget I told you so.* It is now understood that the marker flags were probably those of 1 Light Horse Brigade, who had briefly captured a trench on their flank.

Brazier ordered the third wave forward, this time men from Western Australia, 10/LHR, who met the same fate as their predecessors. Knowing that it would be certain death, many fell flat to the ground as soon as they had left the trenches, which helped to reduce the casualties suffered in this assault. Brazier again tried to prevent a further wave going over the top, and this time he found Brigadier General Hughes, commander of the brigade, who agreed that sending more men would be futile. Unfortunately, before the message was sent to the last wave to inform them that the attack has been cancelled, part of the fourth wave went over the top. The two principal incompetents in this debacle were Brigadier General Hughes and Colonel Antill. As Les Carlyon wrote,

> 'Hughes was the brigade commander and didn't command; Antill wasn't the brigade commander and he did. Responsibility rattled Hughes and, either consciously or unconsciously, he walked away from it. Antill behaved as he always did, like a bull strung up in barbed wire.'

The tragic deaths suffered at The Nek were the result of bad Australian decision making, and not that of the British command, upon whose shoulders the blame for this tragic event is often erroneously placed.

By the time the Australian commanders realised the futility of the attack, four waves had gone over the top in a little more than fifteen minutes. The ground separating the trenches, little bigger than three tennis courts, was covered with dead and dying light horsemen. The 8/LHR suffered the highest casualties losing 234 of its 300 men, 154 of them fatal; the 10/LHR suffered 138 casualties, eighty of them fatal. For Australia, The Nek was a disaster on an epic scale, but it should be remembered that it is but one incident in a catalogue of almost unmitigated disaster at Gallipoli. For example: The Nek, 372 casualties in one morning; in one night the Australians at Fromelles suffered 5,533 casualties! But The Nek has rightfully been condemned by history as not only a tragic but also a futile attack.

By 6.30 a.m., 7 August, the attacks inside Anzac had come to an end. These had all been in vain and provided no assistance to the New Zealanders, who at this time had not even begun their renewed advance on Chunuk Bair. Bean commented, *For sheer bravery, devoted loyalty, and that self-discipline which seldom failed in Australian soldiers, they stand alone in the annals of their country.*

Chunuk Bair

Whilst the fighting at Lone Pine was ensuring, two columns of infantry under the direction of Major General Alexander Godley began their night attack in an attempt to break out from the old Anzac perimeter. The plan centred on these columns striking north along Ocean Beach and, at a pre-designated point, turning at right angles, to head in an easterly direction. They would then split into three assaulting columns: 4 Australian Brigade's objective was Hill 971, 29 Indian Brigade's was Hill Q and the New Zealand Infantry Brigade's was Chunuk Bair. Sari Bair needed to be captured by dawn on 7 August.

Major General Alexander Godley.

An advance over unopposed but tortuous mountainous terrain in daylight is a difficult task, but doing this at night against opposition was almost impossible. This was exacerbated by the condition of already battle-worn men, laden with heavy loads and weakened by dysentery. The left column, under the command of Brigadier General Herbert Cox, soon found itself in difficulties. Disorientated during the night movement,

57

they failed to follow the correct routes to their objectives. Meanwhile the right column, under the command of Brigadier General Francis Johnston, pressed on as planned up Rhododendron Spur. Although this was a slightly easier route, Johnston was also behind schedule, putting the dawn capture of Chunuk Bair at risk.

As the day dawned Johnston was about 500 metres short of the summit. Unsure of enemy opposition, he halted and waited for rest of the column to catch up. This would be a costly mistake. At this precise moment, the Australian Light Horse were attacking The Nek, believing that the New Zealanders would be pressing on from their newly capture positions in support. Godley ordered Johnston to resume the advance, but by then the charge at The Nek had failed and the Turks had spotted the New Zealanders below. The Auckland Battalion was hurriedly sent forward to storm Chunuk Bair, but in the daylight took heavy casualties. Johnston then ordered the Wellington Battalion to follow, but their commanding officer, Lieutenant Colonel William Malone, refused. He would attack at dawn.

So it was that at dawn on 8 August Malone led his Wellington men up onto the summit of Chunuk Bair as promised, supported by two British battalions, the 7/Glosters and 8/Welsh. With the summit captured, there followed a series of fierce counter-attacks and murderous enfilade fire from Hill Q to the north, and Battleship Hill to the south. The new defenders were almost annihilated, and had to pull back to the reverse slope. The open crest of the summit afforded no protection, and to dig down into the rocky soil proved impossible under such a heavy fire. Evacuating the crest allowed the Turks to use the now dead ground on the forward slope to edge their way forward. Without Hill Q or Battleship Hill captured, holding on to Chunuk Bair was proving an impossible task.

On 9 August Godley once again renewed the attack. Cox's 29th Indian column needed to take Hill Q to give Johnston the best chance of success and similarly Monash's 4 Brigade needed to take Hill 971. For support, Brigadier General Anthony Baldwin's 38 Brigade was ordered forward. The day brought little success; units, over-tired, lost, demoralised and lacking water, failed to reach any of their objectives with the exception of one. However, the single glimmer of hope that day, the achievement of 6/Gurkha Rifles, went unnoticed.

Major Cecil Allanson, commanding 6/Gurkhas, had managed to get his battalion very close to the summit of Hill Q, where he waited fruitlessly throughout 8 August, under fire, for support. On 9 August he decided that he could wait no longer. At 5.00 a.m., after a pre-planned bombardment had lifted, he made a heroic assault on the hill.

After desperate hand-to-hand fighting his men gained the summit, but then a salvo of shells fell on top of the position. As quickly as the hill was captured, it was lost again. With so many casualties, Allanson, now wounded, pulled back from the crest and returned to the reverse slopes whence he had come. Controversially the shells were believed to have come from either a Royal Navy vessel or a New Zealand field artillery battery. Godley was totally unaware that Allanson had briefly gain Hill Q, as were the neighbouring New Zealanders on Chunuk Bair.

Major Cecil Allanson, Gurkha Rifles.

At nightfall, Malone's New Zealanders were finally relieved, but not before very heavy casualties and the loss of their commander. Malone, it is believed, was also a casualty of friendly artillery fire. The battered New Zealand survivors, the Wellington's alone having suffered 711 out of 760 men, were relieved by two British battalions, 6/Loyal North Lancs and 5/Wiltshires, but their stay was to be brief. Just before dawn, on 10 August, unsupported by artillery, Kemal led a surprise bayonet attack that overwhelmed those on Chunuk Bair. The 6/Loyals fought a brave last stand action, but nothing could stop the speed and ferocity of Kemal's attack which pushed the intermingled British, Indian and New Zealand troops from all along the Sari Bair Ridge. The counter-attack was costly; during the eight hours of fighting some 9,000 Ottoman casualties were recorded; but the action was decisive. Never again during the campaign would British troops stand upon

Lieutenant Colonel William Malone, Wellington Regiment.

Sari Bair. The August offensive had failed, an attack that had, it must be admitted, only ever had a slim hope of success. Even if it had the capture of Sari Bair would not have been final. There would have still been a hard, long and costly slog to reach the Dardanelles. Kemal held the high ground but could not push the Anzacs into the sea, whilst if the Anzacs had held the high ground they would have faced similar issues trying to push the Turks into the Dardanelles.

Little to show for the fighting – Turkish machine guns captured by the New Zealanders during the August breakout.

By the end of August the allies were virtually back where they began: in the trenches at Helles, on the foothills at Anzac and on the beach at Suvla. The offensive had battered itself to a stalemate, which many believe was inevitable. Hamilton had played his last card and lost. The August offensive gained large expanses of territory; but without the heights the gains gave minimal tactical advantage to the British. Hamilton's force was dwindling by the day in fighting strength and physical ability, with little hope of further reinforcements, whilst the Turks continued to become stronger by the day. Evacuation was once again on the lips of the MEF.

Anzac – The Tours

These trails are divided into two parts; the landings area and the ridges. Both can be completed within a day by vehicle, or over two days by foot. The starting and finishing point for the drive is the **Gallipoli Presentation Centre (*Çannakale Destanı Tanıtım Merkezi* – 40°12'25.5"N 26°16'52.0"E)** near Gaba Tepe; for the landings trail it is the Anzac Commemoration Site.

Getting to Anzac: From Eceabat, follow the road north for two kilometres until you reach the roundabout near the coast, signposted for Anzak Koyu (Anzac Cove). Turn left and drive about eight kilometres across the peninsula. This will bring you to the Aegean coast, with the road turning north. Follow the coastal road for one kilometre until you reach the Gallipoli Presentation Centre (Çannakale Destanı Tanıtım Merkezi).

    The Gallipoli Presentation Centre consists of various galleries telling the Turkish story of the campaign, through the use of 3D films, from the early naval attacks to the evacuation. Screenings are in various languages and last approximately ninety minutes. There are battlefield relics on display, a souvenir shop and toilet facilities. If you have not been to Gallipoli before it is a recommended stop as it will give you an insight into the modern Turkish view of the campaign and how its legacy still endures today. Allow two hours for this visit.

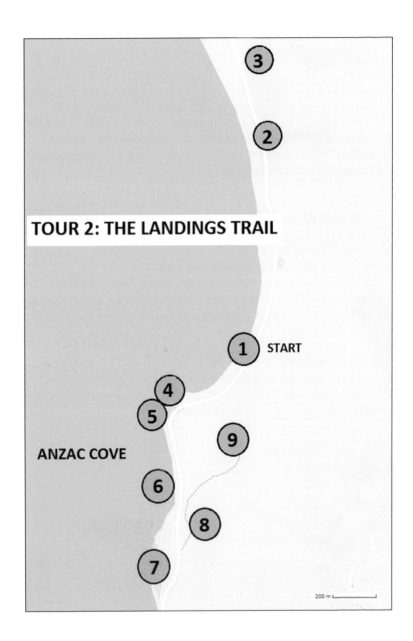

TOUR 2: THE LANDINGS TRAIL

START

ANZAC COVE

200 m

Tour 2

The Landings Trail

Begin this six kilometre walking tour at the **Anzac Commemoration Site (1) (40°14'26.8"N 26°16'52.4"E)**, where the Anzac Day Dawn Service is held. The site contains campaign information panels, and offers amazing views of the eroded sandy outcrop known as the Sphinx and the lower ridges of the Anzac area. It was this sight, in the dim light of dawn, that ominously welcomed the covering force as they rowed ashore on 25 April 1915.

Official Australian war correspondent and later official war historian, Charles Bean, described this spot:

> 'The ridge led down to the sea in only two places, at either end of the semicircle, by the steep slopes of Plugge's on the right, and by a tortuous spur (afterwards known as Walker's Ridge) on the left. Between the two, exactly in the middle of the semicircle of cliffs, there had once been a third spur, but the weather had eaten it away. Its bare gravel face stood out, for all the world like that of a Sphinx, sheer above the middle of the valley … To the Australians from that day it was the Sphinx.'
>
> *The Story of Anzac*, pp 267–8.

It was on this beach where the first boats landed. After the landing this area became a vital operational base, although it was exposed to shell

Anzac Commemoration site in the shadow of the Sphinx.

and sniper fire for much of the campaign. It was only after the August offensive that North Beach became less dangerous due to the front line being pushed back some distance. On the flat areas hospital tents were erected; even a post office could be found! North Beach not only witnessed some of the first men ashore, but also the last. During the evacuation of Anzac some of the last men to leave were by the piers that stretched out from the beach to waiting lighters to carry them away.

Leave the commemoration site and continue north towards Fisherman's Hut. Following the beach road northwards for 1 kilometre, you will pass Canterbury Cemetery and the CWGC base and cottage, which is in front of the area known as No.1 Outpost. Continue on until you reach **Fisherman's Hut (2) (40°14'58.2"N 26°16'55.8"E).** It is marked today as it was in 1915 by a small stone hut. A second hut was originally situated on the inland side of this sandy knoll, called Shepherd's Hut, but sadly this no longer exists. On the morning of 25 April, four boats carrying men from 7/AIF landed in front of Fisherman's Hut. A well-disciplined platoon, under the command of Second Lieutenant Ibrahim Hayreddin, withheld fire until the boats were close to the shore, and then opened up on the small crowded boats. Lieutenant Herbert Layh told Bean, *as we drew near we could see that the water was being churned up by the bullets and that we were in for a hot time. The rowers pulled hard, and we entered the beaten zone at a good pace. The bullets zipped around us like bees.* One by one the rowers were hit, although that did not stop the boats as others immediately took over their oars. In one boat five out of the six oarsmen were shot. Layh jumped over the side and into the water, where he was immediately shot through the hip, and seconds later through the leg. Those who could move or were not hit scrambled to the shore and took shelter behind grass-tufted sand hummocks that fringed that area of the beach. Out of the 140 men that tried to land here, only around 35 reached the beach unscathed or lightly

A panorama drawing of the main Anzac positions in July 1915.

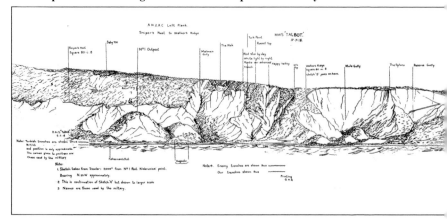

wounded, the remainder lay in the boats or on the beach, dead or dying. By the time the survivors had rejoined the rest of the battalion, only eighteen remained.

About 250 metres further on is **No.2 Outpost Cemetery (3) (40°15'08.0"N 26°16'55.7"E)**, situated in front of the position that was called No.2 Outpost. This cemetery contains the known graves of thirty-two soldiers from New Zealand, seven from Australia, three from the UK and sixty-two who could not be identified. There are special memorials to sixty-six soldiers who are known to be buried in this cemetery. Of the graves, twenty-eight have been identified as soldiers from 7/AIF who were killed or died of wounds during the landing at Fisherman's Hut. One of these was 20-year old Private Alexander McArthur (Sp. Mem. 27), a red-head from Ascot Vale, Victoria, who was mortally wounded,

shot through his femoral artery. He continued to row as a colleague tried to staunch the flow of blood until McArthur was reported to cry, *I'm done!* before collapsing. Several of the burials have their date of death stated as 25 April – 2 May 1915, as it was not clear when those who were mortally wounded died, and it was not until early May that they could be buried.

Retrace your steps along the road; if you prefer to walk along North Beach, follow this back past the commemoration site and on to **Ari Burnu Cemetery (4) (40°14'19.8"N 26°16'37.7"E)**. Several boats from the initial wave of the covering force

Ari Burnu CWGC Cemetery.

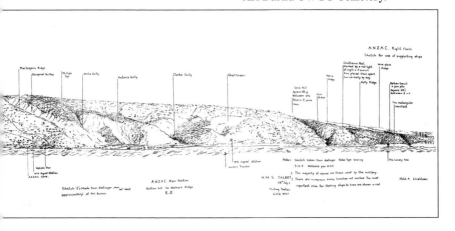

actually beached here, just before 4.30 a.m., on 25 April. The cemetery contains the graves of 151 Australians soldiers, 35 New Zealanders, 27 from the UK, one from the Maltese Labour Corps, 37 unidentified and five Special Memorials. Of the graves, 82 are Australian Light Horse, including several from 8 and 10/LHR who fell during the ill-fated Nek attack. These include the West Australian Chipper brothers, Lance Corporal Lindsay (*E.19*) and Trooper Ross Chipper (*E.15*). Several light horse officers who died in the attack are also buried here, including Lieutenant Colonel Albert Miell (*A.17*), commander of 9/LHR, who was shot dead whilst directing fire support for the assault. Another notable grave is that of Lance Corporal Vivian Brooke (*G.20*), 12/AIF, who fell wounded and was later captured on 25 April. Brooke, a 27-year-old bank clerk from Tasmania, was a well-known amateur athlete, footballer and cricketer. Tragically, on 29 April, Brooke was wounded once again, this time by a British shell that accidentally hit a building in Maidos that was being used as a Turkish hospital. Brooke died of his wounds on 4 May, and was buried locally in Biga; he was moved here after the war.

Leave the cemetery, noting the bronze Ross Bastiaan Plaque (No.1), and stop at the **Atatürk Memorial (5)**, found just outside the cemetery. It was unveiled on Anzac Day 1985 and the inscription is based on Kemal Atatürk's 1934 address to the Allied pilgrims. The wording includes *Those heroes that shed their blood and lost their lives, You are now lying in the soil of a friendly country.*

Ataturk Memorial – *Those Heroes that shed their blood ...*

Leave the memorial and walk 500 metres along the road above the now famous **Anzac Cove (6) (40°14'04.4"N 26°16'38.9"E)** (*Anzak Koyu*). During the campaign this small and sheltered cove of barely twenty-five metres width and 600 metres length was the main rest area during the first months of the campaign, although it was never safe. From the first day to the last a gun, nicknamed 'Beachy Bill', would fire on the beach and was believed to have caused some 1,000 casualties. At the time of writing the safest way to reach the beach is via the steps that lead down from Ari Burnu Cemetery.

Anzac Cove today.

Continue along the coastal road for 400 metres, passing the signs to Shrapnel Valley and the parking area, to **Beach Cemetery (7) (40°13'58.7"N 26°16'35.3"E)**, noting the Ross Bastiaan Plaque (No.2). Until the centenary, these markers were the only information panels to be found on the battlefield; since then the CWGC have erected information boards at their cemeteries and memorials, recently supplemented by further information boards that the Turkish Directorate of Gallipoli Historical Site (Çanakkale Savaşları Gelibolu) have placed at key battlefield points. The cemetery was begun on the day of the landings and continued to be used throughout the campaign. It contains 285 graves of Australian soldiers, 50 (including sailors and RND) from the UK, 21 from New Zealand, three from Ceylon and 21 whose bodies are unidentified; and special memorials that record ten Australians and one New Zealander who are believed to be buried here.

Beach CWGC Cemetery.

Notable burials include Lieutenant Colonel Lancelot Clarke DSO, *(I.B.13)*, commanding officer 12/AIF, who was sniped on 25 April near The Nek whilst writing a field message to Sinclair-MacLagan. Officers and NCOs were often conspicuous because of their command duties and were vulnerable to snipers, who sought such prized targets. Captain Edward Bage *(I.D.7)*, who was a member of the famed 1911-13 Mawson Antarctica Expedition, is also buried here. He was amongst a small group of the Expedition that volunteered to remain behind to wait for Sir Douglas Mawson to return. Bage was killed on 7 May whilst surveying ground in front of the Australian trenches near Lone Pine. Also resting here is Major Charles Villiers-Stuart *(I.H.4)*, 56th Punjabi Rifles. An Indian Army officer, he was attached to General Birdwood's Anzac Corps HQ as chief intelligence officer. Villiers-Stuart had played an important part in gathering intelligence for the landing, having conducted an air reconnaissance of the Anzac landing site on 14 April 1915. Villiers-Stuart was killed by a shell on 17 May whilst sketching near Anzac Cove. Another officer killed by a shell was 'the bloke with the eye-glass', Commander Edward Cater Royal Navy *(II.G.5)*, Assistant Beach Master. Cater commanded a small beach party that was responsible for directing incoming boats and supervising beach parties at Anzac. He had won the respect of all for his cool disregard of Turkish shellfire whilst he assisted others on the beach. He was well known to the Anzacs, and stood out

68

because of the large monocle he wore. The story goes that some Australians approached him one day with their identity discs in their eye. Cater looked at them, threw up his monocle into the air, caught it in his eye and said, *Do that, you blighters!* He was killed on 7 August.

A mass grave in Beach Cemetery.

One of the most legendary Australian figures buried here was actually an Englishman from South Shields in northern England, Private John Simpson Kirkpatrick *(I.F.1)*, 3/Field Ambulance, who was killed, aged 22, on 19 May. He was famed as 'the Man with the Donkey'. Serving under the name of Private 'Jack' Simpson, he landed early on 25 April with his unit and began to work the beaches and inland slopes, bringing in wounded men. The following day he found a lone donkey that he used from then on to move the

Simpson, the man with his donkey.

wounded. It is thought that he used two different donkeys that went under several names, including Murphy, Duffy, Abdul and Queen Elizabeth, all depending on what mood he was in. As with many soldiers, he became

69

Jack Simpson, one of the most visited graves at Gallipoli.

fatalistic and paid little attention to the shelling and sniping along his route from the ridge to the beach. On the morning of 19 May, during the Turkish counter-attack, he was killed by machine-gun fire.

On a clear day, looking from Beach Cemetery directly out to sea, you will see the Turkish island of Gökçeada (Imbros), the island that Hamilton used as his headquarters. During the campaign Imbros was a rest area for the troops on Gallipoli, where it housed a multitude of tented camps, casualty clearing stations, field bakeries, airfields and supply depots. Nestled behind this island to the north-wet is the Greek island of Samothrace.

From Beach Cemetery return along the main road, retracing your steps about 200 metres, and take the small track on the inland side of the road that is signposted to 'CWGC Shrapnel Valley Cemetery – Plugge's Plateau Cemetery'.

70

Shrapnel Valley CWGC Cemetery.

Shrapnel Valley Cemetery (8) (40°14'02.3"N 26°16'42.2"E) contains 527 soldiers from Australian, 56 from New Zealand, 28 from the UK, 72 unidentified graves and 23 Special Memorials. There are 24 burials here that date from the landings. Note the Ross Bastiaan Plaque (No.3). The cemetery is the largest of the original cemeteries at Anzac; Lone Pine Cemetery contains more burials today but was created after the war. It was made soon after the landing and was enlarged slightly after the Armistice when nearby isolated graves were concentrated into it; but generally the layout of the cemetery today is the same as it was in 1915.

There are many graves that are of interest here. These include Major Hugh Quinn *(III.C.21)*, 15/AIF, who was instrumental in setting up the Post that would be named after him. Quinn, a pre-war militia soldier and keen boxer, was killed on 29 May at Quinn's Post. At 3.20 a.m. that morning the Turks detonated a mine that destroyed part of the Post, and followed this up with an attack that captured most of it. It was whilst Quinn was reconnoitring the ground for a counter-attack that he was shot in the head and died instantly. The planned charge went ahead and the Post was retaken. Quinn's body was recovered and he was laid to rest in this cemetery. A few rows away is the grave of Private George Grimwade *(II.D.34)*, 6/Field Ambulance. Grimwade, aged 20, was a medical student

71

from Melbourne who was studying to be a doctor before the war. On 23 September, while on guard duty at a water tank, he was hit by shrapnel; mortally wounded, he died within minutes of reaching the aid post. His fellow Melbourne Grammar boys dug his grave that evening, refusing to let anyone else perform this duty. In 1922 his parents visited his grave and placed a stone by it from their Melbourne home, inscribed in 'ever loving remembrance'. Two of his brothers also served their country; a younger brother served in the Royal Navy, and an elder brother was a member of the Royal Flying Corps in England.

Buried close by is another Melbourne boy, Corporal James Burns *(II.D.37)*. He was an exemplary student and sportsman, with a gift for writing. By 1913 he was the editor of Melbourne's Scotch College magazine and had a number of his articles and poems published. At the time that Burns applied to university the war had begun. Along with many others he joined up, enlisting in 21/AIF. With little more than six months training, the battalion were on their way to Egypt. It was about this time, in May 1915, that Burns composed a poem for which he would be famed, *For England*. The poem gives an insight into the patriotic response that came from the far-flung corners of the Empire when Britain's call to arms went out. Many of the young men who joined from Australia and New Zealand felt a duty and loyalty to their mother country that today some find difficult to comprehend. The powerful sense of comradeship and sharing a common cause with England saw thousands volunteering, many of whom, like Burns, never did get to see the 'mother country'. Burns, who survived the torpedoing of the transport ship HMT *Southland* whilst on the way to Gallipoli, was barely ashore a fortnight before he was mortally wounded near Courtney's Post. He died at 5/Field Ambulance a few hours later, on 18 September.

Shrapnel Valley, which was known to the Turks as the Valley of Fear (*Korku Dere*), became the main highway for the Anzacs from the beach to the trenches, so the area was always under constant shelling and sniper fire. Confronted with this constant danger, men quickly became 'fatalists', working on the basis that a particular shell or bullet had a man's name and number on it and so, until it arrived, it was best to ignore them and carry on as normal. This is the valley along which Jack Simpson and his donkey brought wounded from the front. The upper part of the valley was called Monash Gully.

Follow the sign and path by the seaward side of the cemetery up to Plugge's Plateau. When you have reached the sign marked '570m', you have done the easy bit; the walk gets rather harder as the path winds its way steeply to the top. The strenuous twenty-minute walk will take you along MacLagan's Ridge and then to the top of Plugge's Plateau (a

Plugge's Plateau CWGC Cemetery.

hundred metres high) and its associated CWGC cemetery. This hill was named Treacherous Hill (*Hain Tepe*) by the Turks and Plugge's Plateau by the Anzacs, after Lieutenant Colonel Arthur Plugge. He commanded the Auckland Battalion NZEF during the landings and had established his HQ there during the first day. Once on the plateau you are rewarded by some spectacular views of the surrounding battlefield; all over the plateau are remains of trenches, walled sangars and field gunpits, although many others have eroded away or have become covered by dense prickly scrub. It is worth spending some time exploring the plateau as there is much to see.

Plugge's Plateau Cemetery (9) (40°14'15.0"N 26°16'49.1"E) is the smallest cemetery at Anzac, containing just twelve Australian graves, eight from New Zealand and one that is unidentified. Of these casualties, twelve were killed on 25 April, some of the first Australians to die at Gallipoli. Private Frank Batt *(B.8)*, 10/AIF, was killed in action. He was from Cornwall in England, but lived in his new home town of Broken Hill, NSW. He had served as a regular soldier in the East Surrey Regiment, seeing service in the Boer War, then emigrated and worked in Australia as a miner. Many of the soldiers serving in the Australian and New Zealand forces were in fact of British origin.

Return by the same path to Shrapnel Valley Cemetery, and then return to your vehicle/start point, where this tour ends.

Tour 3

The Ridge Trail

Begin this fifteen kilometre driving/walking tour at the **Gallipoli Presentation Centre (10)** (*Çannakale Destanı Tanıtım Merkezi -* **40°12'25.5"N 26°16'52.0"E)**, a visit to which is not included in the timings of this tour. Leave the site and follow the signs north to Anzac; after 750 metres take the ridge road immediately to the right. This road was built by the Turks soon after the evacuation and rises from the bottom of Legge Valley up on to Pine Ridge, 400 Plateau and Second Ridge. **NB!** Note that this road is one-way.

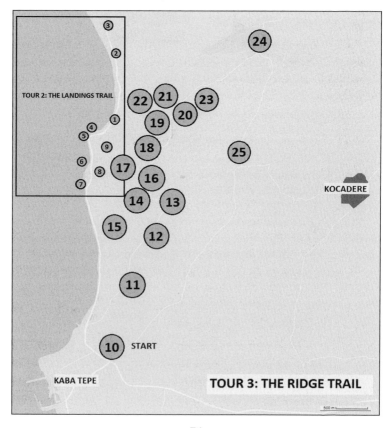

Respect to the Turkish Soldier Memorial.

After just over one kilometre you will reach the nearby **Respect to the Turkish Soldier Memorial (11)** (*Mehmetcige Derin Saygi*) **(40°13'12.3"N 26°17'05.4"E)**, depicting a Turk carrying a wounded Australian officer. The statue represents an event that allegedly took place near this point on 25 April.

Situated on the southern spur of Pine Ridge, during the first day of the landing the ridge was held by various units, including those of 6/AIF, before their position was overrun. After the war skeletons covered in ragged uniforms were identified by the red and violet sleeve patch as men from 6/AIF, lying in groups of three and four down the length of Pine Ridge. Ahead are the grassy plains of Legge Valley that rise up onto the Third Ridge.

After another kilometre you will arrive at the **Karayörük Stream Cemetery (12)** (*Karayörük Deresi*) (40°13'36.4"N 26°17'23.9"E), reached by steps extending down into the valley. This contains the graves of 1,152 men from 48, 63, 72 and 77 Ottoman Regiments.

Continue on 300 metres until you reach the **Kanlisirt Memorial (13)** (40°13'44.9"N 26°17'28.3"E), which stands on the Turkish slope of Lone Pine, known to the Turks as Bloody Ridge (*Kanlisirt*). The memorial's inscription refers to the defence of Lone Pine during the August offensive. It was close to here that Australians overran a Turkish gun battery in The Cup during the morning of 25 April; after fierce counter-attacks in the late afternoon the position and guns were lost. On 6 August Australians fought their way close to this position once again but were forced back later in the battle.

Continue on 500 metres until you reach the **Lone Pine Memorial and Cemetery (14)** (40°13'49.6"N 26°17'13.7"E). Note the Ross Bastiaan Plaque (No.5). Lone Pine is the southern spur or lobe of 400 Plateau; it derived its name from the song *The Trail of the Lonesome Pine* and from a single pine tree that stood on this plateau during the early days of the campaign. Because of this position's tactical importance, overlooking Gaba Tepe to the south, it saw fierce fighting during April and August 1915 as both sides jostled for its capture. Fortified by the Turks in May, it remained in their hands until its recapture on 6 August, an action which resulted in seven Australians winning the Victoria Cross.

Lone Pine Cemetery originally contained only forty-six graves but it was enlarged after the Armistice by concentrating many of the scattered battlefield graves in the area and casualties buried in the Brown's Dip cemeteries. Today the cemetery contains 1,167 graves, of which 651 are Australian, two New Zealand, fifteen from the UK and 499 men who could not be identified. There are special memorial tablets in the cemetery that commemorate the names of 182 Australians and one from the UK who are believed to be buried in this cemetery. There are seventy-three identified graves of men killed during the first few days of the landings.

Amongst these is Lieutenant Colonel Richard Nelson Bendyshe *(III.D.6)*, commanding Deal Battalion, Royal Marine Light Infantry (RMLI), who was tragically killed on 1 May. Bendyshe, a relation to Lord Nelson, saw action at Dunkirk and Antwerp in 1914, before arriving at Gallipoli. He landed with the battalion on 29 April, when they relieved

Lone Pine Memorial and Cemetery.

AUSTRALIAN LIGHT HORSE
1ST REGIMENT

MAJOR	TROOPER
REID J. M.	ADELT C.
	BAKER H. L.
CAPTAIN	BOSEMAN J.
COX W.	BULMER A.
	BURNS H. M.
LIEUTENANT	CAMPBELL H.
NETTLETON B. P.	CLARK A. J.
TINSON G. E. I.	COOPER C. T.
	CRICHTON W. D.
SQD. QMR. SERJT.	DE LEPER VANCHE R. C.
CARR R. M.	FOLLENT J. M.
	FRASER D. A.
SERJEANT	HAMILTON H. P.
BARRY W. J.	HENDERSON D.
CAILLE E.	HILLS C.
SERVED AS	JEFFREY J.
ELLIS G.	KANE F. W.
GIBSON R. W.	KEMPE R. S.
GREEN J.	KOLTS H. F.
KERR H. Y.	LAUNT L. C.
YOUNG F. R. C.	LEE S.
	LUTTRELL F.
CORPORAL	MC KAY J. L.
CLUETT E.	MC MASTER A. H.
MC DONALD K. V.	MAGEE E. W.
	MAGRATH G. W.
LANCE CPL.	MANNING A. G.
CRISP F. G., D. C. M.	MARTIN J.
WHEATLEY T. C.	NEWTON G. E.

**The memorial panel to the 1st
Australian Light Horse Regiment**

the 6/AIF. Bendyshe was being escorted through the trenches by the Australian commanding officer, Lieutenant Colonel Walter McNicholl, who, unshaven, heavily tanned and wearing a torn and tattered uniform, was in direct contrast to the smart English officer. One jumpy Royal Marine, suspicious that McNicholl might be a disguised Turk, raised his rifle to his shoulder and fired at McNicholl but the bullet missed, and struck Bendyshe in the stomach, killing him. Pandemonium then broke out with men running along the trench, towards the spot, firing wildly. A RMLI Sergeant Major and two other men were also shot. McNicholl was attacked with bayonets, one he deflected with his hand, through his tunic, entering at the button and out by the shoulder but only grazing the skin and another, which left a triangular hole in his left sleeve. Another sergeant took charge and shouted at the men to get back to the parapet. They knocked McNicholl to the bottom of the trench on his back, the sergeant telling the nearest man 'Put your bayonet on his chest and if he speaks a word, pull the trigger'. They then searched their 'spy' removing his notebooks and revolver and then tied his hands and blindfolded him and marched him under armed escort down a communication trench. The first man they met was the 6/AIF's Adjutant, whose language on recognising his commanding officer was reported to be 'in the finest tradition of the AIF'.

Thirty identified men of 24/AIF and a further ten from 23/AIF are buried here who were killed during a bombardment of Lone Pine on 29 November. The position had come under increasingly heavy fire throughout the morning and, a little after midday, as the men of 24/AIF were making their way along the deep and narrow trenches and shallow tunnels of the approach trenches to relieve members of 23/AIF, the bombardment intensified. Witnesses watched the men enter a tunnel just before heavy enemy shelling found its mark and caused the tunnel to collapse, burying the men alive. Amongst those trapped in the cave-in was a 19-year-old engineer, Private Frederick Stevens (*I.C.29*), from Victoria, who had left Melbourne. Sergeant William Vale of his company told the Red Cross Missing and Wounded Enquiry Bureau that the men of 24/AIF had not been able to locate all of those buried by the shells. Stevens' body, however, was one of those found and was buried in Brown's Dip Cemetery before being moved after the war to Lone Pine.

Lone Pine looking across onto Johnston's Jolly, Sari Bair and the rear of the Turkish line.

Within the grounds of the cemetery is the Lone Pine Memorial, which commemorates 4,936 Australian and New Zealand servicemen who died in the Anzac area and whose graves are not known or who were buried at sea. The New Zealanders have other memorials to the missing, in line with the country's approach of having such memorials as close to the location of the action in which these men were killed. Here the NZEF names are those who died prior to August 1915. For the Chunuk Bair offensive and subsequent fighting in the area the names are commemorated on the Chunuk Bair Memorial. There are further New Zealand memorials at Hill 60 (North Anzac) and Twelve Tree Copse (Helles).

Amongst those commemorated is Lieutenant Colonel Douglas Stewart (*Mem:73*), commanding officer of the Canterbury Battalion, who pre-war was a shipping agent/accountant from Christchurch. He was killed in action near The Nek on 25 April, in an action that cost the lives of many New Zealanders from the Canterbury and Auckland regiments. A soldier originally from Malta, Private Charles Bonavia (*Mem:33*), 11/AIF, is also commemorated on these panels. Charles was the son of Emanuel, who was the registrar at the Malta Law Courts. He lived in Valetta and studied at the University of Malta before immigrating to Perth, Australia in August 1911. He was employed as an assistant surveyor with the Lands Department before enlisting in 1914. He was initially reported missing on 25 April, but later presumed killed. His service record states that *he was very much loved, and considered very clever by his regiment.* Malta played a significant role in the Gallipoli campaign, providing labourers who later served under Maltese officers,

a naval base and also hosted hospitals and convalescent depots that looked after many thousands of casualties from the Gallipoli campaign.

Captain Alfred Shout VC MC (*Panel 12*), 1/AIF, was a New Zealand born Boer War veteran. He won a Military Cross for gallantry during the Anzac landings and for his actions in the fighting at Lone Pine was awarded the Victoria Cross. On 9 August, during the action, he was mortally wounded by a bomb that prematurely exploded in his hand. He died on a hospital ship and was buried at sea. Another of the Lone Pine VCs commemorated here is Corporal Alex Burton (*Panel 28*), 7/AIF, who was killed early on 9 August whilst defending a barricaded sap. Lieutenant Colonel Alexander White (*Panel 5*), 8/LHR, and many of his men from the disastrous charge at The Nek are named here, as are those from 10/LHR (*Panels 5-10*). These include the Harper brothers, Troopers Wilfred and Gresley, the inspiration for the main characters 'Archy' and 'Frank' in Peter Weir's film *Gallipoli*. Charles Bean, the Australian official historian, stated that Wilfrid was *last seen running forward like a schoolboy in a foot race with all the speed he could compass.*

Among the missing listed on the memorial is Australia's youngest soldier, Private James Martin, 21/AIF. Martin was from Melbourne and enlisted on 12 April 1915, aged 14 years and three months. Like many boys anxious to play an active part in the war, he lied about his age, claiming to be 18, and he even obtained his parents' consent to enlist. Martin landed with his unit on 6 September and the following day took up a position in the line. It was not to be enemy action that killed Martin, but sickness. Through constant work, food shortages and illness, the battalion's numbers dwindled; amongst those evacuated sick on 25 October was Private Martin, suffering from enteritis. He died on board the hospital ship *Glenart Castle* and was buried at sea the same day.

Optional Walk

Shell Green (15)

(40°13'32.7"N 26°16'48.5"E)

The Shell Green CWGC Cemetery is approximately one kilometre down a rough track from Lone Pine. The track follows the original route of Artillery Road, which was built during the campaign. Shell Green, originally a sloping cotton field on the seaward side of Bolton's Ridge, was captured by 8/AIF on 25 April and passed as the battalion advanced up onto the ridge in front. Being so close to the front line, the area was subjected to frequent shelling. At the time of the evacuation, the flat open area in front of the cemetery was used for a cricket match held on 17 December to deceive the Turks in thinking all was well. The cemetery was used from May to December 1915. Originally two separate cemeteries, they were brought together after the Armistice, along with various isolated battlefield burials and graves that were moved from Artillery Road, Artillery Road East, Wright's Gully and The Eighth Battery cemeteries. There is also a Kelia Liman Plot, comprising post-war graves that were removed from Kelia Liman Cemetery in 1927, situated near Maidos (Eceabat). There are a total of 409 burials, of which eleven are unidentified. Of the identified, twenty-two are listed as being killed during April. Note the Ross Bastiaan Plaque (No.4).

Shell Green CWGC Cemetery.

Playing Cricket on Shell Green, December 1915.

Buried here is the uncle of the war correspondent Alan Moorehead, the author of a classic account of the campaign, *Gallipoli*. Private Frank Moorehead (*Artillery Rd. Plot.19*), 8/AIF, was killed between 25-28 April. His epitaph states that *He did his share*. Another early burial is that of 45-year-old Boer War veteran Major John Sergeant (*Artillery Rd. Plot.6*), 8/AIF. Wounded through the hand earlier that day, he was killed on 25 April by a shell whilst leading his company forward from Bolton's Ridge. He was later Mentioned in Despatches. His epitaph reads, *Mate o' Mine*. Other moving epitaphs include those of Private Harold Smith, 12/AIF, who was killed on 20 May - *Mother is proud of her hero though he was only a private*; and that of Lance Corporal Thomas Sage, 8/AIF, who was killed on 26 April and reads *How can man die better, than fighting fearful odds*, a line from the poem *Horatius*, by Lord Macaulay.
    Return to Lone Pine.

Leave Lone Pine, and continue along the one-way system for about 250 metres, where you will find by the side of the road Australian trenches in various states of preservation. Close by is Owen's Gully, named after Lieutenant Colonel Robert Owen, who commanded 3/AIF. Continue until you reach **Johnston's Jolly Cemetery (16) (40°13'57.6"N 26°17'15.1"E)**. The cemetery is situated on Johnston's Jolly, the northern lobe of 400 Plateau, known to the Turks as Red Ridge (*Kirmizi Sirt*). The Australians named it after Lieutenant Colonel George Johnston, an Australian artillery brigade commander, who placed his field guns opposite this position in order to *jolly up the Turks*. The cemetery was made after the Armistice and today contains 181 graves, fourteen of which are unidentified. One grave from the 6 August Lone Pine attack is that of Lieutenant 'Dickie' Seldon (*Sp.Mem.16*), 4/AIF. He was hit in the face, losing an eye, during the initial charge, and killed whilst leading a bombing party down a trench that led into Owen's Gully.
    Continue along the road for about 150 metres until you reach the sign for 4th Battalion Parade Ground Cemetery. To the right is Wire Gully,

where Lance Corporal Walter Parker RMLI won the first Victoria Cross at Anzac. From Stapleford in Nottinghamshire, pre-war Parker worked at the Stanton Ironworks before enlisting into the RMLI at the outbreak of war. In Wire Gully, a forward area of Maclaurin's Hill, were a series of outposts that were fiercely defended by the marines *without means of reinforcement, replenishment or retreat*, according to their battalion commander. Parker, during the night of 30 April / 1 May, volunteered to take ammunition, water and medical stores to an isolated trench containing about forty men and several wounded. There were no communication trenches leading to the position, which lay off some 360 metres away across bullet swept ground. Several men had tried to reach this position but had been killed in the attempt. He managed to reach the trench, where he treated the wounded and helped evacuate the position early the next morning. Severely wounded during this action, Parker was eventually invalided out of the service in June 1916. Owing to the fact that there were so many officer casualties, the recommendation for gallantry was much delayed, so it took until June 1917 before the award was finally gazetted. His wounds never healed properly and he died, aged 55, in November 1936.

Australian trenches near Johnston's Jolly CWGC Cemetery.

Optional Walk

4th Battalion Parade Ground (17)

(40°14'03.8"N 26°17'09.7"E)

From the sign, follow the 200-metre stepped, steep path to the cemetery. The cemetery was started by 4/AIF at the end of April and was used until the beginning of June 1915. Here the battalion buried thirty-four of its dead, and six from other units. The cemetery is built on the southern slope of Braund's Hill, named after Lieutenant Colonel Braund, who was accidentally shot by a sentry near here on 4 May and is buried in Beach Cemetery. It is off a pathway called Bridges Road that went from Wire Gully down through Shrapnel Valley. After the Armistice the cemetery was enlarged by the concentration of seventy-six graves from two smaller cemeteries that were close by (3rd Battalion Parade Ground and 22nd Battalion Parade Ground) as well as by some isolated battlefield graves.

Two NSW high ranking officers are buried here, including Colonel Henry MacLaurin (*A.10*), commanding 1 (Australian) Brigade. He was shot by a sniper on MacLaurin's Hill on 27 April, the fatal shot coming from Russell's Top, behind the Australian position here. The shot was fired just ten minutes after Major Francis Irvine (*Lone Pine Memorial*), MacLaurin's brigade-major, was killed just a few metres away at Steele's Post. MacLaurin had ignored warnings of snipers – *it's my business to be sniped at*, he said. The following moment, standing in his shirtsleeves, he was shot dead. He was buried near where he fell on the hill that bore his name. The grave was moved into the cemetery after the war. Another commanding officer is Lieutenant Colonel Astley Onslow Thompson (*A.11*), commanding 4/AIF, who was killed on 26 April on 400 Plateau. Originally from Pontypridd, in Glamorganshire, Wales, he was director of several companies in Menangle, NSW. He was buried by a Salvation Army padre, William McKenzie, who later recalled (in the 1949 book *Adelaide Ah Kow*) that

> '… it was a relief to find the body of our colonel … after it had lain out for a full fortnight. We buried it after dark, as it lay in an exposed position. I had to kneel and keep head and body in a crouching posture while reading the service. Hundreds of bullets swept over us while this was going on.'

Return to the road.

4th Bn. Parade Ground CWGC Cemetery sign.

Continue along the road, which rises up on Maclaurin's Hill, and after 200 hundred metres you will come to **Courtney's and Steele's Post Cemetery (18) (40°14'07.4"N 26°17'20.9"E)**. Note the Ross Bastiaan Plaque (No.6). Courtney's Post was named after Lieutenant Colonel Richard Courtney, CO of 14/AIF, who arrived here with his battalion on 27 April. Steel's Post (officially named Steele's) was named after Major Thomas Steel, 14/AIF. Both posts consisted of steep niches, literally a slender foothold on to the ridge, which were defended throughout the

Courtney's and Steele's Post Cemetery.

campaign. The opposing front lines were separated by a No Man's Land the width of the road now running between them. The cemetery, created after 1919, contains 167 burials; seven are of known graves, the others are all unknown. There are fifty four Special Memorials to men who are believed to be buried here. There are four burials of 6/AIF men, killed during the attempt to capture German Officers' Trench on 6/7 August, and a large number of Jacka's men from 14/AIF.

Continue past the cemetery for another 250 metres; where the road bends sharply to the right is the location of Courtney's Post, the site of Lance Corporal Albert Jacka's VC, the first awarded to an Australian at Gallipoli. Jacka repelled several Turks who had broken into Courtney's on 19 May, single-handily recapturing the trench. He stated that he *killed the whole party, five by rifle fire and two with the bayonet.*

Leave Courtney's Post, pass the track on the right to the Turkish Çataldere Memorial and Cemetery *(Çataldere Şehitliği ve Anıtı),* and continue along the road for another 150 metres, stopping at **Quinn's Post Cemetery (19) (40°14'17.3"N 26°17'30.4"E)**. Note also Ross Bastiaan Plaque (No.7). This precariously positioned post was established here on 25 April and was officially named Quinn's Post in May, after Major Hugh Quinn, 15/AIF, who was killed here on 29 May. The Turks later called this area Bomb Ridge (*Bomba Sirt*) because of the concentration of bomb attacks that took place here. From the back of the cemetery there are superb views down to the sea along Monash and Shrapnel Valleys, the main supply routes to this part of the line. To the north-east is a gully that became known as The Bloody Angle, part of Dead Man's Ridge, where the RND attacked on 3 May, and the Australian Light Horse on 7 August. To its left is Pope's Hill, named after Lieutenant Colonel Harold Pope, 14/AIF. This steep razor-backed hill runs in front of Russell's Top and The Nek. Pope had a narrow escape here during 25/26 April when he was nearly captured.

The cemetery was made after the Armistice by concentrating 231 unidentified isolated graves and moving seventy-three graves from Pope's Hill Cemetery (originally located at the foot of Pope's Hill). 179 of the burials are identified. There are sixteen Australian Light Horse casualties from the attacks on Dead Man's Ridge and Turkish Quinn's on 7 August. These include two brothers, now buried side by side, Trooper Fred Sherwood (*C.6*) and Trooper Harold Sherwood (*C.5*).

Leave Quinn's, noting the grave to an unknown *57 Regiment* captain (*Yüzbaşı*) on the opposite side of the road, who was found and buried during the 24 May truce. Continue for another 200 metres to the **57 Regiment Memorial (20) (40°14'24.4"N 26°17'32.7"E)** (*57 Alay Sehitligi ve Aniti*). The memorial park is built on the area known as The

Quinn's Post Cemetery.

Chessboard, named because of the concentration of criss-crossed trenches that were there. The area was held by the Australians on the first day of the landing but was relinquished when Baby 700 fell. 57 Regiment, commanded by Colonel Hüseyin Avni Bey, stemmed the Anzac advance in this area on 25 April, and contained all further attacks. He was killed by a howitzer shell on 13 August; his tomb is in the nearby *Çataldere Şehitliği ve Anıtı*.

57th Regiment Memorial on the Chessboard.

57th Regiment in attack.

Statue of a Turkish Soldier.

The Light Horse attempted to recapture the position during the morning of 7 August, but failed. The park comprises a symbolic martyr's cemetery, with the names of the fallen chosen randomly and displayed as graves or memorial plaques. Note the bronze sculpture of a Turkish veteran, Hüseyin Kaçmaz, with his granddaughter. He was reputed to be the last surviving Turkish veteran of the campaign, dying in 1994 at the age of 110. On the opposite side of the road there is a large statue of a soldier, called *Askerine Saygi Aniti,* which translates as 'Respect to the Turkish soldier'. Behind the monument are the slopes of Baby 700 (*Kiliç Bayir*), where much of the devastating rifle and machine gun fire was directed towards the Australian Light Horse assault at The Nek. Baby 700 was captured by the Anzacs on 25 April; subsequently changing hands several times, it was finally lost under the weight of counter-attacks later that day and never retaken. Near 57 Regiment Memorial is a flight of steps that descends to Kesik Dere Cemetery. A recently constructed cemetery, built in 2006, it records the names of 1,115 soldiers of the 19th Division who fell and are buried in the area. Leave the memorial and continue for 150 metres until the road forks at the head of Monash Valley; take the left-hand turn, which is signposted *Mehmet Cavus Sehitligi,* Nek CWGC Cemetery and Walker's Ridge Cemetery. This will take you onto Russell's Top, captured by the Australians on the first day of the landings.

The Nek CWGC Cemetery (21) (40°14'32.6"N 26°17'25.4"E) was built in No Man's Land. Note also the Ross Bastiaan Plaque (No.8). The Nek, famed for the Australian Light Horse attack, was captured by the

The Nek – *little bigger than three tennis courts, was covered with dead and dying light horsemen.* **Inset: Sergeant Mehmet's Turkish Memorial at The Nek.**

Australians on 25 April, when they overran this area in the early morning before advancing up onto Baby 700 behind. Some of the Australian trenches still remain nearby, close to the cemetery wall. The Nek Cemetery was made after the Armistice and today contains 326 burials, 316 being unidentified. Of the identified burials, four are related to the Light Horse attack of 7 August. Also visit the nearby Sergeant Mehmet's Memorial. The original memorial, to Turks who died when an Australian mine was detonated during the evacuation, was erected not that long after the campaign, built over Turkish trenches at The Nek.

Leave the Cemetery and continue on foot 200 metres along Russell's Top, known to the Turks as *Cesarit Tepe* (Hill of Valour), until you reach **Walker's Ridge CWGC Cemetery (22) (40°14'29.9"N 26°17'18.2"E)**. The ridge was named after Brigadier General Walker, who commanded the New Zealand Infantry Brigade. The cemetery, established during the campaign, contains the known burials of forty New Zealander soldiers, twelve Australian soldiers, one Royal Marine and twelve unidentified graves. In addition, eighteen soldiers from Australia and eight from New Zealand are commemorated by special tablets.

One such commemoration is that of Major David Grant, Canterbury Regiment, (*Sp. Mem. 10*), who died during the afternoon of 25 April. Grant was from Timaru, near Canterbury, on New Zealand's South Island, and had a pre-war career in a large butchering firm. According to the *Auckland Weekly News* he was mortally wounded during a skirmish on

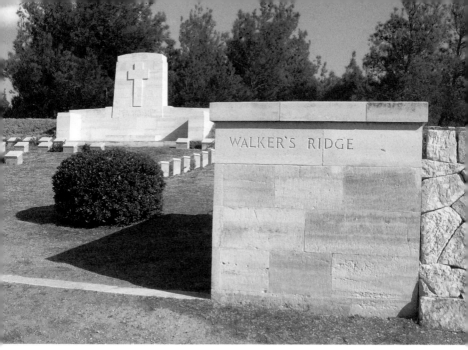

Walker's Ridge CWGC Cemetery.

Baby 700 when he led a group to ambush a machine-gun post. His body was recovered near The Nek during the May Armistice. Interestingly, the CWGC records show he died April 25-29, 1915. There is a memorial to Grant's granddaughter, Rosalind Webb, in the Nurses' Memorial Chapel in Christchurch, New Zealand; she was on a pilgrimage to Gallipoli in 1965 to visit her grandfather's grave when she was killed in a car accident and was buried in the British Consular Cemetery in Çanakkale (see *Chapter 1*).

Amongst the few August burials is English born Trooper Harold Rush (*II.C.4*), 10/LHR, whose last words before charging at The Nek were, *Goodbye Cobber, God bless you*. Also buried here is Major Thomas Redford (*II.C.9*), 8/LHR, also killed at The Nek during the charge. During the night two troopers went out to recover his body and he was laid to rest in this cemetery. An eyewitness of his death wrote:

> 'Our gallant major, whilst lying facing the enemy's trench in front of his men, received a bullet through his brain as he raised his head slightly to observe. He died with a soft sigh and laid his head gently on his hands, as if tired. A braver and more honourable man never donned uniform.'

Trooper Harold Rush.   **"Goodbye Cobber, God Bless You"**

Before you leave Walker's Ridge take a few minutes to take in the spectacular views of the Sphinx and Mule Gully, Ari Burnu, and the north Anzac and Suvla battlefields.

Proceed back to the main road and continue along it, which will take you over the crest of Baby 700. To the right of the road is **Baby 700 CWGC Cemetery and** *Mesudiye* **gun (23) (40°14'33.9"N 26°17'39.7"E)**. Baby 700 was the objective of 3 Australian Brigade on 25 April and was occupied early in the morning by parties of the 11 and 12/AIF. They were joined by 1 and 2/AIF and later by groups of men from the Auckland and Canterbury infantry battalions; however, in the afternoon they were driven off the hill. It was the objective of other attacks, particularly on 2 May and 7 August, but it was never again reached. Baby 700 Cemetery was made after the Armistice. There are now 493 men buried or commemorated in this cemetery. 450 of the burials are unidentified, but special memorials commemorate ten Australian soldiers believed to be buried among them.

Notable commemorations include Captain Joseph Lalor (*Sp. Mem. 4*), 12/AIF, a descendant of Peter Lalor, of Eureka Stockade fame, killed on 25 April; and England and Australian rugby international, Major Blair Swannell (*Sp. Mem. 10*), 1/AIF. He played for the British Lions in two tours of Australia in 1899 and 1904, staying on at the end of the second tour to play for Australia against New Zealand in 1905. One of Swannell's officers, Lieutenant Alfred Shout, would go on to win the VC at Lone Pine in August, but would later die of his wounds. Continue along the road for a hundred metres to a track that is signposted to the *Messudieh* gun. This 15-cm gun was salvaged from the *Messudieh* after it was

91

torpedoed by Lieutenant Commander Holbrook's submarine *B11* in December 1914. The gun was placed here after the evacuation, and rests in a highly defended area still covered with original Turkish trenches. Return to the road.

Ahead is Big 700, named Battleship Hill after the concentration of naval shells that fell on its slopes. The hill is actually 690 feet above sea-level, and was known to the Turks as Straight Hill (*Düztepe*). A small party of Australians, led by Captain Eric Tulloch, 11/AIF, reached the inland slopes of Battleship Hill during the early morning of the first day, but were soon pushed back after the arrival of Mustafa Kemal and 57 Regiment. Charles Bean interviewed Tulloch after the war; he recounted seeing a Turkish officer calmly handing out messages under a single stunted tree just under a kilometre away. We will never know for sure who this officer was, but it has been suggested that it was Mustafa Kemal. He had his troops behind the summit of Chunuk Bair and gone forward on foot to this area in order to evaluate the situation. This is known to have been at around the same time that Tulloch was in position. Before Tulloch withdrew he fired one shot at the officer but missed.

Submarine *B11* and the *Messudieh*.

Continue for 1.5 kilometres over the crest of Battleship Hill, noting the trenches on either side of the road, and on to **Chunuk Bair (24) (40°15'05.4"N 26°18'29.3"E)** *(Conkbayiri)* where there are several memorials, a CWGC cemetery and other sites of interest. On the southern knoll of Chunuk Bair, **Hill 261**, are five large memorial panels that tell the Turkish side of the battles from the landings in April to the last major action on 10 August. Erected in the 1980s, they represent the fingers of an upturned hand praying to God. The position is important as it was where Mustafa Kemal said to the withdrawing defenders on 25 April, *I am not ordering you to attack, I am ordering you to die. If you don't have ammunition, you have bayonets! Fix bayonets! Get Down!* This action was enough to stop the Australian advance that morning, allowing time for 57 Regiment to take up the fight. It was also close to the position where Mustafa Kemal led the counter-attack that eventually forced the British off Chunuk Bair on 10 August.

Re-created trenches on Chunuk Bair.

On the northern knoll of Chunuk Bair (262 metres) you will find the
Chunuk Bair New Zealand Memorial with the inscription *FROM THE
UTTERMOST ENDS OF THE EARTH*. Rising some twenty metres high,
this stone monument, unveiled in 1925, is the site of the official New
Zealand Anzac Day ceremony each 25 April. It should be noted that

Malone's New Zealanders, supported by 8/Welsh, were on the southern knoll. Men from 7/Glosters briefly occupied this summit, but were compelled to withdraw under murderous fire from Hill Q and Hill 971.

Close by is the **Atatürk Memorial,** which shows Mustafa Kemal with his whip clearly seen behind his back. It was with this whip that he launched his decisive counter-attack on 10 August that finally dislodged the British from the top of Chunuk Bair. The memorial also has a reference to Kemal being hit on the right-hand side of his chest by shrapnel and saved from being mortally wounded by his pocket watch. The shattered watch he gave to General Liman von Sanders as a souvenir; he, in turn, gave him his gold watch.

Chunuk Bair New Zealand Memorial and Statue of Mustafa Kemal.

Close-by is the **New Zealand Chunuk Bair Memorial to the Missing and Cemetery**, which bears 856 New Zealand names of those missing who were killed in the Sari Bair operation. Names on the memorial include Lieutenant Colonel William Malone (*Panel 17*), commanding Wellington Regiment, who was killed by a shell on 8 August. Only seventy out of 760 men who went into action in the battalion survived to walk away from that hill. Of those left behind, twenty-one became prisoners. London born Malone, a pre-war barrister, had four sons in the army, two of whom were wounded with the Wellington Mounted Rifles at Gallipoli, and a daughter who served as a nurse in France.

Private Jack Dunn (*Panel 20*), was a machine gunner in the Wellington Regiment, and killed on 8 August on Chunuk Bair. Less than a month before the attack he was sentenced to death for sleeping whilst on duty at Quinn's Post, thus endangering his unit. The sentence was confirmed but later remitted by Hamilton on the grounds that Dunn had not been relieved from sentry duty at the correct time. It also transpired that Dunn had only just returned from hospital, after coming down with pneumonia during the first months of fighting. Dunn was from Wellington and in civilian life was a journalist.

Chunuk Bair CWGC Cemetery was made after the Armistice and contains 632 British and Dominion burials of soldiers killed during the same operations. Only ten are identified. Of these, one is Havildar Limbu Punahang (*Grave 7*), 10/Gurkhas, who was killed on 10 August. Many Gurkhas were in fact Buddhist, even though their religion was listed as Hindu. At Gallipoli it was not always possible to respect the rites of the dead and cremate them, as was customary for the Gurkhas, as this buried soldier shows. Private Edwin Marsden (*Grave 10*), 6/Loyals, was from Chorley, in England. He was reported killed on 10 August during Kemal's bayonet attack and is one of the few identified British bodies recovered and buried here after the Armistice.

Leave Chunuk Bair and continue along the road down the Third Ridge, which gives a good perspective of the battlefield from the Turkish side. After two kilometres stop at **Scrubby Knoll (25) (40°14'07.1"N 26°18'17.3"E)**, known to the Turks at Kemal's Place (*Kemalyeri*), one of the first day objectives of the covering force. The knoll, marked today by a Turkish memorial, is the northern highpoint of the Third Ridge. Two Australian scouts from 10/AIF reached this position on 25 April: Private Arthur Blackburn, an Adelaide-born solicitor (later commissioned and to win a VC at Pozières); and Lance Corporal Philip Robin (killed on 28 April, with no known grave), a bank accountant. They had been sent forward to reconnoitre the Third Ridge. Finding no Turks in the vicinity, both men withdrew to their unit on Johnston's Jolly and reported their sighting. Kemal briefly located his HQ here during the April fighting. It was also the site of a Turkish artillery battery, several of which were dug in all along the Third Ridge, or Gun Ridge, as it became known.

Continue along the ridge road for four kilometres and return to the **Gallipoli Presentation Centre (10)** where the tour ends.

There are additional walks and further detail of the Anzac area mapped out in my Battleground Europe books *Anzac: The Landing*, and *Anzac: Sari Bair*.

Turkish field artillery at the Gallipoli Presentation Centre.

Chapter 3

Helles

The beaches at Helles were little more than narrow strips of sand that lay under the shadow of high coastal cliffs before open farmland gently sloped up to the village of Krithia and Achi Baba. The responsibility for defending Helles fell to 26 Regiment (Ottoman 9th Division), commanded by Major Kadri, who had deployed a battalion in the Sedd-el-Bahr area, another at Kum Tepe to the north and a third in the middle, near Krithia. He was supported by an engineer company that was working on beach defences. These defences comprised barbed wire, trenches, pom-pom guns and field artillery pieces. Trip wire was laid under the surf line, mines were buried on the beaches and any natural obstacle that could afford cover to the attack was in the process of being removed. In the Sedd-el-Bahr area Major Mahmut Sabri's 3/26 Regiment, a single battalion, defended S, V, W and X beaches. Against this defence Hamilton pitched the bulk of the 29th Division, with the objective of taking the tip of the Peninsula and capturing the high ground of Achi Baba, standing 182 metres above sea level.

The amphibious assault was worked in conjunction with the Royal Navy, which would provide the craft to land the army and provide fire support from their 12 and 15 inch guns. Unlike the Anzac landing, the Helles force was to come ashore during daylight, preceded by a dawn bombardment. Although this would alert the defenders to the pending

The Helles battlefield, with Achi Baba in the distance, May 1915.

landing, it was thought that the weight and accuracy of the naval bombardment would afford the best chance of success against the fortified positions.

The covering force's (86 Brigade) objective was to secure the main beachhead, between Sedd-el-Bahr to X Beach, providing a screen for the main force to disembark. On the flanking beaches of S, X and Y, 87 Brigade would land to protect the flanks before all forces would join up for the five-mile general advance to Achi Baba, the first day's main objective. 88 Brigade would provide the divisional reserve. Hamilton said of the landings at Helles that: *no finer feat of arms has ever been achieved by the British soldier, or any other soldier, than the storming of these trenches from open boats on the morning of April 25.*

Y Beach

Y Beach is about four kilometres north of X Beach and just over a kilometre from Krithia and is nearest to the main objective, Achi Baba. The objective was to land a 2,000-man force behind the Turkish defenders and to hold an advanced position until joined by the main force from Cape Helles. Together, they would then assault Krithia and capture Achi Baba. In addition to the physical challenge of the sixty metres steep, scrub-covered cliffs, the beach was little more than a narrow strip of sand, hardly recognisable from sea or shore.

This landing, at 5.30 a.m., was a *coup de main*, a total surprise to the Turks, who did not believe a landing would be attempted here. Because of this it was not defended. Two battalions: Plymouth Battalion, Royal Marine Light Infantry (RMLI) and 1st Battalion, King's Own Scottish Borderers (1/KOSB), supported by a company from the 2nd Battalion, South Wales Borderers (2/SWB) landed here unhindered. The landing was not the problem, the issue was that the force's objective lacked clarity, complicated by misunderstandings and disagreements between the two commanding officers.

The Y Beach operation was controlled by the 29th Division's headquarters on board HMS *Euryalus*, five kilometres south, offshore at W Beach. On the ground, there were two commanding officers, Lieutenant Colonel Archibald Koe (1/KOSB) and Lieutenant Colonel Godfrey Matthews (RMLI). Matthews attended the pre-landing conference and, as he was senior to Koe, GHQ put him in overall command. Koe was ill during this briefing so did not attend, but he believed himself to be in overall command. This did not bode well for the forthcoming operation, not made any better by the vague orders, as an example: to 'make contact' with X Beach. It was not clear if this was meant to be in physical contact or just visually. In the event neither was

Y Beach and Gurkha Bluff

achieved. No contingency plans were made if the advance from the south did not materialise, which it did not, resulting in the force being left isolated and forgotten.

During the spring morning sunshine of 25 April all went well with the landing, the scouts walked to the outskirts of Krithia unmolested, and the few Turks found in the area of Gully Ravine were reported as showing 'no aggressive spirit'. Some distance south of Krithia the soldiers had clear views of Morto Bay and the battleships firing off Cape Helles, but apart from this the area was deserted.

> 'The scouts went on ahead and actually reached the outskirts of Krithia, a small village that we saw but never reached again during the whole campaign. Our scouts came in contact with one or two Turkish scouts during their advance, two were shot dead and one brought in as a prisoner. He looked very depressed. His equipment consisted of a civilian overcoat, and from his size he wore plenty of underclothing, a soldier's head dress, and a white haversack full of loose ammunition and a rifle. His boots were in a very bad state, and rags took the place of puttees.'
>
> Sergeant William Meatyard, Plymouth Battalion, RMLI.

For almost six hours the men at Y Beach were left unmolested. The commanders realised that opportunity was being thrown away and twice asked HQ for orders but received no reply. By 3.00 p.m. Matthews, realising that there was no movement from the south at Cape Helles,

withdrew his patrols and dug a semi-circular defensive perimeter to cover Y Beach. It was barely an hour later that the Turks discovered this force and, realising its threat to their lines of communication, immediately sent their reserve 1/25 Regiment to attack. Fierce fighting went on in the late afternoon and into the night, which made things increasingly difficult for the British. Koe was mortally wounded in the fighting, which at least settled the issue of who was in overall command; but with no reinforcements or any communication with HQ, and under almost constant enemy attack, ammunition had run low and casualties were mounting. As hostile fire increased, and the situation became more precarious, messages were sent back to HQ requesting reinforcements, all of which were ignored. By the morning there was much confusion and although no order was given by Matthews to re-embark, wounded were evacuated from the beach in large numbers, which gave the already beleaguered men holding the perimeter the illusion that a general evacuation was in progress. Without orders, men left their positions and returned to the waiting boats. By the time Matthews realised what had happened it was too late to stop the withdraw. By 11.30 a.m. on the 26th the first evacuation of the campaign had been successful.

Hamilton, who was offshore at the time witnessed this, believing that Major General Aylmer Hunter-Weston must have ordered the withdraw and so did not interfere. Ignored by Hunter-Weston, who never really approved of this landing in the first place, the 29th Division's HQ were focussed on the main events on W and V beaches, leaving Y to its own fate. The Turks, who had all but given up the fight at Y Beach, were amazed to see the evacuation, and wasted no time in securing this area

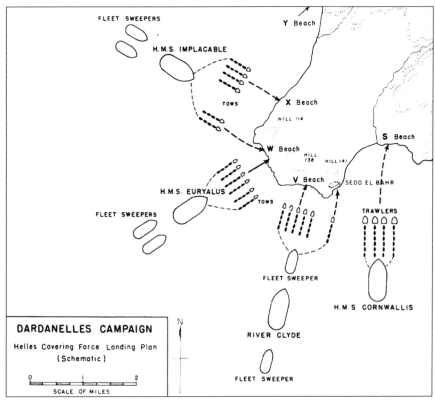

and then moving the rest of the regiment south to engage the hard-pressed British trying to establish a beachhead. All the great opportunities that could have been exploited at Y Beach had been forfeited. The cost was 700 casualties, a third of Y force. It would take a hard month's fighting to reach this position once again.

S Beach

About five kilometres away on the other side of the peninsula, the remaining three companies of 2/SWB, under the command of Lieutenant Colonel Hugh Casson, were landed on S Beach with a detachment of engineers, medics and a few marines from HMS *Cornwallis*. The plan was to capture a Turkish observation post that was defended by a platoon from 3/26 Regiment. The post was sited in a redundant battery known as De Tott's (which dated from the Russo-Turkish War [1768-74], named after Baron Francois de Tott, a French artillery expert then advising the Ottoman Army) and was positioned on a 72-metre promontory known as Eski Hissarlik.

Although the landing was supposed to take place simultaneously with those on V, W, X and Y, it suffered delays due to the landing trawlers struggling against the strong Dardanelles currents. Once the rowing boats were let loose from their tows, they did not ground ashore until 7.00 a.m., over ninety minutes late.

> 'I took up my position in the lower foretop of the *Vengeance*. Our orders were to shell De Tott's Ridge and, if possible, clear out hostile forces that might be in ambush. At 5 a.m., as if the very heavens had been rent asunder, every ship opened fire simultaneously on its allotted area. We simply hammered away for all we were worth. Trawlers and boats, which had been secured to the ship astern of us, now crowded with the South Wales Borderers, made for the end of the sandy patch just inside Morto Bay. They were met by a hail of bullets which killed a number of men, and therefore they withdrew for a short time, during which we increased our rate of fire. The trawlers then came round the south part of De Tott's; at 6.30 a.m., another attempt was made and, in spite of a heavy fire, the men landed and climbed up the side of the cliff. It was splendid to see them with their bayonets flashing in the sun, making the ascent – a sight never to be forgotten.'
>
> Lieutenant Robert Seed, RN, HMS *Vengeance*.

Supported by the guns of HMS *Cornwallis* and HMS *Vengeance*, De Tott's was taken within thirty minutes with very few casualties, 2/SWB losing two officers and twelve ORs killed, three officers and forty ORs wounded. Similar to Y Beach, no consideration was given to reinforcing the success of these flanking positions or directly using them to support the stalled landing at V Beach, which was not going as well. The combined forces at Y and S beaches actually outnumbered the Turkish defenders south of Achi Baba, a known fact that was not exploited. The

HMS *Cornwallis* bombarding the shore.

battalion maintained their position until the French 175th Regiment relieved them during the evening of 27 April. Casson and his battalion then marched over to X Beach, where they prepared for the First Battle of Krithia.

X Beach

Similar to Y and S beaches, the landing at X was largely unopposed. X Beach is situated on the western side of the peninsula and is little more than a shallow gouge in the coastline, about a mile north of Tekke Burnu. The beach is a narrow strip of sand about 182 metres long, about seven metres deep and is at the foot of a steep escarpment some seventy metres high. The task of capturing X Beach was given to a battalion of the covering force, 2nd Battalion Royal Fusiliers (2/RF). The unit was supported by a platoon from Anson Battalion, RND, which would act as a beach working party, and both 1st Battalion, Border Regiment (1/Borders) and 1st Battalion, Royal Inniskilling Fusiliers (1/RIF). The objective of the landing was to secure the beach area and form a defensive flank to the northeast that was to offer protection for the main task, the capture of Hill 114 to the south. Once captured, 2/RF would then link up with 1/LF, who would be advancing towards them from W Beach. A link up to Y Beach would then occur.

The Official History notes: *The morning was absolutely still. The garrison of the peninsula gave no signs of life. A thick veil of mist hung motionless over the beaches. The sea was smooth as glass.* After HMS *Implacable* had dropped off one 1/LF company and Brigadier General Hare (86 Brigade) on W Beach, the battleship continued around Tekke Burnu towards X Beach with her four tows of 2/RF alongside. The cliff-top bombardment by HMS *Implacable* and subsequent covering fire was very effective. The Captain, Hughes Lockyer RN, managed to get to within 450 metres of the shore where, at point-blank range, its mighty 12-inch guns put paid to the twelve defenders from 3/26 Regiment. By 6.30 a.m. 2/RF had landed without loss.

'We got off very lightly while getting ashore; I can only put it down largely to the way our mother-ship plastered the beach for us at close range; however, we had our bad time later on. About 100 yards from the shore the launches cast us off and we rowed in for all we were worth, till the boats grounded, then jumped into the water, up to our chests in some places, waded ashore and swarmed up the cliff.'

Lieutenant Colonel Henry Newenham, 2/RF.

HMS *Implacable* and Royal Fusiliers off X Beach.

When Brigadier General William Marshall, commanding 87 Brigade, came ashore with his headquarters and divisional reserve, 1/Borders and 1/RIF, at about 9.00 a.m., his Brigade Major remarked,

> 'The landing differs from some others. I recollect a bright sunny morning, dead calm sea, not a shot fired. I had a bag in one hand, coat over my arm, and was assisted down a plank from the boat by an obliging sailor, so that I should not wet my boots. The only thing missing was the hotel.'
>
> Brigade Major Cuthbert Lucas.

The landing was a total success. Lieutenant Colonel Newenham, cheered on by the men of HMS *Implacable,* led just over a company towards the objective of Hill 114, where they made contact with 1/Lancashire Fusiliers, who had fought their way up from W Beach. To the north, the remaining Royal Fusiliers fanned out about 725 metres to set up a defensive perimeter. It did not take long before they came into contact with a reserve company from 2/26 Regiment, who subjected the British to almost ceaseless counter attacks. The northern flank soon collapsed and needed 1/Borders and 1/RIF to re-establish the line. However, by the morning of 26 April the Turks had begun to withdraw, having successfully hampered the 29th Division's landing, stifling their advance. The ominous peak of Achi Baba lay in the distance, an objective that still lay largely undefended; an objective that would never be taken.

W Beach

W Beach is on the south west promontory of the Peninsula by the headland named Tekke Burnu. It consists of an arc-shaped strip of deep, powdery sand, about 320 metres in length and approximately twenty-seven metres deep, with steep cliffs each side. The ground then rises up gently through sand dunes that then run up steeply to a low ridge. Trip wires were placed in the surf line and mines planted on the beach. Behind this were two belts of barbed wire, surrounded by trenches that looked down onto the beach from the cliffs and low ridge. Despite some contemporary accounts, there were no machine guns covering W Beach, just a company of rifleman from 3/26 Regiment. Regardless, the defences were formidable.

The Lancashire Landing.

The plan was for 1/LF, under the command of Lieutenant Colonel Harry Ormond, to affect a landing on W Beach and, when secured, to link up with the X and V beach landings, thus extending and then pushing forward the beach head, from where the covering force would provide the necessary protection to allow the rest of the 29th Division to land. To connect these beaches two fortified hills needed capturing; Hill 114, assigned to 2/RF at X Beach, and Hill 138, the objective given to 1/LF.

To give the best chance of success a short but intensive thirty-minute bombardment by HMS *Euryalus* and HMS *Swiftsure* was to precede the landing, to lift some ten minutes before the boats hit the shore. Unfortunately, this lull in the bombardment was to give the Turkish defenders ten unmolested minutes to meet the landing. On board HMS *Euryalus* Hunter-Weston and staff observed the bombardment. He had earlier predicted the difficulties that the amphibious force would soon be facing, warning: *No loss would be too heavy and no risks too great if success would thereby be attained. But there is not in present circumstances a reasonable chance of success.* That said, he was determined to overcome the challenges and encourage all to do their best 'as the eyes of the world were upon them'.

'We all went to the bridge and the bombardment began. The sight now was wonderful – never to be forgotten. A beautiful sunny morning, a glassy sea, on one side of the Peninsula and Asia Minor, apparently uninhabited, being pounded to bits, and in every other direction ships and ships and ships – British battleships round Helles, all the best of the pre-Dreadnought era, cruisers, destroyers, French battleships on the Asiatic coast, like top-heavy walnuts, all bumps and excrescences, the five-funnelled Russian cruiser, the *Askold*, and, in the background, the newest and mightiest, yet so symmetrical as to look quite small and low, 'Queen Bess', one funnelled and one masted with her eight 15-inch guns. All these ships had their allotted areas to bombard, some the coastline, some searching up the valley behind and some dropping their 12-inch and 15-inch shells that burst with mighty columns of smoke on Krithia and on the summit of Achi Baba.'

Captain Clement Milward, Staff Officer, 29th Division.

The sight of the naval bombardment was undoubtedly reassuring, but it was largely ineffective against the entrenched positions; not only did it end ten minutes before 1/LF landed, but the flat trajectory of naval gunnery meant that most of the shells either exploded into the cliffs or fell too far inland.

When the bombardment stopped,

'…all was deadly still and silent, the engines of our ship hardly made a sound. One couldn't help pitying the men sitting there in their boats. It was indeed a hush before the storm. There lay the Peninsula with not a sign of life on it, but the Turks were there all right in their trenches watching our every movement.'

Captain Clement Milward.

The boats unknowingly approached the killing zone where, ninety metres from the beach, a fusillade of rifle fire was unleashed. Those that had not been killed or wounded in the boats gallantly jumped into the water. The men struggled waist-deep, exacerbated by the weight of their equipment, the trip wires and land mines. The Turks continued to fire down from the cliffs into the battalion, who were now held up by a deep belt of wire. Initially the fusiliers could not retaliate as their rifle actions had begun clogged with sand and salty water. The men frantically kicked open the bolts of their rifles in an effort to fire back.

'A very heavy and brisk fire was poured into us, several officers and men being killed and wounded in the entanglements, through which we were trying to cut a way. Several of my company were with me under the wire, one of my subalterns was killed next to me, and also the wire-cutter who was lying the other side of me. I seized his cutter and cut a small lane myself through which a few of us broke and lined up under the only available cover procurable, a small sand ridge covered with bluffs of grass. I then ordered fire to be opened on the crests, but owing to submersion in the water and dragging rifles through the sand, the breech mechanism was clogged, thereby rendering the rifles ineffective. The only thing left to do was to fix bayonets and charge up the crests, which was done in a very gallant manner, though we suffered greatly in doing so. However, this had the effect of driving the enemy from his trenches, which we immediately occupied.'

Major George Adams, 1/LF; he was killed on 11 May 1915.

[Lancashire Landing E 51].

The commander of the Covering Force, Brigadier General Steuart Hare, who was leading the second wave into the shore, witnessed the Fusiliers' plight. He could see that a further landing on W Beach was senseless and, thinking quickly, he ordered the remaining boats to row to the left-hand side of the beach under the cover of the cliffs. Outflanking the Turks, Hare and his men scrambled up a steep slope through a gap in the defenses, forcing the Turks to flee. Unfortunately, when nearing Hill 114, Hare was wounded, but through his initiative, and that of officers like Adams, a landing had been affected. By 8.00 a.m. W Beach had been tentatively secured.

Lieutenant Douglas Talbot, Royal Navy, wrote:

'They all drank our health and the General (Hunter-Weston) said our landing was one of the finest deeds that had been performed, far, far finer than Quebec; in fact they treated us like heroes. He said that every man should have a VC if they had their rights.'

Lieutenant General Sir Aylmer Hunter-Weston

106

In fact six Victoria Crosses were eventually awarded to the Lancashire Fusiliers. In an unusual, but not unprecedented, military decision, the survivors were asked to elect six recipients for the award because it was felt that the Regiment comprised 'equally brave and distinguished people'. The 'six VCs before breakfast', as they famously became known, were awarded to Major Cuthbert Bromley, Captain Richard Willis, Sergeant Alfred Richards, Sergeant Frank Stubbs, Corporal John Grimshaw and Private William Keneally. Three of the above would not survive Gallipoli. The cost to the battalion that landed with twenty-five officers and 918 men was fifteen officers and 411 other ranks; 55% of them became casualties. This feat passed into the folklore of this English county and, as a testimony to the gallantry of the Fusiliers, Hamilton ordered W Beach to be named 'Lancashire Landing' in their honour.

The fighting above Lancashire Landing and X Beach lasted until the weight of British numbers forced a Turkish withdraw. After 1/LF connected with 1/RF on Hill 114, reinforcements landed on the beach in the form of the 1st Battalion, Essex Regiment (1/Essex) and the 4th Battalion, Worcestershire Regiment (4/Worcs). Both battalions pushed out from the beach and made their way towards V Beach and two landmarks, a lighthouse and Hill 138. The hill had been entrenched by the Turks, with the approaches protected in parts by wire. The 4/Worcs, having cut paths through the wire, along with 1/Essex, made a series of bayonet charges against the redoubt, eventually capturing it. However, their path to the beleaguered men on V Beach was still barred by a second hill nestled about 300 metres behind, Guezji Baba. Mistakenly, 4/Worcs believed this to be Hill 141, the hill behind Sedd-el-Bahr, and when they signaled its capture just after 4.00 p.m. on 25 April, there was some confusion at Divisional headquarters until the mistake was realised. Hill 141 would not fall until the following afternoon; but for now 1/Essex consolidated Hill 138 and 4/Worcs Guezji Baba. Counter-attacks halted further movements towards V Beach, and no resumption of the advance occurred until 2.30 p.m. on 26 April, a day behind schedule.

V Beach

The landing at V Beach was undoubtedly the bloodiest of them all. Defensive trenches and wire once again were well placed to disrupt any advance from the shoreline, while a rifle company from 3/26 Regiment, supported by four 'Pom-Pom' quick firing 37mm Maxim-Nordenfelt anti-aircraft guns had established a semi-circular defence between Fort Ertuğrul (Fort No. 1) on the cliffs, along a ridge to Hill 141 and down onto the beach to Sedd-el-Bahr castle (Fort No.3). Two of these guns were located in the castle, and two were near Fort No.1. Reports on the

107

4 March RMLI raid at Sedd-el-Bahr had reported the destruction of four Nordenfeldts, so it is unclear if these guns were operational on 25 April. The Turkish defenders had a clear field of fire from this natural bowl-shaped amphitheatre down on to a 270-metre narrow, gently sloping beach.

The plan was to land four battalions by 8.00 a.m., capture the village of Krithia by noon and to have taken Achi Baba by nightfall. At first light, HMS *Albion* would bombard the defences at V Beach, to be followed an hour later by the landing of three companies from the 1st Battalion, Royal Dublin Fusiliers (1/RDF), towed to the shore in six strings of rowing boats pulled by steam pinnaces. Five would land on V Beach whilst the sixth was directed to land at the Camber, a harbour that was nestled between the castle and village. The plan also included the use of a 4,000-ton converted steam collier, the *River Clyde,* which would be beached and then quickly disembark its hidden cargo of 2,000 men. The *River Clyde* was an extraordinary survivor; she was refloated from V Beach in 1919 and sold to a Spanish owner. Renamed *Muruja y Aurora*, she sailed the Mediterranean until she was finally scrapped in 1966, over fifty years after its distinguished role in the events at Gallipoli. An unlikely candidate, she has become possibly the best known ship that saw service with the Royal Navy during the war.

The idea of using a modern 'Trojan horse' was conceived by Commander Edward Unwin RN, who assumed command of the ship. Sally ports had been cut in her side to allow the men to disembark via gangways, protected under the covering fire of eleven Maxim machine guns of the Royal Naval Air Service (Armoured Car Division). In the hold were two battalions, comprising 1st Battalion, Royal Munster Fusiliers (1/RMF), two companies from 2nd Battalion, Hampshire Regiment (2/Hants) and one company of 1/RDF, supported by a platoon from Anson Battalion and a Royal Engineers field company.

The tows carrying the 1/RDF were meant to land at 5.30 a.m., but embarkation delays and a strong current running out of the Straits delayed the Dublins' approach. As a result the *River Clyde* overtook them. Even the best laid of plans rarely survive first contact with the enemy, but this one appeared to be unwinding even earlier. Commander Unwin, concerned that there would be hellish confusion if he landed first, or if both forces landed simultaneously, turned the Clyde around to allow the Dublin's to land. With so many ships close by, this manoeuvre proved extremely difficult, although ultimately it was successful. He then headed his ship straight for shore, to the utter amazement of the Turkish defenders.

The landing from the *River Clyde*.

'There was a jar that quivered from end to end of the ship, and she was aground. Hardly had the ship come to rest when the little steam hopper with her tow of barges rushed out from under the Clyde's quarter and made for the sandy shore some eighty yards distant. Up till now not a shot had been fired from the shore, and indeed we had begun to wonder whether the landing was to be unopposed, but hardly had the hopper's bow appeared beyond her huge consort when the whole slope leapt into a roar of firing, and a tempest of lead poured down upon the devoted craft and her gallant crew. Disaster overwhelmed her in an instant. Nothing could live in such a torrent of lead and in a moment the middy at the wheel and every sailor on the deck of the little ship was shot down. Devoid of guidance, the hopper went astray and beached side-on while the barges all went out of line, the connecting ropes broke under the strain, and they came to rest in a hopeless muddle lying about twenty yards from the shore. The bridge of boats had failed.'

Petty Officer David Fyffe, 3 Armoured Car Squadron,
RNAS.

Landed by rowing boats, but pinned down on the beach, the Dublins' commanding officer, Lieutenant Colonel Richard Rooth, was already dead, and Father William Finn, a Roman Catholic chaplain, mortally wounded. As the boats drew nearer to the beach the awful hail of machine gun and rifle fire, together with shrapnel, took its toll. Those lucky enough to reach a two-metre high sandbank along the beach sheltered behind it, the only cover that afforded any protection against the ferocious Turkish fire. As more boats rowed to the shore they were met with the same maelstrom of fire, cutting men down before they even reached the beach. Some were killed outright; others drowned or were pulled under by the weight of their equipment. Between the drowning men, boats floated helplessly in the water with their dead and dying crews.

'There were twenty-five in my boat, and there were only three of us left. It was sad to hear our poor chums moaning, and to see others dead in the boat. It was a terrible sight to see the poor boys dead in the water; others on the beach roaring for help. But we could do nothing for them. I must have had someone's good prayer for I do not know how I escaped. Those who were lying wounded on the shore, in the evening the tide came in and they were all drowned, and I was left by myself on the beach. I had to remain in the water for about three hours, as they would fire on me as soon as they saw me make a move. I thought my life was up every minute.'

Private Robert Martin, 1/RDF.

Some of the Dublins who landed on the Camber came ashore with few losses, but ultimately this flanking manoeuvre failed; some of the Dublin men managed to fight their way into the village of Sedd-el-Bahr but were unable to retain a footing and were forced to retire. The survivors eventually fought their way around the fort and joined the rest of the battalion, who were still pinned down on the beach.

The grounded *River Clyde* was powerless, and the bridge of boats had to be formed manually if the men were to run down improvised gangways and over the boats to the beach. It was intended that the flat-bottomed steam hopper, *Argyll*, which was accompanying the *Clyde,* was to move to the ship's port side and move lighters into position. The hopper, commanded by Midshipman George Drewry, was stuck and his six Greek volunteer crewmen, understandably took cover in the hopper's bows, refusing to come out. From the deck of the *Clyde*, Unwin appreciated the hopelessness of the situation and acted. Followed by Able Seaman William Williams, he jumped into the sea and got hold of the lighters and pulled them underneath the bow of the *Clyde* and began to connect them up. The closest piece of dry land was a rocky spit jutting into the sea, and it was towards this natural pier that the men steered the boats. There was

The landing at V Beach.

no way to hold the boats together, other than by grim determination, so Unwin and Williams clung on while the call was made for the infantrymen to leave the ship. Immediately the men of 1/RMF opened the doorways cut into the superstructure and began to run down the gangways towards the lighters.

> 'We could hear splash after splash as the gallant fellows fell dead from the gangway. A few however reached the nearest barge, raced across her open deck and crouched for shelter in the adjacent open boat. One after another the devoted fellows made the dash down the deadly gangways until a considerable number gathered in the bottoms of the open boats or were lying prostrate on the deck of the barge. Then the order was given and up they leapt and rushed for the rocks while a hail of rifle and machine-gun fire beat upon them. Wildly they leapt from boat to boat in that gallant rush while we on the ship cheered wildly at the sight, until they reached the last boat, when they leapt down into the water and started wading towards the rocks that were their goal, holding up their rifles high above their heads. But to our horror we saw them suddenly begin to flounder and fall in the water, disappearing from view and then struggling to the surface again with uniform and pack streaming, only to go down again, never to reappear as the hailing bullets flicked the life out of the struggling men ... We almost wept with impotent rage.'
>
> Petty Officer David Fyffe.

Lance Corporal George Smith, 1/1st West Riding Field Company, Royal Engineers, wrote:

'I landed with a crash on the first barge, bullets spluttering all over the place as our fire had not silenced all the rifles and machine guns on the shore. I lay down at on my tummy and looked around to get my bearings and a terrible sight met me as the barge was crowded with men who had died and lots of wounded men whom we could not help as we had to push on owing to the other fellows coming on behind. Eventually, after crawling along three barges, I came to the place where I could push my face over the gunwhale of the last barge and make up my mind to jump into the sea. I managed it all right, clutching my explosives – I had lost the shovel somewhere – I managed to get to a place where no bullets could reach me and lay down under cover of a small sandbank and at last I was for the first time on the enemy shore.'

Captain Guy Geddes, a company commander in the 1st Munsters, recalled:

'We all made, Dublins and all, for a sheltered ledge on the shore which gave us cover. Here were shook ourselves out, and tried to appreciate the situation, rather a sorry one. I estimated that I had lost about seventy percent of my Company.'

As Geddes made his dash to the right, Unwin and Williams remained chest-deep in the cold water securing the boats; but they were soon exhausted and with Williams now wounded they were forced to let go of the ropes holding the boats together and return to the *Clyde*. In Unwin's absence, Drewry had taken over and with the help of two other men a third lighter had been brought round from the *Clyde*'s starboard side and a bridge of sorts completed. Further attempts were made to land men and three further strings of boats, packed with infantrymen, made for the shore. This time more were able to land but a number were cut down by the burst of three shrapnel shells overhead. Men were sent from the beached collier, and more arrived on lighters, but all were forced to head for the sandbank so that by 9.00 a.m. a few hundred men were huddled there for protection. It was clear that the position was hopeless. The landing had failed.

For these extraordinary acts of self-sacrifice, there were six Victoria Crosses awarded to members of the Royal Navy that day at V Beach: Captain Edward Unwin, Midshipman George Drewry, Midshipman Wilfred Malleson, AB William Williams, Seaman George Samson and Sub Lieutenant Arthur Tisdall.

The extent of the disaster unfolding on V Beach was unclear to Hunter-Weston and his staff onboard the *Euryalus*, who ordered a second

Ruined village of Sedd-el-Bahr.

assault on the beach. Using the limited boats that were still seaworthy, the men met with a similar fate; the dead included men of all ranks, among them Brigadier General Henry Napier (88 Brigade), who had personally led the assault, and his brigade major, who followed him.

> 'We received depressing messages telling us of the death of General Napier, killed on the lighters, and shortly afterwards of the death of Costeker, his brigade major. Colonel Carrington Smith, a fine soldier, of the Hampshires, had taken command, but he was killed on the bridge in the afternoon. Truly the casualties were staggering. General Marshall, too, was slightly wounded. They told us too of how 1,000 men of those on board the River Clyde had attempted to get ashore. About half had been hit in the attempt. So great was the depression that we had great difficulty in dissuading General Hunter-Weston from going himself to V Beach to lead the men to the attack.'
>
> Captain Clement Milward.

The operations were suspended and it was decided to wait until nightfall before a further attempt at landing should be made. Word was sent to the

113

fleet of the failure and the ships recommenced their bombardment of the slopes above the beach and Sedd-el-Bahr. The plan to link up with W Beach was halted, at least for the time being; 4/Worcs were within spitting distance of V Beach, but that was still not close enough. Only with approaching darkness could both sides take a breather and the wounded on V Beach treated. As night finally fell the navy shone searchlights onto the Turkish trenches, dazzling the defenders and, protected by the dark, the men who had been pinned down all day long began to move. Officers began to collect their men and more troops, who had been bottled up in the *River Clyde*, made their way to the shore. By midnight over two thousand men had reached the stretch of sand with hardly a casualty. The Turks were not beaten. They did not withdraw but counter attacked. This ultimately failed, but shocked the British, who now believed that the numbers holding the beach defences were far greater than they actually were. In fact it was just handfuls of men who had successfully pinned the Irishmen and Hampshires to the beach all-day.

Staff officers on board the *River Clyde* realised that it would take a coordinated effort to break this impasse. Colonel Weir de Lancey Williams and Lieutenant Colonel Charles Doughty-Wylie formulated a plan. Williams would lead a party under the lee of the cliffs on the left flank under Fort No.1, Major Arthur Beckwith would advance in the centre, whilst Doughty-Wylie would take a party along the right flank, through the Castle and up through the village of Sedd-el-Bahr.

In action, clearing a path through the wire. Corporal William Cosgrove VC (inset).

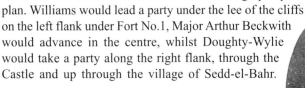

Despite the bravery of soldiers like Captain Garth Neville Walford, a brigade major of the Royal Artillery who was killed clearing Sedd-el-Bahr Castle of enemy, and of Corporal William Cosgrove, 1/RMF, who despite being wounded stood up in clear view of the enemy to clear a path through the wire, progress was slow and casualties heavy. Doughty-Wylie led the remaining men through the village and up to a defended redoubt on Hill 141. This final objective was taken by 2.30 p.m. but at a high cost, Doughty-Wylie being killed at this moment of victory.

Doughty-Wylie, Walford and Cosgrove were awarded the Victoria Cross for their bravery on 26 April 1915. Despite all the courage shown during the daylight landings on V Beach and Lancashire Landing, and what only can be described as lost opportunities on S and Y beaches, it is all too easy to state in **Captain Garth Walford VC.**
hindsight what might have been. What cannot be ignored is that the best part of the 29th Division was thwarted by the unexpected, dogged and determined resistance of 3/26 Regiment. Despite heavy casualties, they had stubbed out any British advance, admittedly aided by lack of effective British command and control. With the loss of so many senior officers, but still outnumbering the Turks, the British units were in bloodied disarray, and by nightfall were worn out, somewhat demoralized and in a confused state of shock. The cost of the V Beach failure should not only be measured in casualties, but also in time; it took over a day for the British to secure Sedd-el-Bahr and thus the plan's timetable had slipped. The advance on the first day objectives of Achi Baba would not begin for another forty-eight hours; after another eight months of the campaign this objective would still not be reached, or even seriously threatened.

The Battles of Krithia

It was clear that the operation was not going to plan. Whilst the superficial causes were obvious, the failure to capture any objectives, the underlying reason, was more fundamental. From the War Cabinet down to commanders of the MEF there was a belief that the Turk was an inferior military fighting man and thus their defence would just collapse. This serious underestimation of the enemy would last throughout the campaign, although respect for the Turkish fighter grew as the battles went on. The 29th Division reorganised itself after the initial shock of the landings and waited for orders to advance. Hamilton realised that he would soon need reinforcements, which angered Kitchener and was not well received by Lieutenant General Maxwell in Egypt, whose garrison was going to be robbed of men to fulfill the request. The 42nd (East Lancashire) Division, a Territorial formation, and an Indian Army brigade were sent. But what was Hamilton or, rather, Hunter-Weston going to do with this fresh injection of men?

Now ashore, the focus at Helles was the capture of the prominent hill of Achi Baba, which still sat unthreatened on the horizon, its gentle spurs tantalisingly stretched out in front, luring the assaulting forces to its summit. Not far away was the white washed stone buildings of Krithia, which shone bright in the late April sun. The original plan should have seen Krithia and Achi Baba in allied hands by nightfall on 25 April but, already two days behind schedule, this did not seem to concern Hamilton too much. As long as both objectives had fallen by sunset on 28 April the overall plan could be salvaged. It was of the utmost importance that a further attack was quickly mounted before the Turks could recover and be reinforced. Achi Baba was key terrain, whose capture would deny the enemy such a wonderful view of Hamilton's forces. It would also be the platform needed for his artillery for the next part of the operation: the capture of the Kilid Bahr plateau. Never during the campaign did a British soldier stand on top of either.

On 27 April the French *Corps Expéditionnaire d'Orient* (CEO), which had made a diversionary landing at Kum Kale on the Asian shore on 25 April, was moved across the straits to Helles to hold the right of the British line. The Turks had pulled back their weakened 26 Regiment, which had so successfully defended the beaches during the first day.

During the late afternoon of 27 April Hunter-Weston ordered an 'advance to contact' that pushed the line forward from the beaches for about three kilometres and over five kilometres width, from the mouth of Gully Ravine to Eski Hissarlik. During the day Hamilton felt confident enough to cable Kitchener about the progress and wrote that *thanks to the weather and the wonderfully fine spirit of our troops all continues to go well.* Hunter-Weston was confident of success, and Hamilton thought the worse was over. Far from it! The weather was cold and miserable and the men, still reacting to their shocking casualties over the last few days, were depressed and utterly exhausted. No one expected the welcome that the Turks had given them, and none were too keen to be thrown into another attack so soon.

French soldiers resting in Sedd-el-Bahr.

First Battle of Krithia

At 8:00 a.m. on 28 April a naval bombardment opened the battle. The hastily prepared plan placed the French on the right, who would hold this ground, while the British line would pivot, capturing Krithia and then rushing Achi Baba from the south and west. Although the initial advance met limited opposition, pockets of resistance and more difficult terrain soon slowed up progress. Defending the new line were the remnants of Major Mahmut Sabri's regiment, recently reinforced by Colonel Halil Sami's 9th Division; the Turks now had thirteen battalions positioned in front of Krithia, three of which were fresh. Hunter-Weston had fourteen British and five French battalions available for the attack, supported by a few field guns and the Royal Navy.

The attack ground to a halt quite quickly; the plan turned out to be overly complex and poorly communicated and so really had little chance of success. The 29th Division's advance also lacked cohesion and, although some blame had been put on Hunter-Weston for siting his headquarters too far back so that he had no control over the events that day, much of the problem was the tiredness of the troops and sapping of morale that had occurred since the landing.

A further issue was that the terrain at Helles, in its own way, was just as challenging as that of Anzac. Helles consisted mainly of open cultivated fields, spread out on the gentle forward slopes of Achi Baba. Like fingers, Achi Baba has four main spurs, divided naturally by four large ravines or nullahs. On the western side was Gully Ravine, which was separated from the Aegean shore by Gully Spur. Moving eastwards is Fir Tree Spur and then Krithia Nullah and then Krithia Spur. East of here was Kanli Dere and then the fields ran up to the Kerevez Spur before the ground falls away into Kerevez Dere, which flows into the Dardanelles north of Morto Bay.

The main thrust of the attack was made along both Gully Spur and Fir Tree Spur, which offered some cover from the bare and exposed slopes towards the middle of Helles. Here 1/Border and 1/RIF (87 Brigade) advanced just short of Y Beach with little resistance before being stopped by a well-positioned machine gun on the bluff above the beach. Only three days previously this area was in British hands; it would take another two weeks before this strongpoint eventually fell and then not to 87 Brigade but to the Gurkhas.

At 3.00 p.m. the Turks made a determined counter-attack that had the effect of stopping the timid advance and even in some places causing a partial retirement. By 6.00 p.m. the by now fatigued and dispirited British were ordered to dig in. They had advanced just over a kilometre from their starting positions; the French on the eastern flank fared no better. The attack, which became known as the First Battle of Krithia, was called off and positions were consolidated. There were 3,000 casualties from the 14,000 troops that participated in the battle. At no time were Krithia or Achi Baba threatened and the modest advance of the line that was made showed that a swift victory would not be forthcoming and that the Turks should not be underestimated.

From the time of the landing the British losses alone totaled nearly 14,000 casualties: 177 officers and 1,990 other ranks killed, 412 officers and 7,807 other ranks wounded, thirteen officers and 3,580 other ranks missing. Most of the missing had in fact been killed. The officer casualties were particularly high. In comments to Captain R. H. Williams, the American military attaché, Turkish officers noted that *The English*

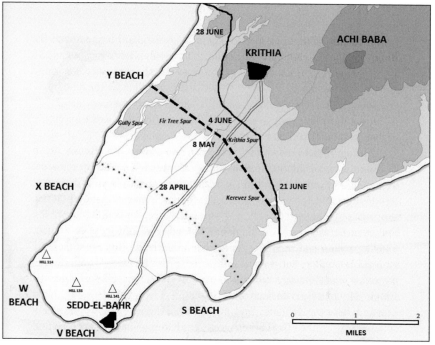

Battles of Krithia.

officers were brave but inexperienced, and did not seem to know how to command or to lead their soldiers into battle.

It is worth noting that until the end of the First Battle of Krithia there were really no trenches to speak of, and much of the field defences were merely shallow scrapings in the ground. On 1 May, 29 Indian Brigade and two battalions of the RND were landed to supplement Hunter-Weston's weakened force. But this would not be enough. Liman von Sanders at the same time created two new formations: at Helles a Southern Group, under the command of Colonel von Sodenstern; and at Anzac a Northern Group, under Esad Pasha. The Turks had defended well and now reinforced by four fresh divisions, they prepared to launch counter-attacks at both Helles and Anzac. There would not be just one of these to be endured but several between 1 and 4 May. Although the Turks did push back the British line in places and overran many of the French positions, the lines were eventually re-established. Sodenstern's night attacks failed with heavy losses, amounting to some 5,000 casualties.

Hunter-Weston wanted to attack Krithia again and quickly, but required reinforcements to do this successfully. Deploying the newly arrived 42nd (East Lancashire) Division, he was able to supplement this with two Anzac brigades that General Birdwood transferred to Helles. In

119

readiness for the next attack on Krithia, 2 (Australian) Brigade and the New Zealand Brigade, around 5,000 men in total, were joined by 125 Brigade of the 42nd Division. The RND would also be available; whilst the 29th Division's contribution would once again be spearheaded by 87 and 88 Brigades.

Second Battle of Krithia

The Second Battle of Krithia began on 6 May. Even though this was a full-scale attack by some 25,000 British and French soldiers, supported by ninety-five guns, the shells (of which there were a woeful lack) that fell on the Turkish lines had little impact. The weakened 29th Division, supported by 125 Brigade and 29 Indian Brigade, formed the left of the line from Gully Ravine to the south-east edge of Krithia. The French, together with the attached British 2 (Naval) Brigade, were to attack the high ridge running north and south above Kerevez Dere. This was key ground, whose capture would afford the best chance to the 29th Division's attack. In reserve Hamilton kept back 2 (Australian) Brigade, New Zealand Infantry Brigade and 1 (Naval) Brigade, which formed a composite division. The Turks themselves had now been reinforced and had strengthened their defences around Krithia and along the spurs that run from the village. In this area the Turks had nine battalions from a mix of regiments from the 5th, 7th, 9th, 10th and 15th Divisions, supported by several field artillery batteries and at least one howitzer battery. Some additional machine guns were added to their defence and were manned by German naval crews from the cruiser SMS *Breslau*.

The initial daylight attempts to carry the village failed. Although the struggle continued until 8 May, little could be shown of any success. Concealed trenches, machine guns and snipers held up 88 Brigade's advance on Fir Tree Spur, as did heavy fire against 125 Brigade to their right. 87 Brigade were held up by a machine gun near Y Beach on Gully Spur, and the New Zealand Infantry Brigade, which was sent up to push through 88 Brigade's lines, only managed to advance the line another 150 metres before coming to a halt under a withering hail of bullets. One last push was made in the late afternoon, supported this time by the Australian Brigade. Brigadier General James McCay, urged his men on with the words, *Now then Australians! Which of you men are Australian? Come on, Australians!* but an advance in broad daylight over a kilometre of open bullet swept ground was a costly exercise for negligible gain. The rough nature of the ground in the nullahs and ravines, to the open fields and slopes in front of Krithia, made the area perfect for defence.

The French on Hamilton's right flank had made brave efforts to advance as their drums and bugles sounded the charge. The French 2nd

Charge of 2 (Australian) Brigade at Krithia. (Charles Wheeler, 1927)

Division initially carried the whole southern face of Kerevez Dere Ridge, but then Turkish gunners directed their fire on the advancing ranks, decimating the Senegalese tirailleurs in their tracks. Both General d'Amade and General Simonin, present in person, rallied the Senegalese and, with support, took the attack back to the Turks.

The 1st Division advanced simultaneously with the 2nd Division and achieved limited success; however the advance was jeopardised when a battalion of Zouaves gave way under heavy shelling. As in the case of the 2nd Division, other battalions restored the situation and in the end the Division carried and held two complete lines of trenches near

General Albert d'Amade.

Zimmerman's Farm and captured the formidable Bouchet Redoubt.

Although an advance of 400-600 metres was made and retained, despite fierce counter-attacks, it looked like Hamilton was still putting a brave face on the dire situation that denied him Krithia and Achi Baba.

'This may not seem very much, but actually more had been won than at first meets the eye. The German leaders were quick to realise the fact. From nightfall till dawn on the 9th-10th efforts were made everywhere to push us back. An especially heavy attack was made upon the French, supported by a hot cannonade and culminating in a violent hand-to-hand conflict in front of the

121

Brigade Simonin. Everywhere the assailants were repulsed, and now for the first time I felt that we had planted a fairly firm foothold upon the point of the Gallipoli Peninsula.'

The attack cost some 6,000 casualties.

The allies had been ashore a fortnight now and, apart from wrestling a slightly firmer footing from the Turks, they had little else to show from these costly daylight frontal attacks. The stubborn Turkish defence had been a complete shock. The poor performing Ottoman army, as witnessed during the Balkan Wars, had been transformed into an organised, well disciplined and efficient fighting force that had frustrated and delayed the landings and now stopped all attempts to take Krithia and Achi Baba. But the offensive spirit had to be maintained. During the night of 12 May, 1/6 Gurkhas pushed the line forward about 500 metres, capturing an important redoubt near Y Beach that had been thwarting previous advances. This placed the British in a slightly better position for renewing the advance on this flank. Similarly, a series of four modest tactical night advances on 18, 23, 24 and 27 May resulted in the Allied line moving forward almost a kilometre with little loss, barely fifty casualties; quite a contrast to the 6,000 casualties paid for a similar distance during the last battle of Krithia.

The military situation in Gallipoli was fast degenerating into that found on the Western Front as open warfare soon gave way to solidified trench lines, meaning battles would soon be costlier in lives, munitions and resources for both sides.

On 24 May Hunter-Weston was promoted to lieutenant general and given command of the newly formed VIII Corps, formed out of the 29th, 42nd and RND. General de Lisle arrived to take over 29th Division and General Henri Gouraud took over supreme command of the French forces from General Albert d'Amade, who was evacuated in bad health.

Whilst the land battles were going on, the allied navies were causing havoc in the shape of submarine warfare. British submarines had been running the gauntlet of the Dardanelles and then disrupting Turkish supply lines to the front. This submarine warfare saw the first

General Henri Gouraud.

submariner Victoria Cross of the war being won by Lieutenant Commander Norman Holbrook, who took the British submarine *B11* up the Straits and through the minefields, where he sank the Ottoman battleship *Messudieh.* Submarine activity continued with varying results, as Lieutenant Commander Edward Boyle's *E14* successfully operated in the Marmara for three weeks, sinking two gunboats and two transports, the most important of which was an ex-White Star liner that had been carrying a battery of artillery and 6,000 Ottoman troops. The loss of French submarine *Joule,* which was sunk with all hands, did not discourage Lieutenant Commander Nasmith in *E11,* who navigated successfully through the Dardanelles on 19 May. Nasmith's ensuing patrol, which lasted two and a half weeks, became a wild rampage among Turkish shipping in the Marmara, culminating on 25 May when Nasmith entered the harbor of Constantinople itself at periscope depth and succeeded in sinking the large transport *Stamboul* just outside the Golden Horn. The effect on the Turks was electric, as the vulnerability of their capital to an attack from the sea sank home. Crowds rioted in the streets, all activity ceased on the docks, and reinforcements for the Gallipoli front were re-routed. Both Nasmith and Boyle were awarded the VC for their actions.

Lieutenant Commander Martin Nasmith VC.

Before the end of the Gallipoli campaign thirteen Allied submarines took part in the Dardanelles operations and, although eight were lost, twenty-seven successful passages were recorded. Turkish losses included two battleships, a destroyer, five gunboats, eleven transports, forty-four steamers, and 148 sailing boats. Beyond the losses of ships and material, however, the effect on the Turkish supply lines was catastrophic. By the end of 1915 the Turks' dependence on tenuous land routes into the peninsula meant that virtually all Gallipoli traffic was forced onto primitive roads along the Sea of Marmara or sent by a round about railway journey of some 600 miles.

The allies were not alone in these limited naval successes as both Turks and Germans were able to create havoc in the Aegean. During the night of 13 May HMS *Goliath* was sunk in Morto Bay by two torpedoes from the torpedo boat destroyer *Muâvenet-i Millîye. Goliath's* commanding officer, Captain Thomas Shelford, along with 570 of her 700-strong crew, were sent to the bottom with her. Then, on 25 May, HMS *Triumph* was torpedoed and sunk off Anzac by German submarine *U21,* commanded by Lieutenant Commander Otto Hersing. Two days later Hersing struck again, sinking HMS *Majestic* off Helles. Although

HMS *Majestic* sinking.

Kapitänleutnant Otto Hersing.

losses were light amongst the crew of these two ships, it shocked the Royal Navy. De Robeck ordered the immediate withdrawal of all capital ships to the safety of Mudros Harbour. In the morning the army ashore looked out to sea and observed the end of their major naval support, inevitably adding to its very low morale.

The Admiralty deployed monitors, basically gun boats, which with their shallow draughts were effectively immune to torpedo attacks as replacements for the capital ships. Once arrived these could provide the necessary fire support for the MEF (in fact actually an improvement, as they could deploy guns that acted more like a howitzer) but they would not arrive until August. Until that time the allied ships would only leave the safety of the protected harbor when an offensive was in progress. Land-based artillery would have to hold the ground in the meantime. At the same time the Turks continued to fortify the slopes of Achi Baba and all the ground around Krithia. Hamilton decided that another general attack was needed before the Turkish defences became impenetrable.

The Third Battle of Krithia
The battle plans for the next battle of Krithia were rather more realistic in the extent of the objective and more innovative; lessons were learnt

from the earlier failures. First, the objective was limited to an advance of about 750 metres, so the notion of capturing Achi Baba was temporarily abandoned. The first step was to capture the Turkish trenches; the second was to advance a further 460 metres and dig a new trench line. Secondly, there was better intelligence of Turkish positions, some provided by aerial photography. Thirdly, to shorten the advance across No Man's Land, the British lines were sapped forward during a series of night digs that brought the jumping off position to within 230 metres of the Turks, as opposed to the previous 1,600 metres.

The Third Battle of Krithia started on a sunny but breezy 4 June, beginning at 8.00 a.m. with a bombardment that would conclude at 11.20 a.m., at which point the troops would feint an advance by cheering and showing fixed bayonet, hoping to draw the Turks back into their trenches as well as getting their artillery to give away their positions. At 11.30 a.m. an intensive bombardment of the Turkish front line would restart, hopefully catching the Turks manning their trenches and with counter-battery fire then suppressing their artillery. At noon the guns would increase their range whilst the first wave of the infantry would go over the top. A second wave would follow up at 12.15 p.m. In support of the infantry four RNAS Rolls Royce armoured cars would advance along the Krithia roads, providing supporting fire from their Maxim machine guns, and, mad as it may seem, they would drive up to the Turkish wire and by the use of grappling hooks literally tow it away.

From left to right the British and French troops were deployed as follows: 29 Indian Brigade would attack along Gully Spur; the 29th Division would attack the other side of Gully Ravine on Fir Tree Spur; the 42nd Division would attack astride Krithia Nullah; 2 (Naval) Brigade

RNAS armoured cars in action.

would attack up Achi Baba Nullah and Krithia Spur, and both the French divisions would attack along Kerevez Spur. Combined, Hamilton had 30,000 men in the assault, supported by additional artillery in the form of six French quick-firing 75mm batteries. Although this was the highest number of men ever allotted to a Helles attack, they were opposed by a much strengthened Turkish line that fielded similar numbers in well prepared positions and with eighty-six guns in support.

The French, the RND brigade and the 42nd Division made a promising start, but this early success was not to last. During the French advance the formidable Haricot Redoubt was captured, but further advances were halted by the heavily defended, deep and wide Kerevez Dere Ravine. A counter-attack forced the French back, recapturing the redoubt and the ground that the French had just taken. This dangerously exposed the RND's right flank, into which the Turks poured murderous enfilade fire. When the RND's advance faltered, the next to be hit were the 42nd Division, which thus far had made some deep advances. Then the 29th Division was hit and, like a domino effect, the once coordinated, broad front, attack quickly collapsed. Most of the ground gained had to be relinquished, leaving the British with little more than a gain of 350 metres in a few places.

The cost was some 5,000 British and 2,000 French casualties, which meant that since the landings allied losses now totaled nearly 39,000 men.

60-pounder of 90th Heavy Battery, RGA.

At the end of the battle, for example, 2/RF only had one officer left out of those that landed on 25 April, whilst an additional ten replacement officers had also been lost. This battalion was not alone: 2/Hants came out of the line with barely a hundred men. One of those men was Second Lieutenant George Dallas Moor, an 18-year-old who had prevented the rout of a leaderless unit. Moor stopped the withdraw and returned them to the line, recapturing the lost trench. It was stated that he had to shoot some of the men in order to stem the retreat; regardless, his decisive action prevented a Turkish breakthrough and gained Moor the VC.

It was apparent to the high command that attacking on a broad front, unless there was a certainty of success at all points, was probably going to fail. Reinforcements in the shape of 52nd (Lowland) Division, under Major General Granville Egerton, brought some urgently needed manpower, but sufficient munitions would also be required. Even the 52nd Division would not be enough to compensate for the previous losses. On 7 June, as the Third Battle of Krithia was being fought to an unsuccessful closure, Lord Kitchener, the Secretary of State for War, sent a telegram to Hamilton confirming the availability of three New Army 'Kitchener' divisions (10th, 11th and 13th Divisions, all from K1). This was excellent news for Hamilton who, whilst waiting for their arrival, ordered the pressure to be maintained on the Turks.

Out of failure comes ingenuity and later in June there were some limited successes. Hamilton authorised two attacks; one on the extreme right flank at Kerevez Dere, the other on the left and Gully Ravine. These divisional attacks had the limited local objective of biting out a key part

An artist's interpretation of French colonial troops charging the heights.

of the Turkish line and holding it against counter-attack. This new 'bite and hold' tactic proved successful and allowed Hamilton to neutralize key Turkish redoubts that had contributed to the failure of the recent Krithia attack.

On 21 June, General Gouraud launched a French attack with two divisions, supported by mass artillery, with the objective of Hill 83, on the crest of the Kerevez Spur, and the head of Ravine de la Mort. The fighting went on into the night of 22/23 June, which resulted in the French finally capturing the Haricot Redoubt and gaining a footing in the Quadrilateral Redoubt on the top of Hill 83. Fighting then continued until 25 June as the French consolidated their gains. For the first time they had won a position that overlooked the Turks. Despite the French successes, they still remained exposed to Turkish fire on their right flank and rear from the Asiatic coast, a problem that they had to endure for the remainder of the campaign.

Turkish casualties were estimated to be nearly 6,000, causing their commander, Weber, to withdraw the weakened 2nd Division from the line, to be replaced by the 12th Division. French losses were 3,200. On 30 June General Gouraud was wounded by a shell that landed near a field ambulance on V Beach whilst he was visiting wounded. The blast of the explosion hurled him over a two-metre-high wall; both his legs were broken and his right arm damaged, later amputated when gangrene set in. (This did not stop his progress up the chain of command; by the end of the war he was a notably successful commander of the French Fourth Army on the Western Front.) General Maurice Bailloud took his place in command of the French Corps.

On 28 June, Lieutenant General Hunter-Weston launched a 'bite and hold' attack at Gully Ravine against the Ottoman 11th Division. The idea was to advance a kilometre on either side of Gully Ravine. The attack was made by the 29th Division, 29 Indian Brigade and 156 Brigade from Egerton's newly arrived, but inexperienced, 52nd Division. The objective was to capture five lines of trenches on Gully Spur, nearest the sea, and two lines of trenches on Fir Tree Spur, on the slope leading towards Krithia. A concentrated artillery bombardment that comprised mainly British and French field guns, some naval gunnery fire and supported by newly arrived trench mortars, began at 10.20 a.m. At 10.45 a.m. the infantry advanced and in two hours had successfully captured all five trenches along Gully Spur. Unfortunately, the attack on Fir Tree Spur was less successful due to insufficient artillery support and, even though a successful advance was made closest to Gully Ravine, 156 Brigade failed, despite their best efforts and enormous loss. The brigade suffered the death of its commander and 1,400 casualties, about half its strength, of

Gully Ravine.

which 800 were killed. Hunter-Weston's callous remark that *he was delighted to hear that the pups have been so well blooded* was not well received by Major General Egerton.

British casualties for Gully Ravine in total were 3,800, and Turkish casualties were as high as 14,000 by the time the battle had fought itself to a close on 5 July. The Royal Scots in the Lowland Division were still recovering from the traumatic loss on 22 May of 210 officers and men killed and another 224 that were injured in the Quintinshill rail crash, near Gretna, out of 500 men (including two of the 1/7th battalion's companies en-route for Gallipoli). In the end only the CO and five officers amongst them were deemed fit enough to proceed immediately. A knock-on effect was that the 1/4th and the 1/7th battalions had been amalgamated.

The success of Gully Ravine put the British almost within touching distance of Krithia, barely a kilometre away, but the village was never the objective for this battle. Following the June battles there was a naive expectation that the Turks would offer little resistance and were, by July, low in morale. This was far from the truth and, although the Turks were on the defensive and had suffered devastating casualties, they were a long way from conceding. Whilst Hamilton waited for the three new divisions to arrive, he needed to maintain the pressure for as long as possible: to gain tactical advantage; to maintain the moral ascendency; and to keep the Turks eyes fixed upon Helles, rather than Anzac. The offensive spirit would be maintained by an unceasing routine of trench raiding, sniping and mining, whilst he prepared for another offensive, this one being the sequel to the action of 28 June.

This new attack would bring to an end the bite and hold tactics at Helles as without adequate munitions and reinforcements the level of loss could not be sustained. On 12 July, 52nd Division, with the French Corps on the right, attacked along Achi Baba Nullah, with the object of straightening 1,800 metres on the right-centre to bring it in line with the advances made at Gully Ravine. Even though this succeeded in capturing two lines of trenches, they found themselves unsupported and exposed to retaliatory fire as the Scots tried feverishly to dig in and consolidate their gains.

Support in the form of men of the battle weary RND were sent forward on 13 July to help consolidate the gains, whilst on their right the French had managed to advance their line down to the mouth of the Kerevez Dere. After two days' fighting the result was an advance of up to 350 metres but at a cost of thirty per cent British casualties, about 3,000 men. The French suffered less; however General Joseph Masnou, commanding the 1st Division, was mortally wounded on 12 July, succumbing to his wounds a few day later. Turkish casualties were estimated at about 5,000.

On 17 July General Hunter-Weston fell ill, supposedly from exhaustion, and a few days later was evacuated sick, although what form the sickness took has remained the object of controversy ever since amongst military historians. He returned to England and found time (in October 1916) to get himself elected to the House of Commons as the Unionist member for North Ayrshire. He returned to the Western Front in March 1916 to command the re-formed VIII Corps. During the opening day of the Somme Offensive on 1 July 1916 his Corps suffered the worst casualties and failed to capture any of its objectives.

Now this over confident, unrelenting and merciless leader had gone (though not entirely without attributes, including considerable personal bravery), the tempo of leadership changed. On 24 July his place was temporarily taken by Lieutenant General Hon. Sir Frederick Stopford, who commanded VIII Corps while awaiting the arrival of IX Corps. The contrast between these two commanders could not have been more different, as we will see. With Stopford ashore, plans were well under way for Hamilton's next offensive. Apart from a diversionary attack at The Vineyard, the main offensive this time would not be at Helles.

Tour 4

The Landings Trail

Even though much of the area can be walked, the expanse of the battlefield really requires a car or similar vehicle if you are restricted in time. Allow a full day to complete all of these tours.

Allow a full morning or afternoon for this eight kilometre tour, starting and finishing at the Helles Memorial, where there is ample parking for a vehicle.

Getting to Helles: From Eceabat it is about 30 kilometres to the Helles Memorial. You can either head in a southerly direction along the Dardanelles coast, passing Kilitbair, Behramlı and Alçitepe, or else head north-west, via Anzac and then take the Aegean coast road south. Both are approximately the same distance. Once you arrive at the village of Alçitepe (Krithia), follow this road south, signposted to Seddülbahir. If you have not already visited Achi Baba and its viewing platform, this is a recommend first stop. See 'Optional Tour – Overview: Achi Baba (Chapter 1).

Please avoid walking through fields with crops; remember that most of this land is private property and this must be respected. If you have to cross a field, always follow the field boundary, preferably a track if one is available.

Park your vehicle at the **Helles Memorial (1) (40°02'44.6"N 26°10'45.0"E)**. From this vantage point you can view the whole Helles battlefield, from the entrance to the Dardanelles, across the killing fields to Achi Baba. To the west is Hill 138 (42 metres), later renamed Hunter-Weston Hill when he established VIII Corps' headquarters on its western slopes. From here the ground slopes down to Lancashire Landing before rising up onto Tekke Burnu and Hill 114 (35 metres). North of Tekke Burnu, along the Aegean coastline, is X Beach, Gully Ravine (now hidden from sight by a tree line) and Y Beach. Achi Baba (182 metres), the initial objective of the Helles landing, sits nestled in the centre, with the village of Krithia on its western spur. To the east is the village of Sedd-el-Bahr (Seddülbahir), with Hill 141 (43 metres) above it, behind

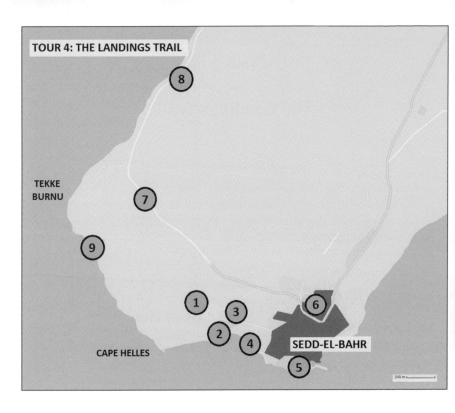

TEKKE BURNU

CAPE HELLES

SEDD-EL-BAHR

200 m

which is the French sector and the Turkish Memorial. At six kilometres deep and three kilometres wide it is not a large battlefield.

Designed by Sir John Burnet, the Helles Memorial was completed in 1924, and was described in by TJ Pemberton, in his 1926 book *Gallipoli To-Day,* as

> 'A symbol of the triumph of human nature over fearful odds; a great nation's willing sacrifice for an idea. Having suffered this splendid failure, Britain has had the courage to ignore the defeat and commemorate in stone those who never questioned the worth or wisdom of the idea. The sacrifice and valour were things far greater than the un-acquired victory.'

The obelisk style memorial stands thirty-three metres high on a hill at the tip of the Peninsula, like a lighthouse for all ships that pass through the Dardanelles to see. The hill was known as Guezji Baba, and to the Turks as Gőztepe (Eye Hill). A redoubt originally stood on this position and, along with Hill 138 (Hunter-Weston Hill), temporarily prevented the forces on W and V beaches joining up as planned.

Helles Memorial.

Guezji Baba was captured by 4/Worcs on 25 April. The memorial is designed to serve two functions: as a campaign memorial and as a place of commemoration for the 20,763 British and Indian forces who died during the campaign and whose burial places are not known. It also includes Royal Naval personnel lost or buried at sea in Gallipoli waters, and those Australian servicemen who died in the Helles region and have no known grave.

Among those commemorated there are several Victoria Cross recipients, two of whom share the same citation: Major Cuthbert Bromley and Sergeant Frank Stubbs, both 1/LF (*Panel 218*). They were two of the six selected by their comrades for singular acts of bravery and devotion to duty whilst storming W Beach on 25 April. Stubbs was killed during the landing; Bromley was drowned when HMT *Royal Edward* was sunk on 13 August. Another landings VC is Sub-Lieutenant Arthur Tisdall, Anson Battalion. Tisdall was decorated for an action on V Beach for rescuing several men from the water under a murderous fire. He was killed on 6 May during the Second Battle of Krithia. Captain Gerald O'Sullivan, 1/Inniskillings, is also commemorated here. Killed on 21 August at Suvla, O'Sullivan, who showed outstanding valour, won the VC; he was recommended twice at Gully Ravine during the night of 1/2

ROYAL WARWICKSHIRE REGT.

LIEUT. COLONEL
PALMER G. H.

MAJOR
SHARP A. G.

CAPTAIN
LOMAX J. H.
REID C. J.

LIEUTENANT
BARRETT G.
GRUNDY G. E.
MALET F. L.

SECOND LIEUT.
GRIGSON F. H.
KEMP A. G.
MARSON E. N.

COY. SJT. MAJOR
TURNER A. F.

SERJEANT
JORDAN A. E.
REID W. J.
WOODS F. J.

CORPORAL
HALL F. W. T.
REYNOLDS A. T.

LANCE CORPORAL
BRADBURY T. W.
BROOKS T.
CRIMMINS J.
CROSS R. W.
EMBREY A. E.
FARLEY F. J.
HODGES W. E.
JOYCE P. J.
LAVIN J.
RACHEL W.
ROTTENBURY H. J.
WOOLFORD W. R.

Panel of the Royal
Warwickshire
Regiment, Helles
Memorial.

July when he saved a critical situation by leading a party of bomb throwers to recapture a lost trench.

Other names of particular interest include two senior officers; Brigadier General Henry Napier, commanding 88 Brigade, who was killed during the V Beach landings; and Brigadier General Anthony Baldwin, commanding 38 Brigade, who was killed near Chunuk Bair when his Brigade HQ was overrun during Kemal's counter-attack on 10 August. Second Lieutenant Hamo Sassoon, Royal Engineers, was the brother of the war poet Siegfried Sassoon; he died of wounds at Suvla on 11 August.

From the Helles Memorial walk down the slope 150 metres to **Ertuğrul Fort (2) (40°02'41.0"N 26°10'52.7"E)**. The fort, also known as Fort No.1, was built in the 1890s, was one of five fortified emplacements guarding the entrance to the Straits, forming the outer defences of the Dardanelles. Ertuğrul and Sedd-el-Bahr forts were destroyed by the Royal Navy and subsequent Royal Marines' landing parties in February/March 1915. Rebuilt to their pre-war look, the original remains of one of the 24 cm Krupp guns can still be seen. Ertuğrul was captured by 4/Worcs just before sunset on 25 April.

Looking down from Ertuğrul are some magnificent views of V Beach, Sedd-el-Bahr Castle and its village. The systematic improvement of defences began in early 1915, when trenches were dug overlooking likely landing points. Barbed wire was stretched across the beaches; in instances where supplies were short, garden and agricultural wire was used. To

134

Ertuğrul Fort.

disguise the new defences the work was done under the cover of darkness, although that scheme did not fool the British who were certainly aware and rightly worried about them. The rock spit is still visible where the *River Clyde* ran ashore, emptying its cargo of 1/RMF and two companies of 2/Hants. The narrow sandy beach where 1/RDF scrambled ashore through a hail of fire, and the high sand bank that saved so many lives, are also clearly visible.

Visit the adjacent cemetery and **Sergeant Yahya Memorial (3) (Yahya Çavuş Şehitlik ve Aniti) (40°02'42.7"N 26°10'57.3"E)** to the Turkish soldiers who defended this area. The statue depicts three Turkish soldiers with a flag unfurled above them, charging with rifles in hand. Sergeant Yahya, 3/26 Regiment, took over the company when its commander was killed. For most of 25 April the sergeant and other isolated pockets of Turks defended the area very bravely. Well-aimed rifle fire pinned the British down on V Beach for the whole of 25 April, to such devastating effect that a RNAS pilot, Charles Samson, who was flying overhead, observed *the water simply whipped into foam by the shells and bullets ... lighters full of dead and the sea stained red with blood all along the beach*. With few exceptions the Turkish cemeteries you will see at Gallipoli are all symbolic, meaning that there are no burials within their walls. Sergeant Yahya actually survived the war.

135

Sergeant Yahya.

Leave the memorial and, turning left by the post-war pillbox and recreated trenches, take the steep road down the hill. After 150 metres turn right, taking the sunken lane that leads you to **V Beach CWGC Cemetery (4) (40°02'38.0"N 26°11'01.6"E).**

The cemetery, beautifully situated on the beach, was begun on 26 April and with the exception of thirteen graves that were brought in after the Armistice for burial in Row O all the other graves date from the landings. There are now 696 men buried or commemorated in this cemetery, 480 of whom are unidentified; special memorials commemorate 196 men known or believed to be buried among them, nearly all belonging to the units that landed on 25 April. They include Captain Garth Walford, who with Lieutenant Colonel Charles Doughty-Wylie led the survivors off the beach. Both won the Victoria Cross but were killed during the fighting. Father William Finn, who was the first RC chaplain to be killed in the war, ironically on a Sunday, is buried here alongside his commanding officer, Lieutenant Colonel Richard Rooth. Father Finn, in the same boat as Rooth, leapt over the side and was almost immediately hit in the chest at about the same time as Rooth. Although badly wounded, Finn went to the assistance of wounded and dying men who were ashore. He was then hit in the arm and leg but despite the pain that he endured, he was seen crawling about the beach talking quietly to the men and trying to give Absolution to those close to death. This was

V Beach CWGC Cemetery.

In life and death, side-by-side: Lieutenant Colonel Rooth and Reverend Finn.

not without the greatest difficulty, according to one account, as he had to hold his wounded right arm up with his left. Suffering from loss of blood and exhaustion, he was eventually killed by shrapnel.

After visiting the cemetery you might wish to take a break and either sit on the beach or visit the Mocamp café, which is open in peak season and serves food, drinks, ice cream and has a customer toilet. There are a few local shops in the village should you wish to supplement your packed lunch for the day. Leave the Mocamp and walk the 250 metres to **Sedd-el-Bahr Castle (5) (40°02'31.1"N 26°11'17.3"E)**.

In early 1915 the castle had ten large guns, antiquated but still effective. It was heavily shelled by British warships on 3 November 1914 and again on 19 and 25 February 1915, when it was finally silenced. Even

View of V Beach and Sedd-el-Bahr castle from Ertuğrul Fort.

though this objective posed no threat to the fleet during the attack on 18 March, it remained a threat for the British soldiers landing at V Beach. Defenders in these ruins could not only enfilade the men who had landed on the beach, but they also helped counter the smaller 1/RDF landing at the Camber. Two staff officers, Doughty-Wylie and Walford, fought their way through the castle and up through the village. Walford was killed exiting the castle whilst Doughty-Wylie pressed on, leading the Irishmen to the fort on Hill 141.

Leave the Castle and follow the steep road that runs up to the west of the village. After 500 metres, you will reach Hill 141, where you will see a sign for **Doughty-Wylie VC Grave (6) (40°02'46.3"N 26°11'21.5"E)**. His grave is by the site of an old hill fort, once circled by a moat. On 26 April increased rifle fire forced Doughty-Wylie's party to seek cover in the fort's moat. Doughty-Wylie, with no thought for his own safety, with initiative, skill and great gallantry, continued to direct the attack, but whilst climbing out of the moat was *killed in the moment of victory*. He was buried where he fell and, uniquely on the peninsula, it is maintained as a solitary burial by the CWGC. Just behind the grave the remains of the moat are still evident, although little can be seen of the fort itself. It

138

The lone grave of Lieutenant Colonel Charles Doughty-Wylie VC.

is believed that his wife, Lilian, visited his grave in November 1915, the only woman to have stepped upon these shores during the campaign.

Leave Doughty-Wylie's grave and take the track back to the main road. Follow this road for about 1.5 kilometres, past the Helles Memorial and Hill 138 on the left. Stop at the **Lancashire Landing CWGC Cemetery (7) (40°03'12.6"N 26°10'24.5"E)**. The cemetery, which is set back from W Beach, was started immediately after the landings. It stands on a small ridge named Karaja Oghul Tepe that leads up to Hill 114 (Tekke Burnu). There is a total of 1,171 graves from the United Kingdom, twenty-seven from Australia, fifteen from New Zealand, two from Canada, one man from the Zion Mule Corps, another from the local Mule Corps and seventeen Greek labourers. The unidentified graves number 135, with eleven special memorials to those who are known to be buried here. There are also graves moved here after the war from the islands of Imbros and Tenedos. The register contains details of 1,101 burials and commemorations. The larger part of the cemetery (Rows A to J and part of Row L) was made between the landing in April and the final evacuation of the peninsula. Row I contain the graves of over eighty men

Lancashire Landing CWGC Cemetery.

Captain Harold Cawley, MP.

of the Lancashire Fusiliers who died in the first two days following the landing. The ninety-seven graves in Row K and graves 31 to 83 in Row L were brought in after the Armistice from the Aegean island cemeteries of Imbros (Imbroz) and Tenedos (Bozcaada).

Amongst those buried is the politician Captain Harold Cawley, MP (*row A, grave 76*), 6/Manchesters, who was killed defending a mine crater (later named Cawley's Crater) near Gully Ravine. Cawley was the fourth MP to die in the war, and one of three sons that the long-serving Liberal MP Sir Frederick Cawley was to lose in the war.

Before his death Cawley had written a letter home to his father that included a scathing criticism of the mishandling of the Dardanelles campaign. As a Member of Parliament, his correspondence was not subject to military censorship, enabling him to convey a frank assessment of the situation. He wrote, for example, of Major General Sir William Douglas, 42nd Division, that:

'He has a third-rate brain, no capacity to grasp the lie of the land, and no originality or ingenuity … He has been in the trenches three times since he landed, hurried visits on which he saw next to nothing … He is always thinking of himself, his food, his promotion, his health.'

140

Interestingly, in 1916 Cawley's father served on the Dardanelles Commission that inquired into the conduct of the campaign.

Also buried here is an Irish Rugby Union player, Lieutenant Vincent McNamara RE (*row L, grave 9*). McNamara was a tunnelling officer. On 29 November he detonated a charge under a Turkish tunnel. When he went down to investigate he was asphyxiated by the resulting gas from the explosion that had not dispersed. Lance Sergeant John Keneally VC (*row C, grave 104*) won the Victoria Cross on W Beach on 25 April. He died of wounds received at Gully Ravine on 29 June.

Lieutenant Vincent McNamara.

Leave the cemetery and follow the road in a north-westerly direction for one kilometre until you see a narrow sign-posted track that leads down onto **X Beach (8) (40°03'43.7"N 26°10'35.2"E)**. X Beach was also known as 'Implacable Landing' because of the close co-operation of HMS *Implacable* in support of 2/RF. Retrace your steps back 750 metres to the rough track on the right of the road. This will lead you past Hill 141, where 2/RF and 1/LF joined up during the morning of the landings. After 400 metres the track will fork. Take the right-hand turn, which leads 250 metres down to **W Beach (Lancashire Landing) (9) (40°03'01.2"N 26°10'06.7"E)**.

The cove is also known as Tekke Koyu, whilst the high ground between the beach and Hill 114 is known as Tekke Burnu. There is little

X Beach.

W Beach, later known as Lancashire Landing.

Wrecked lighters and piers still exist today.

that remains from the landing with the exception of Turkish trenches that still line the cliff tops on both sides of the beach. After the landing, this cove became the main supply base for VIII Corps and evidence of this can still be found, such as the skeletal remains of stone piers and jetties, wrecked lighters, concrete water troughs and remains of dugouts. On the eastern side of the beach there is a large area of rough ground that looks as if a large section of the cliff had fallen away. This was actually caused when the munitions and supply dumps were detonated during the early morning of 9 January 1916, the last day of the evacuation. A large field of rock and boulders still cover the area, clear evidence of the enormous force of this explosion.

It is possible to follow the field boundaries and walk from the eastern side of the beach, up onto the cliffs and over the fields to Hunter-Weston Hill and the Helles Memorial, in the footsteps of 4/Worcs. Alternatively, and an easier route, is to return to the foot track and follow this back two kilometres to the Helles Memorial.

End of tour.

Tour 5

The Gully Ravine Trail

This is a three kilometre walk that begins/ends at Pink Farm Cemetery, but, whilst short, it is over some rough ground. Its purpose is to give you a feel of Gully Ravine and the hive of activity that would have surrounded this area during the campaign. There are several Gully Ravine walks mapped out in my Battleground Europe book *Gallipoli: Gully Ravine*, and so detail is not given here.

To find your way to the mouth of Gully Ravine leave the Helles Memorial, passing Lancashire Landing Cemetery and X Beach. When the road takes a sudden curve to the right, moving away from the sea, you will be above the entrance to Gully Ravine (approximately 4.3 kilometres from the Helles Memorial). Continue another 400 metres to **Pink Farm CWGC Cemetery (10) (40°04'21.9"N 26°11'26.3"E)** where you can park your vehicle off the road, within the shade of the trees.

During the campaign Pink Farm was a ruined stone building, originally called Sotiri Farm, close to a cart track, called West Krithia Road. In a letter from Noel Sergent, who served in 10/French Artillery, he wrote that after he left Pink Farm he *came into the loveliest country. I*

Pink Farm CWGC Cemetery.

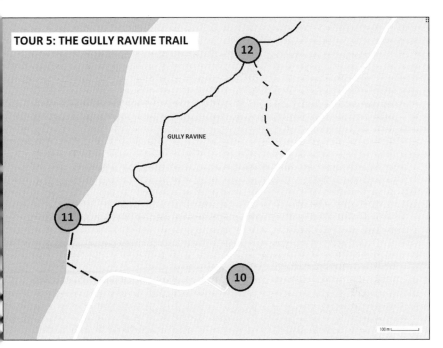

GULLY RAVINE

could hardly believe my eyes; it was just like Valescure. Small tufts of pine trees, thyme, donkey-pepper and heather.[3] Today, little has changed.

Known to the troops as Pink Farm because of the colour of the soil in the area, the area was used as a forward supply dump, serving also as the headquarters for VIII Corps Mining Company. The farm also acted as a collection point for the wounded to be taken down from the front line; from here on they were taken to the field hospitals by mule-drawn ambulance if needed. In the surrounding woods there are also remains of trenches and dugouts.

The grave concentration at Pink Farm Cemetery, begun in late April 1915, brought together several smaller cemeteries after the Armistice. During the campaign there were originally three cemeteries here, Pink Farm No.1, No.2 and No.3. After the war these and six other smaller cemeteries – 29th Division Cemetery, 52nd Division Cemetery, Aerodrome Cemetery, Oak Tree Cemetery, Gully Beach Cemetery and Gully Farm Cemetery – were closed and their occupants reinterred here. Pink Farm Cemetery now contains a total of 602 graves: 209 United Kingdom forces, three from New Zealand, and two from Australia, five from the Indian Army and 164 unidentified. The total number of burials in the cemetery is 383 and special memorial tablets amount to 219. The register contains details of 352 burials and commemorations.

---

3. Sergent, JNB, 'With The French Artillery', *The Gallipolian*, No.67, Christmas 1991, p.20.

Amongst those buried here are Captain Christopher Birdwood (*plot IV, row A, grave 6*), 6/Gurkhas, who was mortally wounded during the Third Battle of Krithia, dying of wounds on 7 June at the 108/Indian Field Ambulance on Gully Beach. He was a distant relation to a fellow Indian army officer, General Sir William Birdwood, the ANZAC commander. A senior officer buried here is Lieutenant Colonel George Stoney DSO (*Spec. Mem. 204*), commanding 1/KOSB. He had only just returned from Suvla with his battalion when he was killed by a shell. Stoney, one of four brothers who joined the army, was Military Landing Officer at V Beach on 25 April, where he had organised parties of the Dublin and Munster Fusiliers on the beach in preparation for the attack to clear Sedd-el-Bahr and Hill 141.

Leave Pink Farm on foot, walk in a westerly direction for 400 metres, back to the curve in the road, where you will find a couple of rough tracks that lead down to the beach. Follow the track to Gully Beach and the sea.

Gully Ravine was also known as Ziğin Dere, Sighin Dere or even Lone Pine Creek. Along the beach used to run the original beach road, constructed out of sight of the enemy during summer 1915. It ran beneath the cliffs, from Lancashire Landing to Gully Beach, and thence up Gully Ravine to the front line. This beach road, remnants of which survive between Tekke Burnu and X Beach, also served as a route for the evacuation. The beach bustled with activity from May 1915 onwards and anything from Field Ambulances to canteens were soon taking up prime sea view locations. The headquarters of both 29th and 42nd Division were also once positioned here. Two men were 'shot at dawn' on this beach: Private Thomas Davis, 1/RMF, who was charged with quitting his post and was executed on 2 July; and Sergeant John Robins, 5/Wilts, who was charged with wilfully disobeying an order and executed on 2 January 1916. Both received posthumous pardons in August 2006.

Close to **Gully Beach (11) (40°04'30.3"N 26°11'05.0"E)** is the wreck of a British 'X' Lighter. It is the remains of the vessel that was accidentally run aground during the evacuation on 9 January 1916. Beside the lighter are the remains of Gully Pier, used during the campaign for smaller boats to dock in order to transfer supplies and take off the wounded. It was last used during the evacuation. The remains, now just piles of rock, reinforced with iron and concrete, can still be clearly seen emerging from the sea. In the mouth of the ravine itself is a Royal Engineers' water well, which was constructed in 1915. The well is referred to in *Gallipoli As I Saw It*, written by a veteran, Joseph Murray of the Hood Battalion, RND. If you look closely, you can still make out the words '*RE 135 COMPANY*' etched into the top of the concrete. There

Gully Beach today.

was a chronic water shortage at Helles, to the extent that additional water supplies had to be shipped to Gallipoli from Egypt.

Turn your back to the sea and look at the scrubby bushes above the plateau, where there are still various signs of where the troops used to live gently scarring the ridges. Everywhere on the Peninsula you will find fragments of earthenware rum jars, which make a useful path for following the British in battle, particularly here at Gallipoli but also on parts of the Western Front. Some still bear the initials 'S.R.D', officially Supply Reserve Depot, although the troops referred to it as 'Seldom Reaches Destination', amongst many other names. Another legacy of war are the many bullets and bones that are found lying on the surface of the fields or in the nooks and crannies of the ravine, clear evidence of the once heavy fighting in this area, exposed and buried again whenever there is heavy rainfall, which rushes down the gully to the sea.

The Gully is a strange and disturbing place, if ghosts walk anywhere they walk in Gully Ravine.[4] Entering Gully Ravine from the beach you will soon notice, once inside its mouth, that the sea breeze suddenly stops and that the heat and silence of the enclosed gully then hits you. This part of the ravine is fairly wide, but soon the walls close in on you, tall and steep. This is the very same route the troops would have taken during 1915. In dry weather it is perfectly walkable, although there are limited

---

4. Sellers, Leonard, "Incident at Gully Ravine", *RND Magazine*, No.2, September 1997, p.139

Entrance to Gully Ravine today.

options to exit the ravine once committed. For this walk we will be taking the first main exit just over a kilometre into the ravine.

The ravine was a hive of activity during the war, the main communication link for the front line on the western part of Helles. Gully Ravine became a warren for the troops that lived, slept and died through those now distant months of 1915. In the surrounding scrub there are many remnants of the previous occupation, from broken rum jars, glass bottles and jam tins to the odd button, bullet and shrapnel piece. Many of the other small offshoot gullies sheltered everything from Indian and Zion Mule Corps mules to cookhouses, stores, ammunition dumps and field dressing posts. There even sprang up a small Divisional School, where they constructed a rifle range and held bombing classes, both giving useful experience to newly arrived reinforcements.

Continue into the ravine for about a kilometre, keeping a look out for two rough tracks that will lead you out of the ravine. On the right hand, eastern, side, you can see a steep dirt track going up to Fir Tree Spur. This is **Artillery Road (12) (40°04'48.8"N 26°11'31.5"E)**, built by the British during the campaign, which leads to West Krithia Road and Pink Farm. Almost opposite this track, on the western side of the Ravine, another wartime track leads up onto Gully Spur, called Artillery Row, at the top of which British artillery used to be located. Follow Artillery Road out of the ravine and after about 200 metres you will reach the fields on Fir Tree Spur. Cross the field boundary and walk about 100 metres to the road. Turn right, and walk in a southerly direction for about 300 metres, returning to Pink Farm Cemetery to complete your tour.

148

Tour 6

The Krithia Trail

This is a five kilometre walk that begins/ends at Redoubt Cemetery. Its purpose is to give you a feel of the central part of the Helles battlefield, and the ground fought over during the battles for Krithia. There are several Krithia walks mapped out in my Battleground Europe book *Helles: Krithia*, where more detail is given.

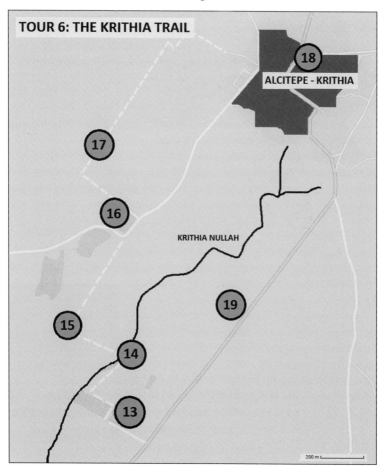

Redoubt CWGC Cemetery.

Redoubt Cemetery (13) (40°04'41.4"N 26°12'53.9"E) is located on the Krithia road that runs between Sedd-el-Bahr and the village of Alçitepe (Krithia). It takes its name from a line of Turkish entrenchments dug during the May fighting, later called the Redoubt Line. It was here that the British and Australian advance was halted during the Second Battle of Krithia. To the north east of the cemetery is the infamous 'Vineyard', today an olive grove that bears no scars of the fighting that occurred here in August 1915 as a diversion for the Sari Bair attack. The cemetery was started by 2 (Australian) Brigade in May and continued in use until the evacuation. After the Armistice, when the battlefields were cleared, graves were brought in from smaller cemeteries: Krithia Nullah No.1 and No.2, West Krithia Nullah, Brown House, White House and Clapham Junction. There are now 2,027 servicemen buried or commemorated in this cemetery. Of those buried, 1,393 are unidentified and there are special memorials that commemorate 349 casualties known or believed to be buried here.

As with almost any CWGC cemetery, it is beautifully planted with small plants and shrubs, and mature trees grow majestically, providing valuable shade on a hot sunny day. Here there is one notable tree, an English oak, which was planted as a special memorial in 1922 by the father of Second Lieutenant Eric Duckworth.

Second Lieutenant Eric Duckworth.

150

Duckworth, an officer in 6/LF, was killed in action near this spot on 7 August during the fighting at The Vineyard. His body was never found. Duckworth wrote his last letter home to his mother on 5 August;

'Little enough did I think 12 months ago today that on the anniversary of mobilisation I should be writing you from a hole in the Gallipoli Peninsula, not having seen you for 10 months, and to the tune of 75mm guns. However, you never know your luck, and I may see you in time to celebrate my 20th birthday at home, but as things look at present there is not much chance of that.'

Lieutenant Colonel Robert Gartside *(I.B.21)*, commanding 7/AIF, was killed on 8 May. An orchardist of Castlemaine, Victoria, he is said to have been rising to lead one of the final rushes, saying, *Come on boys, I know it is deadly, but we must get on*, when he was hit in the abdomen by machine-gun bullets. There is also a grave of a Sikh, Sepoy Saudagar Singh, 14/Sikhs, who was killed at Gully Ravine on 4 June during the Third Battle of Krithia. It is Sikh custom for their dead to be cremated, so this is one of only a few Sikh graves at Gallipoli.

Lieutenant Colonel Gartside, 8th AIF.   Gartside's grave.

Leave Redoubt Cemetery and walk around the western side of the cemetery wall, skirting the woodland for about 100 metres towards Krithia Nullah. The woodland contains deep communication trenches, marked on period trench maps as 'Avenues' and which would have once led up to the front line. Follow the tree lined nullah for 250 metres, crossing the sites of what would have been the Redoubt Line and Burnley Road trenches, established here in May 1915. Near the site of **Wigan Road trench (14) (40°04'52.8"N 26°12'53.3"E)**, the remains of which can still be seen near in the wooded thicket, cross the nullah to its western

151

banks. The trench lines would have continued here with more Manchester region names such as Oldham Road and Ardwick Green, all named after the regiments of the 42nd Division, a Territorial division formed from units from East Lancashire that fought in this area from May 1915.

Once across the nullah, follow the field boundary in a westerly direction for about 200 metres where you will come to a track which once marked the **Divisional Boundary (15) (40°04'57.6"N 26°12'44.2"E)** of the 29th and 42nd Division's in June 1915. This is also the approximate position of the British front line for the opening of the Third Battle of Krithia. It is close to here that one of the most controversial Victoria Crosses of the campaign was won, that of Lieutenant George Raymond Dallas Moor. Moor, only aged 18, was in 2/Hants and in the area during the Third Battle of Krithia. His VC citation read:

Second Lieutenant George Raymond Dallas Moor VC.

> 'For most conspicuous bravery and resource on the 5th June, 1915, during operations South of Krithia, Dardanelles. When a detachment of a battalion on his left, which had lost all its officers, was rapidly retiring before a heavy Turkish attack, 2nd Lieutenant Moor, immediately grasping the danger to the remainder of the line, dashed back some two hundred yards, stemmed the retirement, led back the men, and recaptured the lost trench. This young officer, who only joined the Army in October, 1914, by his personal bravery and presence of mind saved a dangerous situation.'

The action actually took place early on 6 June during the Turkish counter-attack following the battle. Moor 'stemmed the retirement' by shooting four of the men. In the words of the 29th Division's commander, Lieutenant General Sir Beauvoir de Lisle, Moor shot 'the leading four men and the remainder came to their senses'. De Lisle, in a commentary on Moor's VC action, said, 'I have often quoted this young Officer as being one of the bravest men I have met in this War.' Balancing the desperate measures taken by Moor is the certainty that a disorderly rout of a kind that threatened to overtake the British line would unquestionably have resulted in far higher casualties among the retreating troops. Moor was invalided home soon afterwards, suffering from dysentery. He went on to gain the Military Cross and later a bar for bravery on the Western

Front, but died of the Spanish Flu a week before the Armistice in November 1918. He is buried in Y Farm Cemetery, Bois Grenier.

Follow the track in a northerly direction for another 400 metres to **Twelve Tree Copse CWGC Cemetery (16) (40°05'15.1"N 26°12'54.6"E)**. Twelve Tree Copse was originally a small group of pine trees, situated just south of the present-day cemetery, named by the men of the 29th Division when they reached this area on 28 April. The copse is set a few metres north of Fir Tree Wood, to the right of the pre-war West Krithia Road. The contemporary road follows this very closely. The cemetery, which was formed after the Armistice, contains a total of 3360 graves formed by the concentration of smaller cemeteries and isolated graves from the battlefield. These include Geoghegan's Bluff Cemetery, Fir Tree Wood Cemetery and Clunes Vennel Cemetery, all of which had their bodies exhumed by the Graves Registration Unit in 1919.

The cemetery contains the graves of 462 soldiers from the United Kingdom, thirteen from New Zealand, two from Australia, and 1,953 whose unit could not be ascertained. The unnamed graves number 2,226; and special memorials are erected to 644 soldiers from the UK, ten from New Zealand, one from Australia, and two from India known or believed to be buried among them. Of these, forty-seven are to 7/Cameronians (Scottish Rifles) who fell on 28 June during the battle of Gully Ravine, and 142 to the 1/Essex who died on 6 August during the diversionary action at Helles for the Anzac breakout and Suvla landing. There is also a New Zealand Memorial to the missing, one of four on the Peninsula, with 180 New Zealand names of those killed during the Second Battle of Krithia, in May 1915.

Three senior officers of 156 Brigade are buried here: Brigadier General William Scott-Moncrieff (*Special Memorial C. 132*), commanding the brigade, Lieutenant Colonel John Boyd Wilson (*Special Memorial C. 406*), commanding 7/Cameronians and Lieutenant Colonel Henry Hannan (*plot VII, row A, grave 7*), commanding 8/Cameronians. Other notable burials include Second Lieutenant Alfred Smith VC, *Croix de Guerre* (*Special Memorial C. 358*), 5/East Lancs, a pre-war police inspector who was posthumously decorated with the Victoria

Second Lieutenant Alfred Smith VC.

153

Grave of Second Lieutenant Alfred Smith VC.

Cross for an action at Fusilier Bluff. Smith was originally buried in a battlefield grave above Y Beach, but his body was exhumed after the war. Sergeant John Robins, 5/Wilts (*Special Memorial C. 259*), was one of three Gallipoli men executed during the campaign. Robins was 'shot at dawn' at Gully Beach on 2 January 1916, charged with *wilfully disobeying an order given by a superior officer in the execution of his duty.*

Leave Twelve Tree Copse Cemetery and follow the field track that begins on the northern side of the cemetery for about 100 metres. This track marks the approximate position of a trench system named Worcester Flat, the British Front line. Follow the track to the right, which after 50 metres is the site of **Sap 30 (17) (40°05'24.6"N 26°12'51.9"E)**, where Brigadier General Scott-Moncrieff was killed on 28 June whilst watching 156 Brigade suffering heavy casualties in an attempt to capture the Turkish H12 trench line. This position marks the furthest advance the British made towards Krithia. Stay on this track for one kilometre, heading towards the village of Krithia.

Alçitepe, Krithia (18) (40°05'41.4"N 26°13'30.6"E) was an important objective that was never captured during the campaign; the closest British troops came to Krithia was on the 25 April when an officer patrol from Y Beach reached the outskirts of the village. Ottoman Greeks had been settled in the village before the war but were later moved to Anatolia during the military build-up on the Peninsula in 1915. To the east of the village there used to be a small cluster of windmills, used for extracting oil from olives, but all of these were destroyed during the war and never rebuilt. The village, also known as Kirte, was resettled in the 1930s, when it was renamed Alçitepe. The village today has a variety of Kofta restaurants, a few small shops and market stalls, public toilets and probably the oldest campaign museum on Gallipoli: the private collection of Salim Mutlu.

Note: If you are interested in visiting the top of Gully Ravine and Y Beach, you can leave Alçitepe on its western road. This will take you towards Fusilier Bluff via several Turkish memorials: the Son Ok ('Last Arrow') Memorial, that commemorates an action during the Third Battle of Krithia; the Ziğindere Field Dressing Station Memorial and Cemetery; and at Fusilier Bluff the Nuri Yamut Memorial and the nearby Ziğindere Military Cemetery. For further details see my book *Gallipoli: Gully Ravine*.

Leave Krithia by its main, southern 'Krithia road'. After about one kilometre you will pass the site of **The Vineyard (19) (40°04'54.4"N 26°13'15.0"E)**, sign-posted to the west of the road. The area was the sign of very heavy fighting in August 1915 and the place where Lieutenant William Thomas Forshaw, 1/9 Manchester Regiment, won his VC. Forshaw led his company in a forty-one hour fierce defence of a captured Turkish position close to where you are now standing. His citation reads:

'For most conspicuous bravery and determination in the Gallipoli Peninsula from 7th to 9th August 1915. When holding the northwest corner of the 'Vineyard' he was attacked and heavily bombed by Turks, who advanced time after time by three trenches which converged at this point, but he held his own, not only directing his men and encouraging them by exposing himself with the utmost disregard to danger, but personally throwing bombs

The Vineyard.

continuously for 41 hours. When his detachment was relieved after 24 hours he volunteered to continue the direction of operations. Three times during the night of 8th-9th August he was again heavily attacked, and once the Turks got over the barricade, but, after shooting three with his revolver, he led his men forward and recaptured it. When he re-joined his battalion he was choked and sickened by bomb fumes, badly bruised from a fragment of shrapnel, and could barely lift his arm from continuous bomb throwing. It was due to his personal example, magnificent courage and endurance that this very important corner was held.'

After the action Forshaw was reported to look yellow as a result of cordite and cigarette fumes, and visibly shaken. He survived the campaign and war, later serving in the Home Guard during the Second World War. He died of a heart attack in 1943, aged only 53.

Return the last 800 metres to Redoubt Cemetery.

End of the tour.

There are additional walks and further detail of the Helles battlefield mapped out in my Battleground Europe books *Helles: Krithia*.

An artists impression of the 'Cigarette VC'.

Lieutenant William Forshaw VC.

Chapter 4

Suvla

The landing at Suvla Bay was planned as part of the August offensive, what turned out to be Sir Ian Hamilton's last throw of the dice to try and break the deadlock at Gallipoli. This new amphibious landing took the Turks by surprise but, despite initialing facing light opposition, the landing at Suvla was mismanaged from the outset and the situation quickly reached the same stalemate that prevailed on the Anzac and Helles fronts. After a week of indecision and inactivity, the British commander at Suvla, Lieutenant General Sir Frederick Stopford, was dismissed; his performance in command is often considered one of the most incompetent feats of generalship of the First World War. Suvla, known to the Turks today as the Anafartalar battles, was a great victory for them against overwhelming odds. The dynamic leadership of Mustafa Kemal, such a contrast to the British generals, defeated Britain's last hopes for a successful outcome to the Gallipoli campaign.

Suvla, just north of Anzac, is a beautiful crescent shaped bay about three kilometres long, with two rocky promontories forming the horns of the bay: Suvla Point to the north, Nibrunesi Point to the south. Towards the southern end, nearly touching the sea, is a large salt lake, which in summer 1915 was practically dry. Between the Salt Lake and sea is a narrow causeway of sand, the same pure white sand that covers the beaches of this eclipse shaped shore. The country inland is generally flat, a semi cultivated valley but covered with low sand hills and under features, with patches of scrub, broken by ravines and gullies, drainage ditches and farms. This plain is encircled by hills, covered with thick, thorny, dwarf oak scrub, almost resembling woodland in places.

'[It is] a bay of exquisite beauty. Think of the most lovely part of the west coast of Scotland; make the sea perfectly calm, perfectly transparent and deep blue; imagine an ideal August day; add an invigorating breeze; and you can picture our impression of the coast of Gallipoli.'

Captain William Wedgwood Benn,
1/1 County of London Yeomanry.

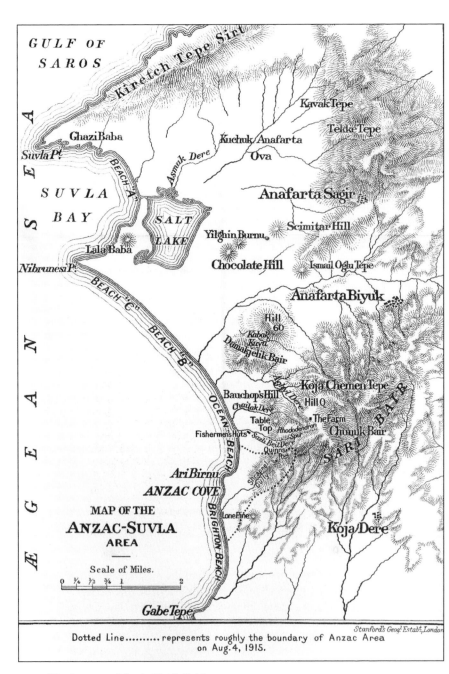

The Anzac and Suvla Battlefields.

Its beauty today is in contrast to the horrors witnessed there in 1915. Suvla was to become a name that brought sorrow into many households, a name associated with lost hope and failure.

The Background

On 7 June, as the Third Battle of Krithia came to an unsuccessful closure, Lord Kitchener, the Secretary of State for War, sent a telegram confirming the availability of three New Army 'Kitchener' divisions (10th, 11th and 13th Divisions) to the MEF. Initially an all-volunteer army, the New Army was formed in the United Kingdom following the outbreak of hostilities in 1914. Eventually totaling thirty fighting divisions, these New Army men were blooded at Gallipoli and went on to prove their worth on the battlefields of Salonika, Palestine, Mesopotamia, Italy and also France and Flanders, where they tested their mettle during the battles of the Somme and Passchendaele. In addition, Kitchener planned to send two additional Territorial Army divisions, the 'Saturday Night Soldiers' as they were known – men with some weekend military training, summer camp attendance but not professional soldiers. Hopefully this reinforcement would allow Hamilton to make a decisive break through and end the campaign once and for all.

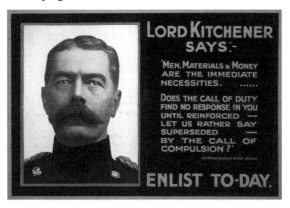

Recuitment Poster: *Lord Kitchener Says Enlist Today.*

As planning progressed for the Anzac offensive, a problem arose: how to accommodate five new divisions, and then manoeuvre them in battle when the Anzac area was already congested. Supply was also a concern for the MEF, in no fit state to support a long drawn out operation. Anzac had a small and congested beachhead where movement was difficult, not only due to its size and difficult terrain but its beaches were exposed to enemy fire and the mercy of the weather. With autumn approaching and

159

Suvla Panorama.

with the threat of a winter campaign, the need for a safe harbour became paramount. The August plan was widened to include a new landing at Suvla Bay, which was suitable as a port and future base for subsequent operations.

As the newly formed IX Corps landed at Suvla Bay, it was hoped that the Anzac assaulting columns would be closing on the Sari Bair heights, to capture them by dawn on 7 August. This Anzac movement would be critical as without seizing Sari Bair the whole success of the operation would be in jeopardy. The primary objective of IX Corps was the capture of Suvla Bay and the establishment of a supply port for the Anzac breakout. In order to achieve this it was expected that the Corps would capture both Chocolate and W Hills before daylight. Once these objectives were secured, the ring of hills that surrounded the Suvla plain were to be captured, from the village of Anafarta Sagir in the south to Ejelmer Bay in the north. Only after this would Suvla Bay be truly secure.

According to intelligence collected in late July, it was estimated that the Turks had approximately 30,000 men north of Kilid Bahr, of which 12,000 were in the trenches opposing the Anzacs. The majority of the remaining 18,000 were known to be concentrated in reserve about Boghali, Koja Dere and Eski Keui. Closer to Suvla were about five battalions, three in the area around the villages of Anafarta, one at the W Hills and another at the Chocolate Hills, with outposts at Lala Baba and Ghazi Baba. It was also known that the surrounding hills were garrisoned by the Gendarmerie, with an artillery battery positioned at W Hills and Chocolate Hills, protected by trenches and a little barbed wire, but nothing that was thought to prove a significant obstacle. It would be a race to capture these objectives before the Turks could bring forward their reserves from Bulair. It was estimated, soon to prove accurate, that the road march from Bulair to Suvla would take approximately thirty hours, which meant that Turkish reinforcements would arrive sometime on 8 August. Thus it was vital to be in possession of the high ground by that time.

160

To achieve the Suvla objectives the plan was to simultaneously land the three infantry brigades of 11th (Northern) Division, a total disembarkation of 13,700 men and twelve guns. The landing was scheduled for the night of 6/7 August, when it was known that it would be pitch black, thus helping mask the initial landing, and before moonlight at 2.00 a.m., which would then assist the men to advance from the shore. In the morning a further 7,000 infantry from 10th (Irish) Division would land, followed by forty-four additional guns, not forgetting all the associated horses, mules, ammunition, vehicles and stores of an army corps. It was hoped that the first ten thousand men would be landed in about an hour, put ashore from purpose-built motorised armoured lighters, each capable of holding 500 soldiers. Nicknamed 'beetles', because of their black paint and prominent antennae like prows that held the landing ramp, they would allow the quick disembarkation of the troops. Their official name was 'X' Lighters, and were part of an original order by the Admiralty in February 1915 for a proposed landing in the Baltic. The shallow draft craft, powered by heavy oil engines with hull constructions similar to the London barges, were designed with a spoon-shaped bow and a drop down ramp to allow easy access to and from the shore. The beetles, the forerunner of the modern landing craft, soon became the workhorse of the Royal Navy at Gallipoli and were used to carry troops, horses, field guns and stores; some were even converted to carry and pump water, and they were used for the remainder of the campaign, including helping in the final evacuation. What Hamilton did not want was a repeat of the April landings when, due to these craft not being ready in time, he was forced to use open rowing boats and tows with the subsequent high casualty cost and delays in getting troops ashore.

Command of the landing flotilla was put in the safe hands of Captain Edward Unwin VC, hero of the V Beach landings, who was still serving alongside the faithful Midshipman George Drewry VC. Unwin planned to use three landing beaches, code named A, B and C. Both B and C beaches were to the south of Nibrunesi Point, whilst A Beach was inside Suvla Bay. At first light the plan was to perform a full reconnaissance of

161

Two over crowded 'Beetles' landing the Essex Regiment at Suvla.

Suvla Bay in order to find the best beach in which to land the main force. This force would then be disembarked on barrel and trestle piers that were to be constructed on the main landing beach within the bay. The success of this scheme would be dependent on the bay being secured before daylight, namely stringing out an anti-submarine net to safeguard the fleet and for the covering force successfully to drive back the enemy from the area.

IX Corps initially comprised two brigades of the 10th (Irish) Division and the entire 11th (Northern) Division. The 13th Division and 29 Brigade (10th Division) were detached and sent to reinforce Birdwood at Anzac. Command of IX Corps was given to Lieutenant General Sir Frederick Stopford. Stopford was chosen not because of his experience or his energy and enthusiasm but because of his position on the list of seniority. Hamilton wanted either Sir Julian Byng or Sir Henry Rawlinson to have the command, both of whom were experienced Western Front corps commanders. However this would not be possible, even if Kitchener could prise away either of these men from the Western Front, as both officers were junior to Lieutenant General Sir Bryan Mahon. Mahon, commander of the 10th Division, was favoured by Kitchener for promotion; however Hamilton thought he had reached his peak as a divisional commander and so rejected him. As time would tell, this was probably a costly mistake. If it was not to be Mahon, Kitchener stipulated that whoever commanded IX Corps must be senior to him. The British

Army at the time still used this much outdated practice of seniority, whereby the system placed its faith on the date of the commission listing as opposed to evident talent. This this left only two lieutenant generals, Lieutenant General Sir John Ewart and Lieutenant General Sir Frederick Stopford. Hamilton ruled out Ewart due to *his constitutional habit,* stating that he would not *last out here for one fortnight.* So, by a process of elimination, this left only Stopford.

Lieutenant General Sir Frederick Stopford, GOC IX Corps.

The relatively elderly Stopford was 61 years old and, although a career soldier, by 1915 had been retired for six years due to ill health and was the Lieutenant of the Tower of London. From a predominantly staff background, with little active service experience, his new posting as a corps commander of raw troops on what was one of the most demanding battlefields of the war was to be a stark contrast to his ceremonial London posting. However there was no alternative at that time, and this recipe for disaster was to result in Stopford, who lasted only a week on the battlefield, becoming a scapegoat for the failure of the August Offensive.

When Stopford first saw the plan on 22 July, he acknowledged that, *it is a good plan. I am sure it will succeed and I congratulate whoever has been responsible for framing it.* Emphasis was on the use of surprise, and a rapid advance from the beaches to secure the surrounding hills. Suvla was only lightly defended, with entrenchments at the Karakol Dagh, Hill 10 and Chocolate Hills, and the outpost on Lala Baba. Apart from these unconnected positions, Suvla lay virtually undefended. Stopford's chief-of-staff, Brigadier General Hamilton Reed, was not so enthusiastic and his doubts and prejudices succeeded in swaying Stopford. Reed, an artillery officer who had served on the Western Front, believed no assault on entrenched positions could be made without artillery support even though intelligence proved that there were no fortifications at Suvla. Stopford, after listening to Reed, watered down the objectives of the landing, thereby removing the original notion for the speed and ferocity of the initial assault, a key component of the attack whilst IX Corps had the surprise.

Due to the poor operational security during the April landings, Hamilton considered secrecy for the August offensive was so essential that it had to be restricted to a few trusted staff officers. Because of this, knowledge of the forthcoming operation was only shared at the last possible moment, which had a detrimental effect on its success. The 11th Division, who would act as the spearhead, were only issued orders during

OPERATIONS AGAINST SUVLA

THE LANDING OF THE XIᵀᴴ DIVISION

Karakol Ridge

I TURKISH BATTALION OF GENDARMERIE

TURKISH POST

Ghazi Baba

Suvla Point (Biyuk Kemikli)

TURKISH POST

Hill 10

Intended landing place of the 34ᵗʰ Brig

● Theseus *(after landing troops)*
● Grafton
● Talbot *(joined later after landing had begun)*

S U V L A

LANDING PLACE OF 34ᵀᴴ BRIGADE

Beagle, Bulldog and Grampus with three motor lighters in tow

B A Y

SALT

LAGOON

TURKISH POST

Lala Baba

Nibrunesi Pt

Grasshopper, Basilisk, Arno, Foxhound, Scourge, Racoon and Mosquito each towing a motor lighter

LANDING PLACE OF THE 32ᴺᴰ & 33ᴿᴰ BRIGADES Nibrunesi Beach

● Endymion

Trawler towing 4 horseboats ●
● Theseus
● Trawler towing 4 horseboats

Trawler towing 4 horseboats ●
● Aster towing 4 horseboats

1000   500   0   1000

Scale of Yards

the evening of 5 August, less than twenty-four hours before they were due to land on hostile shores. Even then the plan was still being adapted; at the last moment Stopford ordered that 34 Brigade was to be landed within Suvla Bay itself, despite the advice of the navy. Landing inside the bay would give the advantage of reducing the distance to the objectives of Hill 10, Karakol Dagh and Chocolate Hills, so it was a risk that he was happy to accept. What could not be confirmed was whether the Salt Lake, which was visibly dry, would support the weight of troops crossing it, so using the lake as a short cut was ruled out. Landing and securing the immediate beach area was of course a priority, but it was expected that a rapid advance into the hills would follow whilst the element of surprise was with the British. With vague and changing orders, and GHQ's constant watering down the part to be played at Suvla, the operation's objectives were becoming blurred. It was actually to Stopford's credit that he enforced the need to capture Chocolate Hills and W Hills, which had been removed from Hamilton's earlier draft. Likewise, Anafarta Ridge would be key to the attack and security of the base, so this was put back into the final orders drawn up for IX Corps by Stopford.

General Liman von Sanders was aware that a new landing was imminent, as he had been receiving reports of troop build-ups in the Greek islands; however he was unsure of where the landing would be made. He thought that Hamilton might attack south of Anzac at Gaba Tepe, or make a new landing either at the Gulf of Saros or maybe on the Asian coast. To protect the shores, von Sanders was forced to locate three divisions on the Asian side whilst a further three were positioned about fifty kilometres north of Suvla, at Bulair. Suvla was not thought a likely place for an attack and was only defended by three battalions of the Anafarta Detachment, under the command of a Bavarian cavalry officer, Major Wilhelm Willmer. These comprised the Bursa Gendarmerie and Gelibolu Gendarmerie battalions and the regular Ottoman 31 Regiment, a total of approximately 3,000 men. Willmer's task was to delay any enemy advance until reinforcements arrived; but to do this he had no machine guns, hardly any wire and few field artillery pieces. Making the most of what resources he had available, Willmer constructed three defensive strongpoints along the coastal hills; one at the Karakol Dagh to the north, one on Hill 10 in the centre and one on the Chocolate Hills, near the south-eastern end of the Salt Lake. Smaller pickets were also positioned elsewhere, including on Lala Baba, a small hill between the beach and the Salt Lake. Here they waited, keeping a careful eye on any activity out to sea.

A painting of the landing by official war artist Norman Wilkinson.

The Landing

The August offensive opened on 6 August with diversions at Helles (The Vineyard) and Anzac (Lone Pine). The Suvla landing commenced at 10.00 p.m., an hour after the two assaulting columns had broken out of Anzac, heading for the Sari Bair heights. 32 and 33 Brigades (11th Division) began to come ashore at B Beach, south of Nibrunesi Point, shortly before 10.00 p.m. on 6 August. The first wave of armoured beetles grounded at the water's edge and lowered their ramps. Four battalions were safely landed without a casualty, leaving the beetles to return for the next load.

> 'It was uncanny, the troops got ashore in record time and then came batteries and mules and munitions. I could not understand it, I stood on the beach and saw guns being landed and horses, and behind us a few yards away was the dark bush, containing what? There was little firing, now and then a sharp rattle quite close and then silence. I thought of Helles and then wondered if we had landed by mistake at Lemnos.'
>
> Midshipman George Drewry VC, Royal Navy.

As planned, 33 Brigade landed on the southern extremity, where they immediately began to entrench a line from it to the edge of the Salt Lake

166

in order to protect the right flank. The only resistance reported was from two Turks who fired their rifles from about half a mile inland before making a hasty retreat into the night. To the left, 6/Yorks and 9/West Yorks (32 Brigade) also came ashore virtually unmolested, with the exception of some rifle fire from further up the beach. One company of 6/Yorks was dispatched to set up a piquet line on the southern end of the Salt Lake whilst another was sent to clear the Turks from the small knolls near Nibrunesi Point. The two remaining companies prepared themselves to assault Lala Baba, supported by 9/West Yorks.

In the first action fought by any unit of the New Army, two companies from 6/Yorks attacked and captured the small hillock of Lala Baba, defended by a Turkish company. Although Lala Baba was taken, as a result of inexperience the casualties were heavy, especially amongst the officers. From the three companies, all but three of the Yorkshires' officers became casualties, as did a third of the men. Nevertheless, both 32 and 33 Brigade were ashore successfully with Lala Baba captured. One could not have asked for a better start; however, this is where misfortune struck, and any advantages gained during the landing were close to being lost.

As the Yorks were beginning their attack on Lala Baba, 34 Brigade had already entered Suvla Bay, where their lighters were set free to continue the last mile to the beach under their own steam. Their objective was the capture of Hill 10, which overlooked the beach, a task allotted to 9/LF, whilst 11/Manchesters, after clearing the enemy post at Ghazi Baba, would climb Kiretch Tepe Ridge, clear another post at Karakol Dagh and advance along the ridge for three kilometres before digging in. When the remaining two battalions of the brigade landed (8/NF and 5/Dorsets) they were to join the Lancashire Fusiliers on Hill 10 and advance together, no later than 1.30 a.m. on 7 August, to seize the Chocolate Hills by first light.

34 Brigade's attempt to land did not go well; the destroyers (HMS *Grampus* and *Bulldog*) that conveyed the brigade anchored almost a kilometre too far south and on the wrong side of the channel, the Cut, that drained the Salt Lake into the bay. This not only separated them from their objective, but also placed them in the area where there were known sandbanks. Two lighters grounded about forty metres out and the men had to wade ashore with water up to their necks. In the darkness 9/LF found themselves pinned down between the beach and the salt lake by sniper fire and shelling. They lost their commanding officer and another six officers killed and seven wounded. The 11/Manchesters were a little luckier and came ashore with fewer problems, which allowed them to clear their first objective of Ghazi Baba and then fight some distance along Kiretch Tepe for the loss of fifteen officers and nearly 200 men; a

high price, but a valuable position had been won. With the exception of the Manchesters success, there were no other movements inland.

The plan had been for a rapid advance but due to the bedlam within Suvla Bay this did not happen. By 3.00 a.m. the moon was beginning to rise, but below there was confusion caused by the night landing, with intermixed units and officers unable to locate their position or their objectives in the dark.

After four hours, 34 Brigade had only landed two battalions, whilst 8/NF and 5/Dorsets were still at sea, either on their transports or in lighters stuck on the sandbanks. Ashore, 9/LF were faring badly. Its companies were in two disconnected groups just north of the Cut and, now illuminated by the moon, their white armbands were proving good targets for the Turks. The battalion had yet to find, let alone capture, Hill 10. When 34 Brigade eventually made it ashore, it was about 3.30 a.m. The hillock that 9/LF understood to be Hill 10, was in fact a large sand dune and the actual Hill 10 lay another 350 metres to the north. It was held by approximately a hundred men of the Bursa Gendarmerie; outnumbered by the British, they withdrew further inland. The Turks had done what was requested of them, holding back the British advance until the last moment. By 7.00 a.m. Hill 10 was finally in British hands.

Daylight had come and instead of 11th Division securing Suvla Bay and the surrounding hills, all it had really captured was the beach. Out of twelve battalions of the division, only three had directly engaged the Turks (6/Yorks, 9/Lancashire Fusiliers and 11/Manchesters); the others were sitting virtually idle, awaiting orders. Hammersley's Divisional Headquarters and the Corps Commander knew nothing of what was happening at this stage, so no direction, when it was most needed, was forthcoming.

About the same time Colonel Hans Kannengiesser, commanding the Ottoman 9th Division, had been informed that enemy troops had landed north of Ari Burnu.

'Suvla Bay lay full of ships. We counted ten transports, six warships, and seven hospital ships. On land we saw a confused mass of troops, like a disturbed ant-heap, and across the blinding white surface of the dried salt sea we saw a battery marching in a southerly direction. With glasses I ... saw English troops on Lala Baba and, on the flat, in certain places, entrenching. Nowhere was there fighting in progress.'

The Campaign in Gallipoli, pp. 205-6

Both 32 and 34 Brigades were badly intermixed; only 33 Brigade was in any cohesive order and they were holding the line from the Salt Lake to the edge of B Beach. The two brigades that had recently landed from the 10th Division only added to the congestion. It was of the utmost importance that Chocolate and W Hills were captured quickly; although patrols reported very few Turks were in that vicinity, command prevaricated. With the plan in danger of falling apart, the race against time was being lost. The plan was a real opportunity to exploit the concentration of force at Suvla, but the lack of offensive action was bringing fatal results. Things were bad but not unrecoverable for the Brigade and the Division as a whole. At this time Stopford was offshore in his headquarters yacht *Jonquil*, fast asleep. He had previously reasoned that he could exercise more control from aboard the *Jonquil*, but with the limited communications to the shore at this time it is difficult to imagine a commander being in less control.

Delays that were in the main caused by conflicting orders, lack of cohesion and co-operation, delayed the capture of the Chocolate Hills until 7.00 p.m., the sole gains of the first twenty-four hours of the operation. Turkish commander, Major Willmer reported back to von Sanders that *no energetic attacks on the enemy's part have taken place. On the contrary, the enemy is advancing timidly.* Von Sanders now ordered the 7th and 12th divisions, under the command of Feizi Bey, to march from Bulair south to Suvla to help contain the British advance. The British staff had estimated that it would take such reserves thirty-six hours to reach Suvla, so

Major Wilhelm Willmer.

therefore they would arrive around the evening of 8 August. This gave Stopford almost a whole day to take advantage of the situation. The British were only five kilometres away from their goal; the Turks fifty! No one stood in between.

Hamilton sent his first message to Stopford to try and encourage a rapid advance:

'Have only received one telegram from you. Chief glad to hear enemy opposition weakening, and knows you will take advantage of this to press on rapidly. Prisoners state landing a surprise, so take every advantage before you are forestalled.'

Stopford appeared more concerned about the position of his Headquarters and, having landed overnight, established himself near Ghazi Baba.

On 8 August, Cecil Aspinall-Oglander, a staff officer at the time and the future British official historian for the Gallipoli campaign, commented:

> 'Following a quiet night, the morning of the 8th was absolutely still. Out of a cloudless sky the sun was shining fiercely. The enemy's guns were silent. Apart from an occasional rifle-shot on Kiretch Tepe there was not a sound of war. The sand-dunes near the Cut were crowded with resting troops. The shores of the bay were fringed with naked figures bathing... It was now broad daylight and the situation in Suvla Bay was verging on chaos.'

Hamilton grew more disheartened by the lack of progress and could see precious time slipping away. Hamilton sent two of his staff officers to Suvla to discover first-hand what was happening as clear reports from the shores were not forthcoming. The reality they found was not good. Stopford was reported to be in excellent spirits, wholly satisfied that he had IX Corps ashore, but was almost dismissal of having not reached the high ground, namely Tekke Tepe Ridge. Stopford blamed the paralysis on the Turks, claiming they were *inclined to be aggressive*. Did Stopford think it was going to be a walkover, without the need for a real fight? The fact that the Turkish reserves from Bulair were estimated to be there that evening, and with time being of the essence, seemed to have not registered as a priority. By the time Hamilton had arrived on the scene during the afternoon of 8 August, almost twenty-four hours after the landing, it was too late. He pushed one brigade forward that evening to Tekke Tepe, but due to the rough and unfamiliar terrain and a march of three kilometres at night, they did not reach the ridge until 4.00 a.m. on 9 August. It was an effort too light and too late. By the time 32 Brigade neared their objective the Turkish reserves were upon them, annihilating the leading battalions. Tekke Tepe had lain virtually undefended for two days and now this prize was lost. The Turks had won the race. Colonel Hans Kannengiesser wrote in his book (p. 220): *during the whole of the 8th August the goddess of victory held the door to success wide open for Stopford, but he would not enter.*

Hamilton had observed the British being thrown from the foothills of Tekke Tepe, so close, but too late. He wrote in his diary: *My heart has grown tough amidst the struggles of the Peninsula but the misery of this scene well nigh broke it... Words are of no use.*

Fighting escalated on 9 August as the Turks counter attacked, but a line was just about held about halfway between the beach and Tekke Tepe. By this stage both the 10th and 11th Divisions were utterly exhausted and demoralised by the lack of water and sleep. Along with a growing casualty rate and confusion, many of the units were still fragmented across the battlefield, where gaps in the line still needed filling.

Whilst a brigade from the 10th Division tried to extend the Manchesters advance along Kiretch Tepe, the focus of the day was on Scimitar Hill. This indistinct, curving sandstone ridge, shaped like a scimitar, was to be the scene of a new chaotic battle that would rage for the next two days. The hill, only held twenty-four hours before by the British, was needlessly relinquished in the chaos of the previous day. By the time IX Corps realised the mistake, the hill had already been recaptured by the Turks. To make matters worse, just after midday a scrub fire broke out that quickly engulfed the hillside. Private John Hargrave wrote: *The gorse and dry holly-oak scrub, even the dead grass on the surface and the tough ilex and juniper roots beneath it, were ablaze, so that soon Scimitar Hill was a roaring, crackling mass of flames.*

The blaze soon forced the total abandonment of Scimitar Hill, as those who could made their way back through the choking smoke and flame. Unfortunately a lot of the wounded had to be left to their fate. This prompted Captain Percy Hansen, 6/Lincolns, to call for volunteers to assist him in rescuing the wounded, in danger of being consumed by the

Captain Percy Howard Hansen, 6 Lincs, VC.

Captain Hansen rescuing wounded as the flames sweep Scimitar Hill.

171

scrub fire. Six times Hansen went into the inferno and rescued a total of six men. His was the first VC to be awarded for the Suvla operations. Ashmead-Bartlett, who was watching the attack from Lala Baba, witnessed the British wounded trying to escape the flames:

'I watched the flames approaching and the crawling figures disappear amidst dense clouds of black smoke. When the fire passed on little mounds of scorched khaki alone marked the spot where another mismanaged soldier of the King had returned to mother earth.'

Even with the newly landed reinforcements of the 53rd (Welsh) and 54th (East Anglian) Divisions, giving Stopford the best part of four divisions, albeit with little artillery, there was still limited progress made. Territorials straight off the boat from the 53rd Division were hurriedly thrown piecemeal into a renewed attack on Scimitar Hill, but with little effect. The attack was a failure.

The fighting at Suvla had ended for now. IX Corps, as well as the Turks, were exhausted, having fought themselves to a standstill, which allowed 11 August to pass uneventfully for both sides. For the Turks they probably thought the offensive was over, but the British planned another attack for the following day. Although Hamilton realised that the Anzacs were in no fit state to continue the attack on Sari Bair, he put his hope in the 54th (East Anglian) Division to change the balance at Suvla. Unaware of the scale of the defeat, he still believed that there was a chance to pry Tekke Tepe from the grip of the Turks. Using this only available reserve, Hamilton needed the 54th Division to get IX Corps off the Suvla Plain before the Turks had sealed the British into Suvla forever. Recent aerial reconnaissance showed that Tekke Tepe had not been entrenched or held in any great strength, so it was hoped that an attack delivered with speed and force would take the high ground once and for all.

On 12 August 163 Brigade was ordered to make a daylight advance across the exposed plains of Suvla towards the foothills of Tekke Tepe. This ground, known as Küçük Anafarta Ova, was an area that comprised a flat, cultivated plain interspersed by ditches and dry water courses, clumps of trees and scattered farm buildings; exactly as it remains today. Ideal for defence, the Turks used this to their advantage. It was hoped that once the line has been pushed forward about 2,000 yards and consolidated by a supporting brigade from the 53rd Division, this would allow the rest of 54th Division to make a night advance and be ready for a dawn attack. On either flank both the 10th and 11th Divisions would cooperate in the attack.

The assaulting battalions in 163 Brigade only received their orders two hours before the advance was to begin, so there was no time for reconnaissance. Turkish strength and defensive dispositions were unknown and the location of the objective was a mystery; maps arrived late, few of which covered the area of the advance – all spelt disaster.

After a completely ineffective bombardment as the gunners were also unsure of the targets or even the positions of the British front line, the infantry advanced. This started reasonably well and with few casualties; however, after several hundred yards the line began to falter, enfilade machine gun and rifle fire coming from Kidney Hill on the left flank and shrapnel fire from the direction of the Anafarta Spur over on right flank. The Brigade gained another 300 yards but then became disjointed, the 1/5 Norfolks veered over to the right and outpaced the 1/8 Hants and 1/5 Suffolks to their left. The heat and growing casualties continued to take their toll, soon causing the attack to break up. The ground also made it difficult to maintain cohesion, as the crisscross of dry water courses, hedge rows, scrub and dust all contributed to slowing the advance. Some of the trees, scrub and fields caught fire, the rising smoke clouding visibility. On the right hand side of the attack, the Norfolks suffered less from rifle and machine gun fire and so were able to continue their advance as the Suffolks and Hants came to a halt. Although advances were still significant, in places up to 1200 to 1500 yards, the Suffolks and Hants could do no more, and fell back to a defensive line along a ditch.

Over on the extreme right a party of fourteen officers and about 250 men, mainly from the 1/5 Norfolks, continued forward with their colonel

Officers of the 'Lost Battalion'.

but, unsupported and without protection on their flanks, their effort was doomed. As dusk was closing in, the Turks launched a counter attack that surprised, surrounded and quickly overwhelmed the Norfolks. Stories circulated after the battle of the mysterious disappearance of this battalion, although later reports put the missing down to 137 men, not the whole unit.

The Brigade's casualties were heavy, especially amongst officers. The war diaries state that: 1/5 Norfolks lost twenty-two officers and 350 other ranks; the 1/8 Hants nine officers and 290 other ranks; and the 1/5 Suffolks, eleven officers and 178 other ranks.

With the exception of 163 Brigade's attack on 12 August and bitter fighting by the 10th (Irish) Division on Kiretch Tepe during 15/16 August, which cost them nearly 2,000 casualties, the remainder of IX Corps were still trying to reorganise. The earlier shortage of water had been resolved, as wells were discovered or dug across the Suvla plain. Stores were reaching the shore in greater volume and rations and ammunition were making their way by mule to the front. With the line established and supply problems largely reduced, Hamilton prepared the next attack. This time he wanted the effort to be concentrated on the W Hills and Anafarta Spur. Hamilton was pushing for the attack but Stopford was concerned that, after the failure of 163 Brigade's previous attack, there would not be sufficient time to make the 54th Division ready. Stopford was worried that the 54th Division were *a danger* and might *bolt at any minute,* and he was also increasingly concerned about the loss of morale in the 53rd Division who, under the shelling, were getting shaky to the extent that local commanders thought that they could break and seriously jeopardise the line. It was not a good start for the Territorials.

The Turks had retained the high ground, leaving IX Corps to their gains along part of Kiretch Tepe, Lala Baba, Hill 10 and the Chocolate Hills. To the right flank of IX Corps, Chunuk Bair had been captured and lost, with the Anzacs fighting themselves to a standstill. At Helles the diversionary attacks failed to keep the Turks in the area engaged. The plan had failed on all three fronts, with an estimated 25,000 British and 20,000 Ottoman losses.

Hamilton cabled Lord Kitchener on 14 August, reporting that the IX Corps generals were unfit for command. He had finally had enough of Stopford and his generals:

'The result of my visit to the IX Corps, from which I have just returned, has bitterly disappointed me. There is nothing for it but to allow time to rest and reorganize unless I force Stopford and

Royal Irish Fusiliers in the trenches.

his divisional generals to undertake a general action for which, in their present frame of mind, they have no heart. In fact, they are not fit for it. I am exceedingly reluctantly obliged to give them time to rest and reorganize their troops.'

The Irish fight a desperate defence.

Kitchener swiftly replied:

> 'If you should deem it necessary to replace Stopford, Mahon and
> Hammersley, have you any competent generals to take their place?
> From your report I think Stopford should come home. This is a
> young man's war, and we must have commanding officers that
> will take full advantage of opportunities which occur but seldom.
> If, therefore, any generals fail, do not hesitate to act promptly. Any
> generals I have available I will send you.'

Kitchener immediately made available Lieutenant General Sir Julian Byng for the command of IX Corps. But this was a week too late. If Hamilton had had Byng originally the August campaign could have had a different outcome. Byng was the complete opposite to Stopford and possessed the qualities of a commander that Hamilton so sorely needed at Suvla. By 15 August the old Suvla senior commanders began to disappear. Hamilton dismissed Stopford while Byng was travelling from France and temporarily replaced him with Major General Henry de Beauvoir de Lisle, commander of the 29th Division at Helles. Hamilton intended to retain Mahon in command of the 10th Division, as he was probably the only general in IX Corps that was *fit for it*. However, Mahon was infuriated that de Lisle, whom he disliked, was appointed above him and quit, saying: *I respectfully decline to waive my seniority and to serve under the officer you name. Please let me know to whom I am to hand over the Division.* On 17 August the commander of 53rd Division, Major General Lindley, voluntarily resigned, on the grounds that *his Division had gone to pieces and that he did not feel it in himself to pull it together.*

Lieutenant General Sir Bryan Mahon.

The culling of the Suvla generals was a little too late. General Stopford is blamed for the failure of the Suvla operation; but responsibility ultimately lay with Kitchener, who had appointed the elderly and inexperienced general to an active corps command,

Major General Frederick Hammersley.

and Hamilton, who had failed to impose his will on his subordinate. Hamilton, who had now acknowledged the failure of the August offensive, cabled Kitchener on 17 August to inform him that his *coup had so far failed*. Not only this, but the Turks now outnumbered him, their morale was good, they possessed all the advantages of position and munitions supply did not appear to be a problem. Without an extra 95,000 troops, which would give Hamilton superiority, the offensive would be a failure; with no reinforcements and resources to sustain them, Hamilton would be forced to reduce the Suvla perimeter to an area only slighter larger than Anzac.

To improve the Suvla situation Hamilton saw hope in the experience and leadership of de Lisle, along with reinforcements from the 29th Division and 2nd (Mounted) Division (minus their horses), which would support IX Corps' depleted brigades. A lot rested upon de Lisle's shoulders. He was not liked by many and had a reputation for a brute force approach. Arriving, he was in strange surroundings and in command of a disorganised and exhausted Corps, with officers and men with whom he was unfamiliar. Casualties had been heavy, morale was low and what they had to show for themselves was little more than an exposed beachhead. De Lisle's immediate task was to organise the Corps quickly so that it was in a position to renew the battle.

Major General Henry de Beauvoir de Lisle.

The objective was no longer the Anafarta Spur and Tekke Tepe, as these were deemed in Hamilton's eyes not to be necessary anymore. Hamilton faced the problem of mounting casualties through combat and disease and no hope of any early reinforcements, so at best by capturing the W Hills, and hopefully, Scimitar Hill and Hill 60, this would allow his defensive line to be shortened, if necessary, thus resulting in an enlarged Anzac area that IX Corps would share.

The 21 August attack commenced at 3.00 p.m. to take advantage of the setting sun. This time of day would allow the infantry to advance with the sun at their backs, thus aiding the artillery whilst also blinding the defenders with the glare. Unfortunately for de Lisle a midday haze had developed over Suvla that masked the Turkish positions. It was no surprise that the British bombardment was ineffective, exacerbated by the limited supply of munitions and knowledge of the enemy positions. The bombardment achieved little and at worse resulted in alerting the Turks of the pending attack; a heavy retaliatory bombardment now pulverised the British trenches, packed with troops waiting for zero hour.

The first objective of the 11th Division was a trench that ran from Azmak Dere to Hetman Chair. Behind this trench was another at the base of the W Hills, joined by a communication trench; these were first objectives for the leading waves and which had to be taken before W Hills could be climbed. As the bombardment had failed in most places, the Turkish lines were relatively untouched. As the first battalions rose in attack they were met by an immediate fusillade of bullets. The ground they had to cover was flat, open and with over 500 metres to cover, the men becoming easy targets. Reserves attempted to provide support, but became victim to shelling and heavy small-arms fire. The shelling was so intense and the scrub so dry that the brush caught fire, hampering the attack as it tried to edge its way forward. Despite a small section of the front line being captured, the attack became confused, lost direction, faltered and came to an abrupt stop in front of the Turkish positions. Further attempts were made into the evening to take the objectives, but to no avail.

The 29th Division, who were attacking Scimitar Hill, also made little progress. Shellfire was already falling upon the British lines by the time the leading waves left the trenches, and it was not long before the dry, scrub covered slopes of Green Hill had also caught alight. Although this hindered the movement forward in some places, the smoke generated had the effect of helping to cover the advance of the leading companies into No Man's Land. However the following waves fared poorly as heavy small-arms fire soon broke up all efforts to get forward. The only success was on the northern slopes of Scimitar Hill, which afforded a little more cover and allowed elements of the 29th Division temporarily to take the crest. As the top of Scimitar Hill was so exposed, holding onto this gain proved impossible, and once again the British troops had to withdraw.

As both Scimitar Hill and W Hills mutually supported each other in defence, it proved difficult to take one of these objectives without at the same time capturing the other. This was not fully appreciated at the time, so once again men were sent into the attack with little hope of success. Next would be the turn of the Yeomanry.

But first the 2nd (Mounted) Division, de Lisle's reserve, had to be brought into the battle zone; they were over three kilometres

My Kingdom for a Horse.

Yeomanry advancing across the Salt Lake.

away near Lala Baba. One by one the five brigades, each consisting of just under a thousand men, began to cross the open expanse of the dry Salt Lake. Reminiscent of a parade, they advanced; regiments followed each other in squadron order, each squadron then in line of troop order at set regular distances, advancing with echoes of the Charge of the Light Brigade minus their horses. Their morale and enthusiasm was high, this would be their first action, in fact the first time under fire for most.

> 'The spectacle of the Yeomen of England and their fox-hunting leaders, striding in extended order across the Salt Lake and the open plain, unshaken by the gruelling they were getting from shrapnel, which caused many casualties, is a memory that will never fade.'
>
> Hans Kannengiesser, *The Campaign in Gallipoli*, p.220.

The yeomen were a target that the Turkish gunners could not miss; however, the shrapnel was set to burst too high and casualties were not as heavy as they might have been. By 5.00 p.m. the whole division had reached the cover of Chocolate Hill. Within half an hour the brigades were on the move to their new jumping off positions, with little knowledge of the task ahead of them or of what had already befallen the 29th Division. All the brigadiers had been briefed; however, two of them still did not know exactly what they were meant to do. If the brigadiers did not know, this left little hope for their officers and men.

At 5.15 p.m. the cream of Britain's rural volunteers were sent into the attack. There would be no exploiting success, as there was not any to exploit; the Yeomanry were expected to push through and capture the

The terrible fires around Scimitar Hill.

Scimitar Hill engulfed in flame.

same objectives that had held up the battle hardened 29th Division and, in places, the 11th Division. The Yeomanry, with no battle acclimatisation, little briefing, poor maps and really no idea what was happening, were sent forward into the burning scrub to retake Scimitar Hill. The mounted division was now firmly committed to the chaos of the last attack; bodies were lying all over the ground in front, whilst wounded continued to dribble back from the mist ahead. The scrub was still aflame in many places and the acrid smoke added to the general haze that still covered the battlefield. The continuing din of battle only added to the confusion. All knew that there was only an hour of daylight left; progress had to be made quickly. Just before 6.00 p.m. the Yeomanry pushed onto the crest of Scimitar Hill but, once again, when the troops gained the top, enemy enfilade fire fell upon them. In the failing light the trench line along the crest was evacuated, either by order or panic, as witnesses wrote of Yeomen running back, shouting that they had the order to retire. This in turn took with them other units who were clinging to the top of the hill, the line soon withdrawing to a position further down the slopes, whence the battalions had earlier advanced. It proved impossible to retain Scimitar Hill whilst Hill 112, the high point of the W Hills, remained in Turkish hands; the concentration of these combined strong points was too great. Ian Hamilton noted:

'By 6.30 it had become too dark to see anything. The dust mingling with the strange mist, and also with the smoke of shrapnel and of the hugest and most awful blazing bush fire formed an impenetrable curtain. As the light faded the rifles and guns grew silent.'

On 23 August, Lieutenant General Sir Julian Byng arrived to take over command of IX Corps. Byng, the general that Hamilton had originally requested back in June for the Suvla operation, had arrived too late. Aspinall remarked: *the experienced pilot has arrived but the ship is already on the rocks.* It was also too late for Hamilton; his downfall came on 15 October when he was sacked. There would be no more offensives at Suvla; activity soon receded into sporadic fighting until Suvla was evacuated by the British in late December. The last battle was on Hill 60, which formed an important junction between Suvla and Anzac. Here bitter fighting raged until 29 August, when most of the hill was taken by a composite force of British, Irish, Indian, New Zealand and Australian troops. British historian Robert Rhodes James was caustic: *For connoisseurs of military futility, valour, incompetence and determination, the attacks on Hill 60 are in a class of their own.*

Sir Ian Hamilton departing Gallipoli after his recall – 16 October 1915.

Conditions during the summer had been appalling because of heat, flies, and lack of sanitation. On 15 November there was a deluge of rain and again, on 26/27 November, a major rainstorm flooded trenches, in some places to over a metre deep. This was followed by a snow blizzard and two nights of heavy frost. At Suvla 220 men drowned or froze to death and there were 12,000 cases of frostbite or exposure.

Stopford, Hamilton and Kitchener had many negatives, and Suvla

Ambulances on the Anafarta Plain.

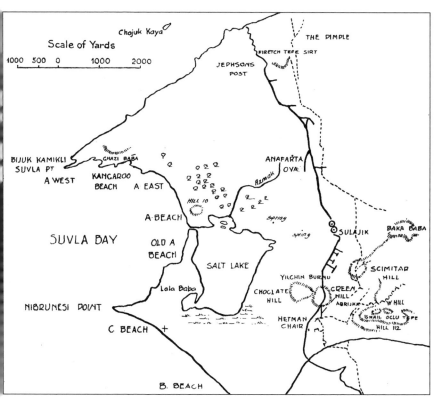

Final position at the end of August.

many problems, but these have become over exaggerated in subsequent years. What must not be forgotten is a landing on an enemy shore was achieved and a port, although it remained far from secure, was established in most trying circumstances. The August offensive was undoubtedly flawed and both Suvla and Anzac relied on at least one of the offensives breaking through; however both fell short of the mark. The British were no nearer to their objectives than they were during the April landings, or even after the naval attempts at forcing the Dardanelles. There was genuine anger after the failure of the August offensive, as high expectations were dashed as opportunities were seen to have been frivolously thrown away. There will always remain doubt as to the margin between failure and success, points that are still debated between historians today.

183

Tour 7

Suvla Bay Trail

Even though much of the area can be walked, the expanse of the battlefield really requires a car or similar vehicle if you are restricted by time. Allow a full day to complete the full tour of over thirty kilometres.

Getting to Suvla: From Eceabat, follow the road north for two kilometres until you reach the roundabout near the coast, signposted for Anzak Koyu (Anzac Cove). Turn left and drive about eight kilometres across the peninsula. This will bring you to the Aegean coast, with the road turning north. Follow the coastal road past the Gallipoli Presentation Centre (Çannakale Destanı Tanıtım Merkezi). This road will take you north, along the Aegean coast before turning inland to the road junction near **Hill 60 (*Bomba Tepe*) (40°16'34.0"N 26°17'14.0"E)**, a distance of nine kilometres. You have now entered the Suvla battlefield.

The first part of this tour will cover the main landing beaches used by Kitchener's New Army on 6/7 August 1915, and the subsequent captures of Lala Baba, Hill 10 and Ghazi Baba. The second part will visit the main in-land battlefield areas. The tour will end in the village of Büyükanafarta, from where you can return via the Hill 60 junction to Anzac, or return through a pictureque fifteen kilometres route to Eceabat via Bigali, where Mustafa Kemal (Atatürk) was once housed during the campaign.

Leaving the Hill 60 junction, take the left-hand turn (heading in a northerly direction) towards Suvla Bay. What you see today is similar to how it was in 1915; open ground, cultivated with many irrigation ditches, hedges and an abundance of wells (the Turkish word *kuyu* meaning well). The wells in this area became tactically important and the fighting intense in the battle to dominate the water rich ground. In and around this area were many important wells, including Susak Kuyu and Kabak Kuyu, which were fought over in late August. Even though in summer months the area becomes hot and arid, drinkable water can be found about five metres beneath the surface, as the many water pumps and wells bear witness today. After about 250 metres, on the left, take the track sign-posted to Lala Baba CWGC cemetery. Follow this track for 4.7

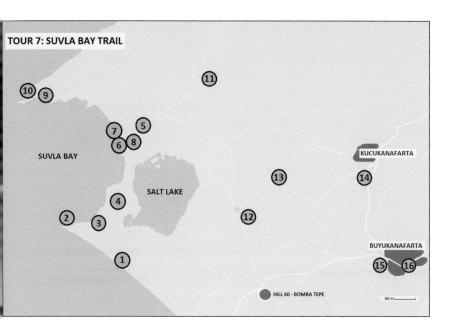

SUVLA BAY

KUCUKANAFARTA

SALT LAKE

BUYUKANAFARTA

HILL 60 - BOMBA TEPE

500 m

kilometres. At one point, you will cross the Azmak Dere, but the track surface and ford should be passible in dry weather and without the need of a 4x4 vehicle. Depending on the time of year all of the tracks can be in a poor condition so please take note, especially if it has been raining, which is a fortunately rare occurrence in Gallipoli.

As you approach Lala Baba you will pass an old well head, surrounded by stone sarcophagi. Used by generations of ancient Greeks and Ottomans, the British found this an unhealthy spot due to Turkish sniper fire. If wells could talk! Soon you will come into view of the small

An old well near Lala Baba.

rise called Lala Baba (49 metres), which was also known as Yorkshire Hill, after 6/Yorks, who captured it during the night of 6 August. The sign post to the CWGC cemetery is to the right. Continue on the track, without turning off, until you reach the beach; here you can stop and park.

The open 1,600 metre stretch of sandy beach is **C Beach and B Beach (1) (40°16'56.5"N 26°15'01.6"E)**. To the south note the Anzac Sari Bair ridge. A last-minute change in orders amended the original sequential naming of the beaches from A, B and C to A, C and B. B Beach was then 'moved' to the south of C as the original area within Suvla Bay was thought to shoal by the Royal Navy. The moving of beaches only added to the chaos during the initial landings. At about 10.00 p.m. on 6 August the beetles grounded on B Beach, bringing ashore the first elements of 11th Division; 33 Brigade landed with no casualties and then advanced to entrench a flanking position from the edge of the Salt Lake to the coast whilst 32 Brigade landed to their left and attacked Lala Baba. Both beaches were also used to land artillery, mules, horses and general supplies, as well as men, and remained in use until the evacuation. Along this shore there were numerous brigade field ambulances and casualty clearing stations, an important part in the casualty evacuation chain that brought the sick and wounded from the front line and treated them, either to return to duty or to enable them to be taken by hospital ship to a base hospital (situated on Lemnos, Malta and Egypt).

If you would like a scenic two kilometre circular walk, take the rough foot track that runs in a northerly direction on to Little Lala Baba spur, in the direction of Nibrunesi Point; or else return to your vehicle and drive

C and B Beaches today, looking towards Nibrunesi Point,

Coming ashore on C Beach, looking towards Anzac. (Norman Wilkinson)

directly to Lala Baba Cemetery. **Nibrunesi Point (2) (40°17'21.5"N 26°13'47.2"E)** is known as Small Rib Point (Küçük Kemikli Burnu), so named as it is the lesser of the two promontories of Suvla Bay. It was here that the first British troops came ashore during the night of 6 August, as it was also witness to the last British troops leaving during the evacuation on 20 December. 6 August was not the first time that British troops had ventured into this area. Five days before the 25 April landings the Royal Navy landed a small party at Nibrunesi Point to destroy a telephone wire. Later, on 28 April, the Royal Navy shelled Lala Baba as an artillery battery had been sighted in the area. At dawn, on 2 May, a New Zealand reconnaissance party under the command of Captain Charles Cribb, Canterbury Battalion, landed at the point. This small force thoroughly searched the area for guns but found none. Several startled Turks were killed or wounded and, at about midday, the party returned to Anzac with no casualties and a prize of fifteen prisoners. Leave Nibrunesi Point and walk along the field boundary to **Lala Baba CWGC Cemetery (3) (40°17'24.4"N 26°14'22.6"E).**

The cemetery is situated on a spur from the hill called Little Lala Baba and, along with Nibrunesi Point, was cleared of Turks by Major William Shannon, 6/Yorks, during the night of 6 August. The cemetery contains 200 graves, of which fifty-three are unknown and sixteen are special memorials. During the war many little cemeteries like this grew in size over the course of the campaign, their graves marked by an assortment

Lala Baba CWGC Cemetery.

of markers made from wood and tin packing cases, inscribed by purple field service pencil or engraved with the help of a soldier's clasp knife. Today the originals have long since gone, replaced with stone-faced pedestal grave markers carefully engraved by the stonemasons of the Commonwealth War Graves Commission.

One senior officer buried here is Brigadier General Paul Kenna VC (*II.A.1*), 21/Lancers. Educated at Stonyhurst College and then Sandhurst, he was commissioned initially into the West India Regiment, before transferring to the Lancers, where he served in Egypt during the 1898 Nile Expedition. He was awarded the VC for rescuing a fellow officer whose horse had been killed during the charge at Omdurman. During the Boer War he commanded a cavalry column, and gained the DSO; after South Africa he

Brigadier General P. A. Kenna VC and his grave.

188

took part in the action at Jidballi with the Somaliland Field Force. A personal friend of Winston Churchill, he was appointed to command 3 (Mounted) Brigade in 1911, being promoted brigadier general in August 1914. On 29 August, whilst inspecting the lines at Chocolate Hill, he was mortally wounded, dying the following day.

Another notable burial is Irish botanist Private Charles Ball *(II. A. 8)*, 7/RDF, who was killed on 13 September. His friend and fellow soldier Herbert Cowley, the editor of *The Garden*, wrote a short and touching obituary for the October 1915 edition. Ball was, a *delightful companion, unassuming, sincere and a most lovable man*... He had worked in both Kew Gardens and the Royal Botanic Gardens in Dublin. He was also editor of *Irish Gardening* and a friend and fellow travelling companion to Bulgaria with Kew colleague and Alpine plant enthusiast Cowley. It was Cowley's wife who chose the Biblical inscription on his headstone: 'Greater Love Has no Man than This'. At Gallipoli, Ball was often found *sheltering behind a rock under fire, digging away at 'weeds' with his bayonet to send back home seeds to his botanic garden colleagues.* Numerous seedlings from the vicinity of Suvla Bay were reported as growing in Glasnevin from seeds he had sent home. A plant, *Escallonia*, is named 'C.F. Ball' in his memory, a beautiful shrub with dark green leaves and bright red flowers.

Leave the cemetery and, by following the field boundaries close to the cemetery entrance, walk 200 metres to the track by **Lala Baba (4) (40°17'35.7"N 26°14'34.7"E).** Dominating the surrounding area, it was captured by 6/Yorks just before midnight on 6 August. This would be the first attack made by a Kitchener's New Army battalion in the First World War. The hillock was garrisoned by a company of 2/31 Regiment, which

Lala Baba, view from Nibrunesi Point.

Kitchener's men soon put to flight. It is possible to walk around most of Lala Baba by using the various tracks, the very same that were prominent on British Army maps of the time, and still used today by the local farmers. Original trenches and dugout remains can still be found on and around the hill. After its capture the 11th Division temporarily sited its headquarters here, although later it became a popular area to house British artillery, thus a little too warm for some when it attracted more than its fair share of shelling.

Leave Lala Baba and return to your parked vehicle, and retrace your route back to the main Suvla road. Continue in a northerly direction for five kilometres, passing Green Hill Cemetery (Chocolate Hills), and follow the signs to Hill 10 Cemetery. This road runs just behind the old British front line, with the Salt Lake to the left and the Suvla Plains (Küçük Anafarta Ova) to the right.

Hill 10 CWGC Cemetery (5) (40°18'45.0"N 26°15'08.6"E) is positioned on Hill 10 (*Softatepe* – Fanatic Hill), a ten metres high mound that is barely discernible against the landscape. The hill was another of the fortified positions organised by Major Willmer to help defend against a landing. One Gendarmerie company defended the hill from narrow slit trenches that overlooked the beach, supported by a field gun. There was no barbed wire, although on the beach mines, connected to trip wires, were laid. It was an initial objective of the landing, a task assigned to 34 Brigade, but was not captured until the morning of 7 August.

The cemetery, with the exception of three graves, was made after the war when isolated battlefield graves and small cemeteries (88 Dressing Station, 89 Dressing Station, Kangaroo Beach, B Beach, 26 Casualty Clearing Station and Park Lane) were consolidated. Today there are 699 men buried or commemorated in the cemetery, 150 of the burials are unidentified. Amongst the graves is that of Lieutenant Colonel Harry Welstead (*V.D.1*), commanding 9/LF. He was shot and wounded whilst wading ashore and soon after found dead on the beach with a bullet in the back of his neck. He is buried close to his fellow battalion officers who were killed capturing Hill 10; these include Lieutenant Leslie Osborne (*I.C.15*), whose headstone, interestingly, bears an inscription to his brother, Second Lieutenant William Osborne (*Helles Mem. Panel 58-72*), who was wounded the same day, died of wounds and was buried at sea. The Osbornes were born in China. Leslie was in Germany at the time war was declared, arrested as a spy but soon released and expelled from the country. Another pair of brothers, buried side by side, is Second Lieutenant Duncan Hook (*I.C.18*) and his older brother, Lieutenant Robin Hook (*I.C.17*), again killed whilst capturing the hill. The Hooks were working as civil engineers in Canada when war was declared,

Hill 10 CWGC Cemetery.

immediately offering their services to King and Country, were commissioned into the Lancashire Fusiliers on the same day and, tragically, killed on the same day.

Second Lieutenant Edmund Priestman (*I.H.14*), 6/Y&L, is also buried here. A slection of his letters were published in 1916: *With a B.-P. Scout in Gallipoli: A Record of the Belton Bulldogs*. Priestman was a pre-war scoutmaster; during the attack on Hetman Chair on 21 August he wrote that he had the opportunity to do some *real serious scouting work with people's lives depending on it.* Priestman was killed on 18/19 November during a night patrol to capture a position near Jephson's Post. An article was printed about his death in a Sheffield newspaper in February 1916:

'Our trenches ran along the coast, near Jeffson's Post [sic: Jephson's], and orders had been received for us to work along the furthermost sap to enable us to gain a portion of higher ground on the left of our sap. In order to do this, it was necessary to leave our trenches at night, run forward with sandbags to the place marked, and dig in as rapidly as possible. On this particular night, Lieutenant Priestman and about thirty NCOs and men were detailed to make good this position. Leaving the trenches at about 1am, they gained the position without incident, and commenced to entrench as quietly as possible. Shortly afterwards the Turks rushed the position. Lieutenant Priestman did not retire, but

191

Grave marker of Edmund Priestman.

A B-P Scout in Gallipoli –
Lieutenant E. Y. Priestman.

opened a rapid fire, which kept the enemy at bay for a while but, coming on again with a combined rush, they decimated the whole of the gallant little band. Lieutenant Priestman fell, fighting till the last, and Regimental Sergeant Warr was also killed whilst taking up a message to him. We attacked the position again in larger force next night, and succeeded in holding it. The bodies of Lieutenant Priestman and several men were discovered, all the wounded having been removed by the enemy. The captured position was named 'Priestman's Post' by Headquarters to commemorate the gallantry of this young officer, who was respected by all who knew him.'

Regimental Sergeant Major Frederick Warr (*I.I.11*) also lies here; however, there is no record of what happened to the wounded.

Also killed near Jephson's Post was an Australian sniper from 8/LHR; Lance Corporal Herbert Peters (*I.I.18*), who died on 30 August. From Victoria, Australia, he was a prominent member of the Stratford Rifle Club, joining the Australian Light Horse when war was declared. Later attached to 161 (Essex) Brigade, Peters was manning a position with another scout, where they had been sniping at the Turks. They were at dinner at the time when Peters was killed by a shrapnel bullet. Originally buried at Park Lane Cemetery, he was reinterred at Hill 10 after the Armistice. Also from Victoria, Chief Petty Officer Edward Perkins (*Sp.Mem.47*), Royal Australian Naval Bridging Train, was killed on 6 September when his dugout received a direct hit by a shell; he is the only one of the unit's four fatalities to be buried in Gallipoli as the other deaths occurred at sea or on Lemnos Island.

By the time of this book's publication there may well be a memorial to the Newfoundland Regiment in place, a caribou, as found in five locations on the Western Front. The regiment (not then 'Royal') fought at Gallipoli as part of the 29th Division, landing as reinforcements in September. A memorial has been mooted for many years, marking the regiment's first overseas action; in April 2018 the Park authorities gave its blessing to the project. There are eight members of the regiment commemorated in the cemetery, including Private Hugh McWhirter *(I.A.4)*, who holds the dubious distinction of being the first of the regiment to be killed in the war.

To make an optional visit to A Beach, leave your vehicle at Hill 10 Cemetery and following the track that runs alongside the cemetery, continue on foot for just over a kilometre. Whilst walking you will have some of the most beautiful views of the Salt Lake (Tuzla Gölü), which is now permanently open to the sea, so it should never crust over as soldiers experienced in 1915. It is not unusual today to see pink flamingos on the lake, or eagles soaring above. Follow the track that skirts the lake's sea inlet on to **A Beach (6) (40°18'19.0"N 26°14'50.6"E)**.

This is where 34 Brigade landed but not before suffering delays after grounding on the sandbank during the night of 6/7 August. Walk on to the beach and, in a northerly direction, walk approximately 150 metres, where you will find the remains of a beached **X Lighter (7)**

The author in a wrecked lighter on A Beach.

(40°18'26.3"N 26°14'48.9"E), one of the few that still survive today from the Gallipoli campaign. Leave the lighter and follow the sandy path towards the large grass-covered **Sand Dune (8) (40°18'24.7"N 26°14'55.0"E)**, which was the one misidentified as Hill 10 and mistakenly 'captured' by the 9/LF. On top of this trenches can still be found, along with a view of the 'real' Hill 10 further inland and where the cemetery is today. From this rise of land you will get good views of Suvla Bay and in calm sea conditions you may even see the sandbars that caused so many problems during the landing. During the planning and execution of the Suvla landings the beach names caused much confusion. Prior to the landing this beach was code named 'A Beach' but when, due to navigational error, the navy landed 34 Brigade to the south of the Cut, this beach became known as 'Old A Beach', and 'A Beach' was then 'moved' close to Lala Baba. Return to the cemetery along the field boundary, rejoin the track and walk back to your vehicle at Hill 10.

Leave Hill 10 Cemetery and continue on what was named the Sulajik Road for 2.5 kilometres. You will notice A Beach on the left of the road. Where the ground gets rockier are the small coves and inlets known during the war as Kangaroo Beach, Little West Beach and West Beach. Pull off the road and park by the fishermen's cottages. It was near here that elements of the 10th Division landed, although not without some difficulty caused by the shoal rocks that are still visible in the water today. After the landing, the Royal Engineers built up this area, which soon became the main Suvla port, and because of that it was under constant enemy shell fire. During the campaign two steamers, *Pina* and *Fieramosca*, were sunk to form a breakwater and piers were made from rock leading out into the sea. Today little remains, although by the cottages at West Beach Harbour is the wreck of a Horse Boat or **X Lighter (9) (40°19'02.7"N 26°13'26.7"E)**, its metal ribs seen clearly as it rests just below the surface of the water. This boat was probably sunk during the November 1915 storms that wrought havoc along the Gallipoli coastline, destroying piers, washing away stores and sinking shipping.

The Royal Australian Naval Bridging Train was based in this area. This unit was attached to IX Corps during the Gallipoli operations, and by the Armistice in 1918 had become the most highly decorated Royal Australian Navy unit of the war. As early as 9 August it had constructed a 120-metres long pier, which was put into immediate use for evacuating the wounded. Surrounding this were a scattering of field ambulances, medical store depots and casualty clearing stations. One field ambulance member was Private John Hargrave, who wrote of the area in his book, *At Suvla Bay: Notes and Skteches*, published in 1916:

Suvla Harbour area today.

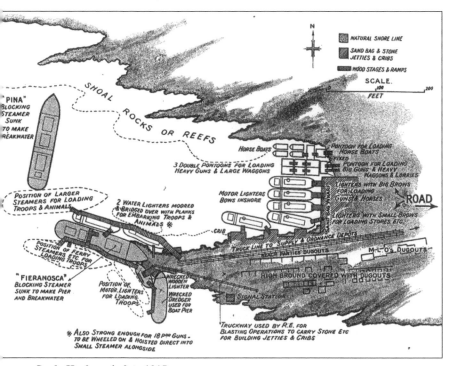

Suvla Harbour in late 1915.

'It was one muddle and confusion of water-tanks, pier-planks, pontoons, huge piles of bully-beef, biscuit and jam boxes. Here we came each evening with the water-cart to get our supply of water, and here the water-carts of every unit came down each evening and stood in a row and waited their turn. The water was pumped from the water-tank boats to the tank on shore. The water-tank boats brought it from Alexandria. It was filthy water, full of dirt, and very brackish to taste. Also, it was warm. During the two months at Suvla Bay I never tasted a drop of cold water, it was always sickly lukewarm, sun-stewed.

'All day long high explosives used to sing and burst – sometimes killing and wounding men, sometimes blowing up the bully-beef and biscuits, sometimes falling with a hiss and a column of white spray into the sea. It was here that the field-telegraph of the Royal Engineers became a tangled spider's web of wires and cross wires. They added wires and branch wires every day, and stuck them up on thin poles. Here you could see the Engineers in shirt and shorts trying to find a disconnection, or carrying a huge reel of wire. Wooden shanties sprang up where dug-outs had been a day or so before. Piers began to crawl out into the bay, adding a leg and trestle and pontoon every hour.

'Here they were laying a light rail from the beach with trucks for carrying shells and parts of big guns. Here was the field post-office with sacks and sacks of letters and parcels. Some of the parcels were burst and unaddressed; a pair of socks or a mouldy home-made cake squashed in a cardboard box – sometimes nothing but the brown paper, card box and string, an empty shell – the contents having disappeared. What happened to all the parcels which never got to the Dardanelles no one knows, but those which did arrive were rifled and lost and stolen. Parcels containing cigarettes had a way of not getting delivered, and cakes and sweets often fell out mysteriously on the way from England.'

Return to the road and continue on about 400 metres to Suvla Point. During 7 August, it was also the task of 34 Brigade to capture an enemy post at Ghazi Baba, a slight area of rocky high ground on the seaward side of the road. Even though they were landed on the wrong beach and had a three kilometres' night march, 11/Manchesters cleared Ghazi Baba of its small picket of Gendarmerie and advanced onto the Kiretch Tepe Sirt, clearing the Karakol Dagh in its wake. At **Suvla Point (10) (40°19'03.6"N 26°13'09.3"E)** (*Büyük Kemikli* – Big Rib Point) is a Turkish monument to the Suvla landing and subsequent evacuation. If

Suvla Point today.

you climb up on to the high ground to the north, the site of a naval signal station and IX Corps headquarters, you will get some wonderfully picturesque views of Suvla Bay.

Return to the road; after about three kilometres you need to take the left hand turn that heads east, signposted to Azmak CWGC Cemetery and Kireçtepe Jandarma Şehitliği. To the left is Kiretch Tepe Ridge (Kireçtepe). From this junction it is about two kilometres to **Azmak CWGC Cemetery (11) (40°19'15.1"N 26°16'16.2"E)**. The cemetery is situated to the east of the Azmak Dere and is approximately 500 metres behind the eventual British front line, on this northern part of Küçük Anafarta Ova. To the east is the Tekke Tepe Ridge, with two dominant peaks, to the left is Kavak Tepe (Poplar Hill) at 274 m and to the right, above Küçükanafarta, is Tekke Tepe (Convent Hill) at 272 m. It was on Tekke Tepe that signallers from 6/East Yorks, who reached it on 8 August, signalled that the hill was unoccupied. Delays in launching the main brigade attack that same day allowed the Turkish reserves to get there first and in their hands it remained, helping to seal the fate of Stopford's beleaguered troops below.

The cemetery was made after the Armistice by concentrating many isolated battlefield graves and sixteen smaller cemeteries from the area (Dublin Cemetery, Sulajik Cemetery, 5th Norfolk Cemetery, Borderers' Ravine Cemetery, Oxford Circus Cemetery, Worcester Cemetery, Kidney Hill Cemetery, Irish Cemetery, Azmak No 1, 2, 3 and 4 Cemeteries, Jephson's Post Cemetery, Essex Ravine Cemetery, Hill 28 Cemetery and Lone Tree Gully Cemetery). Today Azmak Cemetery contains 1074

Azmak CWGC Cemetery.

burials, 684 of which are unidentified. Among the unidentified are 114 officers and men of the 1/5 Norfolks who died on 12 August 1915. Myth has grown up about this battalion due to its Sandringham connection, as a number of men who worked on the Royal estate enlisted in it. All but a few of the Norfolk men allegedly disappeared during the attack, but this was far from the truth. With the exception of those who were killed or captured, most returned to tell their tale. Chaplain Leonard Egerton-Smith, who was attached to the Graves Registration Unit in 1919, wrote of finding the 'missing' Norfolks:

> 'For a long time, all search for these men was fruitless. And quite by accident their bodies were discovered. A private attached to the GRU was purchasing local supplies from a farm situated far over in what was the enemy terrain and found a Norfolk badge. Further search revealed the remainder. Only two were possible of identification, Private Carter and Corporal Barnaby. I rode out to see their bodies brought in.'

Private Walter Carter (*I.C.7*) and Corporal John Barnaby (*I.C.6*) are now buried side by side in Azmak Cemetery. The date of death is given as 28 August, which is incorrect as this is the date that their service records

'Their Duty Done' – Corporal Barnaby.

...and Private Carter, 5th Norfolks.

state that they were posted *missing, presumed killed*; both men were actually killed on 12 August.

Captain Harold Tyler (*Sp.Mem.54*), whose body lay out in the open on the southern slopes of Kiretch Tepe Ridge for nearly two days, was recovered when an unarmed officer and six men with a stretcher volunteered to go out to retrieve it. Under observation by the Turks, they held their fire to allow Tyler to be recovered. He was buried originally in Lone Tree Gully Cemetery before being reinterred here after the war. Corporal Ewart Clifton (*I.F.17*), 6/Lincolns, one of the men who volunteered to help Captain Percy Hansen VC rescue the wounded in Scimitar Hill's burning scrub, is buried here. He was killed in October 1915.

Leave the cemetery, return to the road. I refer you to my Battleground Europe book *Suvla: August Offensive* if you wish to visit the Kireçtepe Jandarma Memorial and walk along the heights of Kiretch Tepe Ridge: Jephson's Post, Kidney Hill and The Pimple, all closely associated with the 10th (Irish) Division.

For the Irishmen of 10th Division Kiretch Tepe would be their first taste of war and also failure. The sun-bleached bones that scatter this ridge today is evidence to the bitter fighting that once raged here. Walking the Kiretch Tepe Ridge, which is marked on some campaign maps as Kazlar Dagh, can be very rewarding, although the dangers of it need to be noted. From a distance the whale-backed ridgeline with its gentle green slopes can be misleading. However, there are no real tracks, other than the odd goat trail, to follow, so the walking is over very rough ground, rocky in places and covered in loose shale. Other areas are interspersed by thick, almost impassable, thorny scrub, some twelve feet high, and by deep ravines and gullies, which all add to the challenge. The area is also known snake territory, some of which are venomous, so be warned. Come equipped with a stick, plenty of water and a mobile phone, and never walk here alone. However, having said all that, the views are wonderful and the atmosphere unforgettable.

Return along the road and back to the junction with the Sulajik road. Head south on this road for 3.5 kilometres until you arrive at the **Green Hill CWGC Cemetery and 10th Irish Division Memorial (12) (40°17'35.0"N 26°16'46.9"E)**, which was part of the Chocolate Hills (Yilghin Burnu). The 53-metre hill to the west of the road is Chocolate Hill, named after the dry and burnt scrub that covered it in 1915; the 50 metre hill to the east is Green Hill, because it remained mainly green. Today it is the site of the CWGC cemetery of that name. The naming of the Gallipoli features can be as confusing today as it was for the men in 1915. Not only did Chocolate Hill burn but also parts of Green Hill and Scimitar Hill, and at one stage all three were known as Burnt Hill. To add to the confusion, both Green Hill and Scimitar Hill were also known as Green Knoll, not forgetting that Chocolate Hill and Green Hill were also known collectively as the Chocolate Hills or Yilghin Burnu.

Chocolate Hill was one of the three defensive strongpoints that Major Wilhelm Willmer had established prior to the August landing, garrisoned by two companies of *1/31 Regiment,* supported by two mountain guns. The Chocolate Hills therefore became one of the primary objectives for the first day of the landing, but were not captured until sunset on 7 August. Both Chocolate and Green Hill remained in British hands until the evacuation.

Looking down on Green Hill CWGC Cemetery.

Green Hill CWGC Cemetery was made after the Armistice when several smaller war-time cemeteries (named York, 40 Brigade, Green Hill No.1 and 2, Chocolate Hill, Inniskilling, Salt Lake and Scimitar Hill) and other isolated graves were concentrated into the picturesque cemetery we see today. There are now 2,971 servicemen buried or commemorated in this cemetery, but only 499 have named graves. Among those identified is Dublin born Brigadier General the 5th Earl of Longford, KP MVO (*Sp.Mem.E.3*), commanding 2 (Mounted) Brigade. A friend of Winston Churchill, he was killed during the attack on Scimitar Hill. Longford was educated at Winchester and Christ Church, Oxford. He succeeded his father as Earl in 1887; commissioned initially into the Life Guards, he served in the Boer War, where he was wounded and captured when a captain with 45th Imperial Yeomanry. He was given command of 2 (Mounted) Brigade in 1912 and promoted to Brigadier General in August 1914. His long-lived son served in a Labour cabinet and was a well-known prison reformer.

Lord Longfords grave.

Brigadier General Lord Longford – died leading his men into battle.

Also buried here is Lieutenant Colonel Henry Moore (*II.B.13*), commanding 6/East Yorks, and Major Francis Brunner (*Sp.Mem.A.8*), 67 Field Company, Royal Engineers, who were involved in attempting to capture Tekke Tepe. Both these officers were with an advanced group, totaling about seven officers and 140 men, who were overwhelmed by the sudden counter attack on 9 August. An account of this action was written by the battalion adjutant, Lieutenant John Still, who was captured along with Moore and Brunner. He survived and later wrote *A Prisoner in Turkey* (1920), in which he described his capture.

'We reached the point where the ravine ended, and in the scrub ahead of us we saw a number of men who fired upon us. For a moment, we thought they were our own, firing in ignorance. Then we saw that they were Turks. We had run into the back of an enemy battalion which held the lower slopes against our supports. They had crossed the range at a point lower than that we had attacked, and had cut in behind our climbing force. We could do nothing but surrender. When we held up our hands some dozen or more of the enemy charged towards us with fixed bayonets. And we began to experience that strange mixture of nature, so characteristic of the Turks, from which we and our fellows were to suffer much in the years to come. The man who took possession of me searched my pockets and annexed everything of military use except my revolver, which had fallen out of my hand a minute before, when I had been knocked down by a bullet that glanced off a rock on to my leg. He took out my purse and saw that it contained five sovereigns in gold (more than I have ever seen since) and a good deal in silver. Then he gave it back to me, and apparently told me to keep it. The pay of a Turkish private is, or was, ten piastres a month, nominally about one shilling and eight pence. My captor was a good Turk. Later on, when I came to know how rare good Turks were, I was filled with marvel. Of those taken with me, one was not molested; one was fired at from five yards' distance, missed, and quietly captured; one was beaten and fired at. Thank God, the man who fired at him hit the man who was beating him and broke his wrist. The fourth, my Colone [Moore]l, was bayoneted. Then, for the moment their fury ceased. I was permitted to tend the Colonel. He did not seem to suffer pain at all, only to be intensely thirsty. He drank the whole of the contents of my water-bottle as well as his own. They even allowed me to carry him on my back; and on my back the Colonel died. May he rest in peace! He was a brave man, and a good friend to me.'

War poet Lieutenant Nowell Oxland (*I.C.7*), 6/Borders is another interesting burial. Oxland, an Old Dunelmian, was a close friend of William Hodgson, who was killed on the Somme in 1916. Oxland, son of a clergyman, entered Durham School as a King's Scholar in September 1903, where he excelled in sports, particularly rowing. In 1909 he went up to Worcester College, Oxford. After matriculation in 1911 he took a prominent part in the life of the College; he was captain of the College Rugby Football Team (he played for Rosslyn Park, Richmond, Middlesex and Cumberland) and had just been elected secretary of the Lovelace

Club when war broke out. In September 1914 he was gazetted into 6/Borders and sailed for the Dardanelles in June 1915.

War poet Lieutenant Nowell Oxland.

He was killed only two days after he landed, on 9 August. Cut off in a forward position, he was hit in the head and chest whilst tending some wounded. His last words were, *I am alright, look to yourself, lad.* He showed promise of becoming a poet and prose writer of distinction. His best-known poem, *Outward Bound,* appeared in *The Times* in August 1915; much of his work was collected and published as *Poems and Stories* in 1917.

Another notable burial is Lieutenant William Niven (*Sp.Mem.F.10*), 1/1 Berks Yeomanry, father of the British actor David Niven. Niven was killed at Scimitar Hill. Niven's body was never found at the time and as for many telegrams that included the word 'Missing' must have left some optimistic hope by the recipients that he might be a prisoner of war. This faded when an eye-witness, Private William Deacon, reported that he and Lieutenant Niven had actually reached the Turkish trenches in the dark and it was then that Niven was killed. It was some seventeen months later that his wife received official confirmation of his death.

In February 1919 she managed to track down another Berkshire yeoman, Private Archibald Calder, who had been captured by the Turks during the same attack. Calder had also witnessed Niven's death and confirmed that he had been shot in the head and killed instantly. David Niven wrote of his father and of receiving the news of his death in his autobiography, *The Moon's a Balloon* (1971).

There were three soldiers 'shot at dawn' during the Gallipoli campaign, one of whom is buried here: Private Harry Salter (*I.G.26*), 6/East Lancs, from Bridgwater in Somerset. He was shot for desertion on 11 December. Private Edward Roe, who was in the same battalion as Salter, wrote in his memoirs, published in 2004 as *Diary of an Old Contemptible*:

This youth, barely nineteen years of age, was shot by twelve of his comrades for taking 'French leave' from his Regiment on two occasions and attaching himself to the Anzacs. Not by any stretch of imagination could my comrades and I catalogue it as desertion, as 'twas impossible to desert from the Peninsula even had he so

Tekke Tepe heights.

desired. Our position in comparison to the position that the Anzacs held was a heaven compared to Hell. He therefore did not seek safety; he absconded because his life was made hell by the CSM [Company Sergeant Major] of my company (D). In barrack room parlance he was 'sat upon'. I was one of the firing party; he was marched from a dugout about eighty yards away, to a kind of disused quarry where the final scene was enacted. A clergyman preceded the doomed youth and his escort, reading prayers for the dying (the mockery of it all). The doomed youth was tied up to a stake, his grave already dug. His last request was, 'Don't blindfold me'. What followed I'll leave to the reader's imagination, in other words, I'll pull the pall of oblivion o'er the ghastly scene – 'If I can ever forget it'.

In August 2006 Salter was one of 306 executed men in the Great War who were posthumously pardoned.

Within the cemetery grounds, on the inside of the wall and by the entrance gate, is the **Green Hill Irish Memorial**, which was unveiled in March 2010 by Mary McAleese, President of Ireland. The memorial is to all the Irish who died at Gallipoli, in particular those of the 10th (Irish) Division. The plaque includes the regimental badges of the Royal Irish Regiment, Royal Inniskilling Fusiliers, Royal Irish Rifles, Royal Irish Fusiliers, Connaught Ranges, the Leinster Regiment, Royal Munster Fusiliers and the Royal Dublin Fusiliers.

Scimitar Hill　　　　Küçükanafarta

Return to the main road and take the road that runs in an easterly direction towards Küçükanafarta. After approximately one kilometre you will come to **Scimitar Hill (13) (40°17'51.5"N 26°17'32.5"E)** (Hill 70 or Burnt Hill), which is positioned towards the lower tip of the Anafarta Spur. The hill was so called due to its long-curved shape that resembled a Turkish sword. The Turks referred to it as Kusufçuktepe, meaning Dragonfly Hill. This key position was captured three times by the British on 8, 9 and 21 August; but it was also retaken three times by the Turks. Capturing this hill was difficult; retaining it proved impossible. It was here that one of the biggest and fiercest battles that ever took place at Gallipoli was fought and lost. The only two Victoria Crosses awarded during the Suvla campaign, to Captain Percy Hansen on 9 August and Private Frederick Potts on 21 August, were both for saving lives on Scimitar Hill. Today three Turkish stone memorials stand on its crest.

Scimitar Hill Turkish Memorial.

Leave Scimitar Hill and drive over the crest towards Küçükanafarta (Little Anafarta or Anafarta Sagir), about three kilometres distant. The road will follow the crest of the spur; to the southern end is Hill 112, the summit of W Hills (Ismail Oglu Tepe). This was the failed objective of both the 29th Division's and the Mounted Division's attack on 21 August, and the same hill that stopped the 11th Division's advance the same day. Even though there are tracks that can take you on to the top of the W Hills, where trenches still exist, it is best to go with a local guide as the scrub and rough tracks can be quite hazardous. The village of Küçükanafarta, with a history that goes back to 1356, was destroyed during the war and later rebuilt; today the means of living are livestock and agriculture. From the British positions in 1915 they could easily make out the village but not quite as one can see it today; its landmarks then were its slender white minaret and a cluster of four windmills. All the latter were destroyed during the war and only the minaret was rebuilt.

At the T-Junction turn right towards Büyükanafarta (Big Anafarta). After 200 metres you will come to the position of an original **Turkish gun battery (14) (40°18'03.8"N 26°19'13.7"E)**. Two 21cm German manufactured Krupp guns, dated 1875 and 1876, remain that were used during the campaign to fire on the British at Suvla and Anzac. One gun is almost intact and sits on its original carriage within the gun pit; the other is badly damaged.

Continue along the road for another two kilometres to Büyükanafarta. Stop at the **Büyükanafarta Ottoman Cemetery and Memorial (15) (40°16'56.7"N 26°19'28.9"E)**, which was constructed in 2005 and lists

Anafarta Turkish Gun Battery.

the names of 749 soldiers commemorated in the cemetery and who are still buried in unmarked battlefield cemeteries in the area. The fallen were from the 3rd Division (31 and 32 Regiments), the 7th Division (19, 20 and 21 Regiments) and also units of 33, 45 and 17 Regiments and the Bursa Gendarmerie. The adjacent old village cemetery contains several military marked graves from the period. These include three 7th Division officers who were killed during the August battles; Lieutenant Colonel (Yarbay) Halit Bey, 20 Regiment, Yarbay Ziya Bey, 21 Regiment and Lieutenant Hasan Tahsin, 7th Division Artillery Regiment and a regimental mufti. The mufti did similar work to the British chaplains, serving with the troops in the trenches, morally encouraged the soldiers in action, said prayers for the dying and wounded and whenever possible wrote home to the next of kin of the slain or wounded.

Continue in to **Büyükanafarta (16)**. This rural village, like its smaller sister, was evacuated by civilians after the landings. Heavily shelled and bombed during the war, it had to be rebuilt after hostilities. Mustafa Kemal stayed here on the occasions he visited the front. Today it has a population of around 400 people, whose main living is also from livestock and agriculture. There is a small café in the village centre. Whilst in the village it is recommended that you visit the small, but very good, **Gallipoli Campaign Museum**, situated between the café and cemetery. This museum contains many exhibits found locally on the Suvla battlefield, serves refreshments, has a toilet and makes an appropriate conclusion to the tour.

There are additional walks and further detail of the Suvla area mapped out in my Battleground Europe book *Suvla: August Offensive*.

Buyukanafarta Turkish Cemetery and Memorial.

207

Chapter 5

The Evacuation

With the failure of the August offensive, the stark reality of the situation at Gallipoli had begun to sink in. Large expanses of ground had been taken at huge cost, but still the tactically important high ground remained in Turkish hands. Even Achi Baba, the first day objective at Helles, remained a hill too far for Hamilton's force. The MEF was dwindling by the day in fighting strength, physical ability and morale. Not only was there little hope of further reinforcements, but the Turks had continued to grow stronger in both reinforcements and munitions supply, which flowed steadily into the area in ever increasing numbers – it was reckoned that by this stage they had 315,000 men compared to the MEF's 150,000.

On 6 September 1915 Bulgaria declared war on Serbia, joined the Central Powers and effectively opened a new front in Salonika, in north-eastern Greece. The Greeks made a plea to the Allies for military support, which was granted. There was no possibility in the short term of finding the manpower required as on the Western Front a new joint Anglo-French offensive (Second Battle of Artois 1915, Battle of Loos) was about to begin. Much to Hamilton's disgust, Kitchener ordered that men be sent from Gallipoli. He was told to send one British and two French divisions, but he successfully argued that he should send only one French, the 2nd, Division and the 10th (Irish) Division. Not only did Hamilton lose these two, but he lost a third in October when the 2nd Mounted Division left Suvla to return to Egypt. Any future operation at Gallipoli was now less likely.

On 11 October, less than a week after the 10th Division began departing for Salonika, Kitchener cabled a question to Hamilton. If Suvla were evacuated, how many casualties did he envision during the operation? Fearing the worst, Hamilton estimated at least 50 percent. The question enraged Hamilton who wrote:

'If they do this they make the Dardanelles into the bloodiest tragedy of the world! Even if we were to escape without a scratch, they would stamp our enterprise as the bloodiest of all tragedies!'

Kitchener did not like the answer and recalled Hamilton to London the following week. With his departure, Birdwood was left in temporary command; he reported that all units were under strength, poorly armed and undernourished. The only hope they had of winning was to push the Turks back so far that their guns could not hit the beaches. However, with the limited resources available and with no hope of receiving additional ones, there would be no chance of this happening. The French had also determined that their resources were better employed at Salonika and were totally opposed to reinforcing Gallipoli. The political scene in London had by now been influenced by British journalist Ellis Ashmead-Bartlett and who now wrote a letter to Prime Minister Herbert Asquith to

Field Marshal Horatio Herbert Kitchener.

alert him to the situation, in which he criticised how the campaign was being run and the conditions the men had to endure. Ashmead-Bartlett was a long-time critic of the campaign and had struck up a friendship with Australian journalist Keith Murdoch. He justified this action on the grounds that *the issue now is to try and save what is left of the army*. This letter was confiscated from Murdoch at Marseilles, so the latter rewrote it in his own exaggerated words; it duly reached the Prime Minister and was in time circulated amongst the cabinet.

Lieutenant General Sir Charles Monro arrived on 28 October to take over command from Birdwood and two days later visited all three sectors. He concluded that there was no realistic chance of capturing the Peninsula. He reported:

'The position occupied by our troops presented a military situation unique in history. The mere fringe of the coast line had been secured. The beaches and piers upon which they depended for all requirements in personnel and material were exposed to registered and observed Artillery fire. Our entrenchments were dominated almost throughout by the Turks. The possible Artillery positions were insufficient and defective. The Force, in short, held a line possessing every possible military defect. The position was without depth, the communications were insecure and dependent on the weather. No means existed for the concealment and deployment of fresh troops destined for the offensive, whilst the

Turks enjoyed full powers of observation, abundant Artillery positions, and they had been given the time to supplement the natural advantages which the position presented by all the devices at the disposal of the Field Engineer.'

It was not so much now a question of whether another British push were possible but rather if they could hold off the next major Turkish attack. Monro cabled Kitchener with his recommendation that Gallipoli be evacuated. Evacuating fourteen divisions (even if they were severely depleted) in winter was going to be an extraordinarily challenge to achieve without heavy casualties. Churchill, on learning of the suggestion, jibed, *He came, he saw, he capitulated*. These were strong and unwarranted words from a man who had once stated that it was impossible to secure the Dardanelles.[5] Kitchener decided to see Gallipoli for himself, and sailed in early November.

Lieutenant General Sir Charles Monro.

Upon his arrival Kitchener joined Birdwood for a three-day inspection and was shocked by what he found. On 15 November he cabled the Dardanelles Committee that he had reached the same conclusion as Monro. If the general conditions at Gallipoli were not intolerable enough, the winter storms arrived just over a week later. Gales and thunderstorms gave way to a short 'Indian summer' before the beginnings of winter showed itself in late November with heavy rain storms. This was such a contrast to the blistering heat of the summer and the lack of water. The men in the trenches who were located up on the hills and ridges meant that they were spared the floods' worst effects as water gushed down the spurs and gullies into the trenches below. Captain Peter Ashton, 1/Herefords, recorded the effect of the deluge; his battalion occupied trenches running across the bed of the Azmak Dere. Normally there was only a barely visible trickle of water in the dry watercourse.

> 'Suddenly, without warning, a brown flood poured in. The water rose as you watched until it was about 3½ feet deep and then stopped. As I didn't want to drown I struggled out of the trench, and met the C.O. emerging from next door where the same thing had happened. It was quite obvious what had occurred. The very

5. Churchill, *The World Crisis, Volume II*, page 908.

heavy rain, probably still heavier back in the hills, had suddenly transformed the Dere into a river again. The water had poured down from the high ground behind the Turks till it had got caught up behind their barricade. This, presumably, had held until there was a respectable weight of water behind it, when it collapsed and the whole tearing flood came rushing down at ours. It didn't gather, or pause for the twinkling of an eye at ours, it simply swept it away as if it hadn't been there, and swept on to the sea, a solid river, 20 yards wide and 8 or 9 feet deep.'

The following morning, 28 November, the wind got up and began to blow in from the north. The temperature dropped rapidly below freezing and, to cap it all, flurries of snow began to fall across the Peninsula. That night the Herefords were relieved and they had moved back into reserve in the open sand dunes behind Lala Baba. Ashton recalled:

'Dawn found it still snowing. We rose with considerable difficulty and started a little circulation back in our frozen limbs. A great many people were unable to get up at all; Holman, for one, was practically unconscious and we thought he was dead. But worse was to follow.

New Zealander in the snow.

Overnight our rations had been sent out to us in a lorry. The folk who sent them out, presumably sorry for those unfortunates in the snow, sent with them a double ration of rum. The wagon drivers, who brought the stuff, apparently before we arrived, finding no one to hand over to, had simply dumped the things by the side of the road and gone home. When morning broke men began wandering about, as men will, and unhappily found the dump. Instead of telling somebody, or even eating the food, which would have been sensible, they broke open the rum jars and started in. The effect on empty stomachs and in that cold was simply devastating. Filled with a spurious warmth, they lay on the ground, and in many cases took off coats, boots, even tunics! Those in the immediate vicinity of the dump were quickly put in the 'bag' but,

211

An Australian 18 pdr gun team under a fresh snowfall.

unfortunately the majority had filled mess tins and water bottles, and crawled into the bushes to enjoy themselves. We fairly combed those bushes all the morning, but by the time we found them all a certain number were dead. I remember finding one man in particular in only his shirt and trousers, holding out an empty mug with a perfectly stiff arm, quite dead. Coming on top of everything else, it was heart-rending.'[6]

There were at least 250 British soldiers who froze to death or drowned in the torrents that flooded the area, and 5,000 more were suffering from frostbite and hypothermia. The Turks were no better off. The winter weather was fickle and would be an important factor in any decision regarding evacuation.

Whilst British politicians in London prevaricated over the decision to stay or go, the consequence of Bulgaria joining the Central Powers had manifested already in the supply of heavier artillery and more reliable ammunition to the Turks. The relative lack of modern Turkish artillery, shortage of munitions and the unreliability of what they had, meant that the MEF previously could continue to exist even though their rear areas were under the intermittent menace of shell fire. All over Anzac and Suvla the shells were now dropping on areas that had been previously considered relatively safe. It was evident that the Turks were being

6. P. Ashton quoted by CH Dudley-Ward, History of the 53rd (Welsh) Division, 1914-1918, (Cardiff: Western Mail Ltd, 1927), pp 47-48 and 49.

supplied with new and heavier guns, and to counter this the British had no answer.

It was not surprising to anyone that on 7 December the Committee finally agreed to evacuate the peninsula, but it would only be partial. Suvla and Anzac would be evacuated; but Helles would be retained and for several reasons. The Royal Navy wished to keep it to help restrict enemy submarine activity in the Dardanelles, whilst Committee members felt that evacuating the whole peninsula would *really* be admitting defeat. Retaining Helles meant that it could still be used as a base for a future operation. In addition there was the practically that there was not enough shipping available to evacuate simultaneously all the three sectors. Nevertheless, the stunning reality of evacuation, despite the planning already underway, was a task that no one relished.

> 'A retirement in the face of an enemy on land where you have plenty of room is a very difficult and critical operation but under the circumstances here, where one is bang up against your enemy, and where you have absolutely no room to sling a cat, and also have to embark in small craft every single man, gun, animals and stores on a beach which is under the enemy's gun fire, and of which they know the range to an inch - and in the case of Suvla can see from their positions - you can imagine what a difficult anxious job it is. We have not only the enemy to contend with, but at any moment, practically in the twinkling of an eye, a south-west wind may spring up.'
>
> Brigadier General Walter Campbell, HQ, MEF.

Stores build-up at Anzac Cove. (State Library of Western Australia 7175-B3)

The challenge was to evacuate from Anzac and Suvla some 83,000 men, 186 guns and as much of their equipment and stores as possible. The evacuation plans envisaged either a fighting withdrawal to the beaches with fresh defensive trenches close to piers, or a withdrawal based on deception and cunning. With the trenches in such close proximity to each other, the danger was the Turks' reaction to an evacuation, which would almost certainly bring increased bombardments of the beach embarkation points as well as disruptive attacks across the whole front line. Because of this the chosen plan favoured deception to try and conceal the evacuation until the very last moments.

Lieutenant Colonel Cyril Brudenell White, ANZAC Chief of Staff.

The main architect of the Anzac and Suvla plan was Lieutenant Colonel Cyril Brudenell White, the ANZAC Chief of Staff. It was undoubtedly a brilliant piece of work that combined rigorously detailed planning with a considerable imaginative effort to 'fool' the Turks. The evacuation was carried out in three stages: a preliminary stage to remove all surplus personnel, animals and vehicles not necessary for the winter campaign; an intermediate stage that would remove all personnel, guns, and animals that were not absolutely necessary for the defence of the positions; and a final stage that required two nights, with the units in reserve and support evacuated on the first while on the final night the rear-guard elements would follow. Throughout every effort would be made to maintain the appearance of normality in everything the soldiers did. The 'final night' was to be the night of 18/19 December 1915.

In order to facilitate the evacuation without giving the plan away, clever means were employed to simulate the presence of men, guns and stores where there were none. Indian muleteers continuously drove their carts, throwing up huge clouds of dust, so that it appeared as if a consignment of stores had just arrived. Rifle and artillery fire was to cease unless there was an attack, in order to get the enemy used to extended periods of relative silence, just as it would in the last hours of the evacuation. Trenches were held by as few men as possible, their presence supplemented by uniformed scarecrow like dummies made out of straw filled old jackets and hats. On the beach the illusion of stacks of wooden ration crates was created by means of constructing an outer framework only, making it appear that the massive piles were solid. Stores that could not be evacuated were buried, rum jars smashed and water tins holed. Even games of cricket were played in the overlooked reserve areas to give the impression that everything was normal. It worked, and the Turks remained ignorant of what was occurring.

'Yes; the evacuation of Suvla is now a reality. I hear to-day that we have now begun the intermediate stage of the evacuation. It has been a reality for some days. The storm only delayed it. We have just completed the preliminary stage. We hear that it will be but a few days now when not a British subject will be left alive here unless as a prisoner. The shelling to-day is in fits and starts. High explosive shells are searching the beach, bursting well and with a louder explosion than in past days. But West Beach is well protected, and the steady shipment of vehicles and ordnance goes on all day. At night, empty ration carts go up to the line to bring back men's surplus kits, blankets, surplus ammunition, and the surplus part of the usual accumulation of baggage that a regiment takes with it to the trenches and to dumps just behind.'

Captain John Gillam, ASC.

A British soldier pays his respects to a fallen comrade.

When the men found out about leaving Gallipoli for good, emotions were mixed. Many felt that they had not been beaten and hoped that with the right level of support a renewed attack could finally win them the Dardanelles. Others were totally disillusioned and could not wait to leave those fatal shores. But all shared the sacrifice and did not want to leave their 'mates' who were buried on the Peninsula. At Anzac, men spent time visiting the graves of friends for what, they assumed, would be the last time. Bean wrote in *The Story of Anzac (Vol II*, page 882):

> 'The consideration which did go straight to every man's heart was the tragedy of confessing failure after so many and well-loved comrades had given their lives to the effort. The men hated to leave their dead mates to the mercy of the Turks. For days after the breaking of the news there were never absent from the cemeteries men by themselves, or in twos and threes, erecting new crosses or tenderly 'tidying-up' the grave of a friend. This was by far the deepest regret of the troops. "I hope", said one of them to Birdwood on the final day, pointing to a little cemetery, "I hope they don't hear us marching down the deres."'

At Anzac, Sergeant Cyril Lawrence, 2nd Field Company, Australian Engineers, records hearing the first news of the evacuation:

> 'It has been rumoured that we are going to evacuate the Peninsula. It must be a rumour only, because no one considers it possible, and work is going on just as usual – and we are working on jobs that will take weeks to finish. If it were true! God! I believe that murder and riots would break loose amongst our boys. Much as we hate and detest the place there's something of an indescribable feeling that comes over one when he thinks of leaving it. Oh, it couldn't be; how could we leave this place now after the months of toil and slavery that have gone to the making of it? And after the blood of brothers and fathers that has been shed in making it OURS. How could we leave those comrades who have paid the price and now lie sleeping under the sod in the cemeteries tucked away in the valleys? Are their lives to be given for nothing and all our striving to go for naught'? No! No! I cannot believe it. Why the boys would go mad with rage. God help the fellow that has to put it to them.[7]

---

7. C. Lawrence (edited by R. East) "The Gallipoli Diary of Sergeant Lawrence of the Australian Engineers, 1st AIF, 1915", (Melbourne, Melbourne University Press 1981), pp.126-127 (Diary entry 10 December 1915).

In the opposing lines where the Turks were close, no reply was given to Turkish bombs throw in, while clever booby traps were designed to delay the Turks should they enter the trenches. Action delayed rifles, utilising water-powered weights, were set up to self-fire after the lines were evacuated to give the illusion that the trenches were still occupied. These 'drip-drip' rifles worked on the principle of water dripping along a piece of rope from the upper container into the lower one, until the weight increased to a level that was sufficient to pull the trigger. Up to an hour after the evacuation shots were still echoing through the gullies. This delayed-action device was invented by Lance Corporal William Scurry, 7/AIF, who was awarded the DCM for its invention. The men themselves would make their way quietly to the beaches with muffled boots, following lines of flour that were laid to direct the men in the right directions.

The Turks, although suspicious in the run up to the evacuation, remained in the dark as to the evacuation date, although they were well aware that evacuation would happen. Openly discussed in London, the debate over the future Dardanelles policy was no secret. Even the Turks in the trenches were aware of the vacillating position of British politicians.

'The postman brings the Tasviri Efkar [newspaper] of 12 November. Contains good news. Debate under way in House of

Scurry's Drip Self Firing Rifle.

Lords concerning eventual withdrawal of English ... This news is 15 days old. It is possible that by today they have reached a decision and have started to implement it ... Newspaper reports a Colonel Repington [the military correspondent of the *The Times* and a noted intriguer] has stated that, from the military point of view, Allied forces need to be reinforced otherwise they will certainly be wiped out ... It is therefore likely that, having realised nothing can be accomplished in Gallipoli, British forces here are being withdrawn to be used as reinforcements in the Balkans. In time, we shall certainly find out what is to be.'

Lieutenant Mehmed Fasih, 47 Regiment.

And just before dawn on 20 December they did find out when the Australians blew mines under The Nek as a defiant last gesture. The mine destroyed part of the Turkish front line trenches and killed several men. To the Turks' surprise no attack followed up the explosion, so a patrol was sent forward to the Anzac trenches, which were found empty. About the same time the Turks spotted large fires on the beaches, by which time the troops at Anzac and Suvla had already gone, evacuated without a single fatality.[8] Anzac and Suvla was Turkish once more.

The last day on North Beach, Anzac: 18th December 1915.

---

8. Staff Sergeant Harry Bowser, 2/Australian Light Horse, died on 20 December of wounds received on the beach and was buried at sea. He was the last Anzac to die at Gallipoli and is remembered on the Lone Pine Memorial. According to Charles Bean, 'on shore one man had been wounded, and a light horseman in one of the boats was hit by a stray bullet from the fusillade caused by the explosion of the mines'. These were the mines that were fired at The Nek at 3.26 a.m.

On 20 December the men at Helles learned of the evacuation via a Special Order of the Day. In addition to describing the successful withdrawals, it noted that Helles would continue to be garrisoned. The reason, it stated, was to maintain

'the honour of the British Empire against the Turks on the Peninsula and [to continue] such action as shall prevent them, as far as possible, from massing their forces to meet our main operations elsewhere.'

'Elsewhere' meant Egypt, Palestine and Mesopotamia. This did not stop rumours spreading at Helles that their evacuation could follow, especially now that the whole weight of the Ottoman army would be concentrating all their energies on the tip of the Peninsula. But could the ruse that was played out so well at Anzac and Suvla be repeated?

The French sector was the first to be evacuated on 21 December when it was handed over to the RND. A week later the 13th Division, after a week's rest and already experienced after their evacuation from Suvla, was landed at Helles to relieve the 42nd Division. At Helles there were now only four divisions remaining, the 13th, 29th, 52nd and the RND. Designed to look as though IX Corps was relieving VIII Corps, the Turks thought life looked as if it were normal. Guns and troops were still being landed during the day; but unknown to the Turks, under the cover of darkness, the garrison began to dwindle. During a clear Christmas Day, the semi-finals of the 'Dardanelles Cup', a VIII Corps football competition that had started back in October, continued to be played on the Corps football ground near Hunter-Weston Hill. This ground, which also doubled as the aerodrome emergency landing strip, was under the full observation of the Turks, who had a grandstand view. Although a shell or two on occasion would bring a temporary pause to the match, on the whole the games continued unmolested. Unfortunately, the final, scheduled to be played on Boxing Day, had to be postponed because of the evacuation, though it was eventually played, on 13 January 1916, on Lemnos.

Not all French troops had left straightaway as their artillery, which the British needed if they were to protect their now-depleted front, was retained in the event of a Turkish onslaught. This was an attack that was anticipated, as Ottoman troops from the northern fronts, along with their artillery and trench mortars, could now be diverted south to Helles.

On 24 December London finally ordered Monro to prepare for the evacuation of Helles. The British at Helles followed the same template as that adopted in the northern sectors so successfully. Once again the

The Dardanelles Cup being played at Helles.

number of men in the line was thinned and guns removed, leaving roughly half of the original force, 17,000 men, to be evacuated on the night of 8 January. But could they once more get away with it? What the British feared was an all-out attack, and their worst nightmares came true on 7 January, just thirty-six hours before Z-Day, the final day of the evacuation.

General Otto Liman von Sanders had planned a large scale attack as he had noticed that the British were reducing their garrisons and removing artillery, as described in his book *Five Years in Turkey* (pp 101-102).

'During the first days of January 1916 it appeared as though the fire of the land artillery at Sedd-el-Bahr was becoming weaker. But one gun was firing from several batteries, frequently changing its position, while the fire from the ships, including the largest calibres, sometimes grew to great vehemence. The removal of guns was observed from the Asiatic side. The scouting parties that were pushed forward against the hostile front at all hours of evening and night invariably met with strong resistance. Of the troops designated for the attack, the 12th Division had arrived in rear of the south front. The division was designated to capture a section of trenches projecting northward opposite the extreme Turkish right, from which the British artillery could have flanked the great attack we were planning. On January 7th I ordered the 12th Division to carry out the attack planned on the extreme Turkish right after two hours of preparation by the heaviest artillery fire and explosion of mines.'

Between Fusilier Bluff and Gully Ravine the bombardment fell remorselessly on the British trenches for nearly five hours, which by that stage were only held by a minimum of men from 9/Worcesters and 7/North Staffs and with precious few guns for support. Ordinary Seaman Joe Murray, who was in the trenches with the North Staffs, recalled the unexpected ferocity of the shelling which fell

'… on both sides of the Gully Ravine. It was soon obvious that this was the prelude to an attack. The question was - "How long did we have to wait?" As the hours passed, thousands of shells crashed into the empty support trenches and those that fell in the front line took their toll. It was by far the most severe and prolonged shelling I have ever experienced.'

When the high explosive and shrapnel bombardment ended and two mines were fired on Gully Spur, there was no doubt that an attack would immediately follow. Fortunately it was a half-hearted attack towards the North Staffs trenches. Some forty Turks left their trenches to be met by a withering fire from the Staffs and the supporting salvos of the Royal Navy. Opposite the Worcesters no Turks left the trenches.

'The Worcestershire lads for some wonderful minutes stood up on the firestep and jeered at the enemy, inciting them to come on. Captain Conybeare, in a fine battle-fury, leapt on to the parapet and stood there, shouting defiance and leading his men in derisive cheers; "All together now: One-two-three—Al-l-l-lah!'[9]

Very soon the firing died away and again all was quiet.

One of the casualties was the North Staffs commanding officer, Lieutenant Colonel Frank Walker. His Adjutant, Captain John Robinson, wrote to the wife to tell her what happened to her husband.

'During all the bombardment your husband was in the firing line. Then the Turks attacked. Their trenches were, at one corner only,

9. Stack, Captain H., *Worcestershire Regiment in the Great War* (1928).

from 10-15 yards away. Some four Turks got onto the parapet of our trench here and Colonel Walker, finding the bay empty, collected three or four [men] and rushed into the bay, into which the Turks were firing. I believe he shot two with his revolver and was then himself shot. But the Turks were driven off. That I think is the plain unvarnished tale. He fell down into the bottom of the trench and two of our men fell dead on the top of him. I feel sure he did not speak and that he felt no pain.'

Lieutenant Colonel Frank Walker.

Walker was buried in Border Ravine, close to his dugout, in a grave marked out with empty shell cases and a solid wooden cross edged in black and recording his name. Despite the efforts of his men, the location of the grave was lost and he is now commemorated on the Helles Memorial.

Lanarkshire Yeomanry packing up before leaving the Peninsula for good.

The British were enormously relieved that this attack had not been pushed home. That day their total numbers at Helles stood at only 17,000, with sixty-three guns in support. Any sustained effort by the Turks would have surely broken through. Everyone feared a renewed assault and the tension remained excruciating. That night another 2,300 men and nine guns were evacuated. Still the Turks seemed oblivious as to what was going on.

All surplus stores and all horses and mules not required for moving the last guns were destroyed and the surplus ammunition was buried or packed into the natural caves at the back of the beach and fused ready for detonation after the last men had left. All the wagons and vehicles that could not be embarked were parked on the cliff edge for destruction by naval guns. Positions were selected for a stand on Hunter-Weston Hill, but the enemy did not take alarm and so these positions were among the last to be evacuated.

Luckily the weather had held again but, as the last troops began to make their way to the beaches, the wind began to pick up and there was a noticeable swell in the sea, threatening the evacuation of the last few men from the 13th Division. Designated to leave by two lighters from Gully Beach, the group included their divisional commander, Lieutenant General Sir Stanley Maude, who only narrowly escaped being left behind. The lighter that was allocated to evacuate the General and a rear section of men from Gully Beach accidently grounded due to the heavy seas. This left the General, members of his divisional staff and about 150 officers and men stranded on the beach. Eventually they made haste to Lancashire

General Sir Stanley Maude.

Landing but when the main party reached this destination and boarded the two remaining lighters, the General and his staff were nowhere to be seen. A General could not be left behind!

At W Beach, Brigadier General James O'Dowda, the military commander of the beach party, found himself in a predicament. Not only was the firing line deserted and thus at any time the Turks could descend on them, more daunting was the fear of being blown up. The fuses to the main magazine dump had already been lit and were set to explode at 4.00 a.m.

'I packed up my dispatch case and, leaving my office, brought up the rear of the last party. Just at that moment a GSO, very disturbed, rushed up and told me that General Maude had not yet arrived. I asked what had happened and was informed that after they had left Gully Beach General Maude had discovered that his bedding roll had been left behind. He said that he was hanged if he was going to leave his bedding for the Turks, got two volunteers with a stretcher and went back for it. The time was now 3.50 am and there was no sign of the missing General. I therefore sent an officer and a couple of men, who knew every inch of the beach, and gave them ten minutes to retrieve him. Fortunately, they found him almost at once.'

The crew and men onboard the lighter were getting jumpy as the dumps along the cliff were already burning and they knew that the main magazine was set to explode. Maude's party was delayed as they came a different way and had been unable to find a gap in the wire until, luckily, a demolition party came along who showed them the way through. The last lighter left the jetty at 3.55 a.m. and was only 200 yards from the shore when the magazine exploded, throwing up thousands of tons of debris into the sky. It was reported that a couple of men were wounded by the falling debris, and one was killed, a member of the lighter crew.[10]

General Maude became a legend soon after the evacuation when a verse was written about him refusing to leave until he had been reunited with his kit. Based on a parody of the Victorian-era parlour song, *Come Into The Garden, Maude,* it became popular with the troops.

> *Come into the lighter, Maude,*
> *For the fuse has long been lit,*
> *Hop into the lighter, Maude,*
> *And never mind your kit.*

By the time that the Turks realized that the evacuation was occurring and began to bombard the trenches and beaches, they were empty. The British warships responded with a last goodbye and gesture of defiance by shelling Achi Baba for one last time. The Turkish bombardment lasted until about 6.30 am, followed up by an infantry advance; but by the time they had got through the trenches, between which all gaps had been closed with barricades and blocked with mines and bobby traps, the transports were already long gone. Helles was once again Turkish. Sanders noted in his book on the campaign (p. 103)

---

10. No name is given of the fatality, although it is mentioned in the *London Gazette,* 11th April 1917 – Admiralty Despatch. Several soldiers were killed in action on 8 January 1916, but as part of the daily attrition, not relating directly to the evacuation.

'The booty was extraordinary. Wagon parks, automobile parks, mountains of arms, ammunition and entrenching tools were collected. Here too most of the tent camps and barracks had been left standing, in part with all of their equipment. Many hundreds of horses lay in rows, shot or poisoned, but quite a number of horses and mules were captured and turned over to the Turkish artillery. Here, as at the other fronts, the stacks of flour and subsistence had some acid solution poured over them to render them unfit for our use. In the next few days the hostile ships made vain attempts to set the stacks and the former British tent camps and barracks on fire. It took nearly two years to clean up the grounds.'

All quite true, of course; but this account glosses over the fact that an enormous military and propaganda coup had been lost.

Lieutenant Charles Black, 1/6 HLI, wrote that *no man was sorry to leave Gallipoli; but few were really glad.*

Lancashire Landing evacuation.

225

Tour 8

Evacuation Trail

Even though much of the area can be walked, the expanse of the battlefield really requires a car or similar vehicle if you are restricted by time. Allow a half day to drive, or a full day to walk the twelve kilometre trail.

This tour is designed to cover some of the rear areas of Helles that were important not only to the evacuation but also includes the French contribution to the campaign. No 'evacuation walk' of Anzac or Suvla has been included in this chapter; the author felt that the ground that would be covered has already been included elsewhere in this volume or in other Gallipoli books in this series. It is also important to note that the evacuation of its nature was one-way and so whilst some of the walk is circular, thus you could start and finish at Skew Bridge or Sedd-el-Bahr, there will be some of the route where you would need to retrace your tracks.

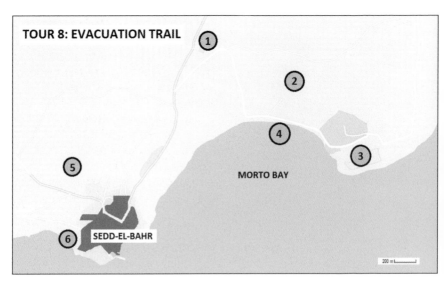

TOUR 8: EVACUATION TRAIL

MORTO BAY

SEDD-EL-BAHR

Sub Lieutenant Ivan Heald, Hood Battalion, RND, was evacuated from Helles in January 1916. A soldier, sailor and airman, Heald was also a poet who wrote the following poignant verse that was published in the 'Liverpool Echo' on 19th February 1916:

Sub Lieutenant Ivan Heald, Hood Battalion, RND.

EVACUATION

Evacuation of the Dardanelles
So quietly we left our trench
That night, yet this I know -
As we stole down to Sedd-el-Bahr
Our dead mates heard us go.

As I came down the Boyau Nord
A dead hand touched my sleeve,
A dead hand from the parapet
Reached out and plucked my sleeve.
'Oh, what is toward, O mate o' mine,

That ye pass with muffled tread,
And there comes no guard for the firing-trench.
The trench won by your dead?'
The dawn was springing on the hills,
'Twas time to put to sea,

But all along the Boyau Nord,
A dead voice followed me.
'Oh, little I thought', a voice did say,
'That ever a lad of Tyne,
Would leave me alone in the cold trench side.
And him a mate of mine.'

We sailed away from Sedd-el-Bahr,
We are sailing home on leave.
But this I know – through all the years
Dead hands will pluck my sleeve.

Alas, there is no happy ending to Heald's story – he was killed when serving in the Royal Flying Corps on the Western Front in December 1916; he is buried in Cabaret Rouge British Cemetery (a huge concentration cemetery north of Arras), XVI.D.11.

Skew Bridge CWGC Cemetery.

Begin this walk at **Skew Bridge Cemetery (1) (40°03'35.1"N 26°11'59.3"E)**, which lies just off the Krithia Road. It was begun in early May 1915 at the time that engineers built a wooden 'skew' bridge across Kanli Dere behind the cemetery.

Skew Bridge Cemetery only held fifty-three graves at the end of the war, after which time it was greatly enlarged when bodies were brought in from smaller cemeteries (Orchard Gully, RND, Backhouse Post and Romanos Well) and battlefield burials. Today it contains 607 burials, of which 351 are unidentified; but special memorials commemorate a number of casualties known or believed to be buried among them. The early graves mostly date from May 1915 and the Second Battle of Krithia, when the RND were engaged in the fighting north of this cemetery. Observation Ridge, down which the Krithia Road runs, still has the remains of trenches and dugouts, whilst locations like Backhouse Post, Romanos Well and the White House, all important in the RND's history, can still be located.

Heald may have known many of the men buried here, for example his old colonel, John Quilter *(II.B.4)*, a Boer War veteran who served in the Grenadier Guards and commanded Hood Battalion, RND. Quilter, while carrying an oversized walking stick, was killed leading his men on 6 May. Prior to

Lieutenant Colonel John Arnold Cuthbert Quilter

the outbreak of war he had served as the military secretary to the Governor General of Australia. The following verse was written in him memory:

> *All honour to Colonel Quilter,*
> *The Battalion mourns his loss.*
> *The only things we could give him*
> *Were a grave and a wooden cross.*

He is joined by three other RND colonels: Colonel Frank Luard (*II.B.3*), Portsmouth Battalion; Lieutenant Colonel Edmund Evelegh (*II.E.13*), Nelson Battalion; and Lieutenant Colonel William Maxwell (*Sp. Mem. B.19*), HQ 2 (Naval) Brigade. All three led by example, demonstrating courage to their men.

Epitaphs are often quite moving and on occasion give information as to how a soldier died. 19-year-old Private Albert Prince (*II.F.4*), Plymouth Battalion, was killed on 15 July, *Shot Rescuing a Comrade*; the line above shows that he was Mentioned in Despatches. The only posthumous awards available in 1915 were Mentioned in Despatches and the Victoria Cross. An Accrington lad, Drummer Joseph Townsend (*Sp. Mem. B.4*), 1/4 East Lancs, was killed on 18 June, aged just 15 years. Joe was the youngest British soldier to die at Gallipoli; he was the son of Company Sergeant Major Townsend, the recruiting officer for his home town. Joe was one of three sons in the same battalion. One of them witnessed Joe's death. He wrote home with the sad news, saying that he saw his brother hit in the chest, causing a severe wound, from which he died within a few minutes.

Leave Skew Bridge Cemetery and make your way towards the French Cemetery, taking the high road that leads up on to the rise above Morto Bay, a total distance of about 1.7 kilometres. Take the track in the woodland on the right-hand side of the road to the **French Cemetery and Memorial (2) (40°03'26.0"N 26°12'36.7"E)**, which is located on the ridge above Morto Bay, roughly between the Helles Memorial and the Turkish Çanakkale Martyrs Memorial. The cemetery contains 2,340 identified graves and four ossuaries containing the bones of 12,000 unidentifiable soldiers.

The remains of several old French cemeteries and memorials can still be found in the surrounding wooded area, all of which have now been consolidated in to this single large cemetery and memorial. It was through these woods that men like Ivan Heald and other small scattered groups of men would have walked in the dark during the evacuation. Heald came out of the trenches in the old French sector and marched down the *Boyau*

French Cemetery and Memorial.

Nord, one of the main communication trenches that provided (relatively) safe passage to the rear lines. There were two *Boyau Nord* trenches, No.1 and No.2, both exiting near the French Military Cemetery at Morto Bay. The remains of these communication trenches can still be traced in the woodland to the north of the French cemetery.

At the southern entrance of the cemetery is an information plaque that gives a brief history of the *Corps Expéditionnaire d'Orient* and the cemetery. There were originally six French cemeteries on the battlefield; Le Cimetière Galinier, Le Cimetière de L'Ambulance, Le Cimetière de la 1re Division, Le Cimetière de la 2e Division, Le Cimetière Zimmermann and Le Cimetière de Kerevez Dere. In 1919 the French began gathering in all their fallen into two newly built ossuaries, named after the French generals Masnou and Ganeval, both of whom died during the campaign. In 1923, after the signing of the Treaty of Lausanne, the French consolidated all the cemeteries and ossuaries into this cemetery. This also included those who were buried on Lemnos and some graves from the Allied occupation of the area. On 9 June 1930 the cemetery was inaugurated by General Gouraud, the original GOC *Corps*

Expéditionnaire d'Orient; at the end of June he was seriously wounded and had to have an arm amputated. He ended his war as a successful commander of Fourth Army.

An ossuary that contains the bones of 3,000 unidentifiable French soldiers.

The *Corps Expéditionnaire d'Orient*, made up of French metropolitan and French colonial African troops, came ashore at Helles on 27 April and fought alongside the British for the best part of eight months. The Corps was responsible for the right of the line at Kerevez Dere, a deep gully about two kilometres north east of this cemetery and the Turkish memorial (Çanakkale Martyrs Memorial). The battles for Kerevez Dere failed with huge casualties, despite a number of attempted advances to take the Turkish positions. Those fighting in places with infamous names such as 'Ravin de la Morte', 'Haricot', 'Quadrilateral' and 'Le Rognon' Redoubts included not only French born soldiers but also men from the colonial parts of the French empire, such as Algeria, Morocco, Guinea, Sudan and Senegal.

Despite several battles that would account for 27,000 French casualties, of which up to 15,000 died, their advances achieved little. The French Military Cemetery is the largest on the Peninsula, containing the graves of some 3,236 men. Each grave is marked by a black iron stake that looks similar to a barbed wire picket, with its ends flared into a *fleur-*

de-lys style design. The graves have a simple metallic plaque that bears the name and a common MORT POUR LA FRANCE (died for France) epitaph. The graves are laid out according to rank; the officers at the top end of the cemetery and the soldiers in the remainder. (Perhaps remarkable for a republic that has *Liberté, Egalité, Fraternité* for a motto.) What is unusual are the number of officer marked graves that still contain their original stone markers, moved from their original cemetery locations before all the French burials on Gallipoli were consolidated here.

The French Memorial.

Close by the officers' graves is the Memorial Wall (*Mur des Souvenirs*). This wall, constructed in 1926, is the main monument upon which numerous marble plaques have been imbedded from the different monuments that used to stand on the battlefield itself. The memorial recalls the loss at the Dardanelles of French sailors from warships like *Bouvet* and the four French submarines that were lost: *Joule, Mariotte, Saphir* and *Turquoise*. Marble plaques to all the French infantry units involved are also shown. In Latin, across the front of the obelisk, is carved *Ave Gallia Immortalis* (Hail Immortal France) above a verse from Victor Hugo's *Anthem*.

There are several senior officers buried here, one of whom is General Marie Ganeval (*Grave 30*), who was killed on 7 June, aged 61. A senior officer, he was criticised for his handling of the French 62nd Infantry Division on the Western Front during the fighting in August and September 1914 in which it suffered heavy casualties. He left this division at the end of September and sailed for Gallipoli in 1915, taking command of the 2nd Infantry Division. On 7 June, accompanied by an interpreter and liaison officer, he visited the British trenches in the Achi Baba

Grave of General Marie François Ganeval.

Nullah sector. Ganeval was in a trench only a hundred metres from the Turks when he was sniped, falling mortally wounded and dying in a dressing station. He was buried the following day with full military honours and in the presence of General Sir Ian Hamilton, General Gouraud, General Bailloud (GOC 2nd Division), Brigadier General Simonin (4 Colonial Brigade) and a number of other senior officers. The guard of honour comprised a detachment of Zouaves. Regardless of rank, nowhere was safe at Gallipoli.

Not too far aware is Brigadier General Marie Xertigny (*Grave 36*), 2 Brigade, who was also 61 years of age; he died of wounds on 7 June. Next to him is Commander Romieux (*Grave 37*), who was killed on 12 July in the Kerevez Dere battles. From a general to a private, there is Private Kone Moussa (*Grave 1156*), 56 (Colonial) Infantry Regiment, who was killed in action at Kerevez Dere on 29 July. Moussa was from Senegal, in West Africa, a recruiting ground for much of the French colonial forces at the time. Captain Gabriel Leroux (*Grave 972*), 176 Infantry Regiment, was a noted pre-war writer, killed on 9 June. Another famous author and poet was Leon Gauthier-Ferriéres, who was killed on 17 July; he has no known grave but is believed to be interred in one of the ossuaries.

Military chaplains also became casualties, and buried here is Marie Lafont de Contagnet (*Grave 2225*), Chaplain to the 2nd Division. He was posthumously awarded the *Legion d'Honneur* and the *Croix de Guerre* with palm. It is said that he had *a quiet and smiling courage and never hesitated to visit the men in the front line, comforting the wounded and dying*. He was killed by shrapnel fire on 9 June whilst in the trenches close to the Ottoman lines. He had only been in Gallipoli less than a month before being killed. Contagnet spent some of his early life in England, where he took his vows as a Jesuit priest in Canterbury in 1897. As a Jesuit, he would have spent thirteen years at least in preparing and training for ordination. He moved to Jersey in 1899 and to Beirut in 1903, where he engaged in Biblical studies and teaching at the inter-ritual seminary and recently established Jesuit university there, before returning to France in 1907. He returned to work in Syria at an Armenian mission in Caesarea in Cappadocia until war broke out; he returned to his mobilisation centre in Briançon, was moved to Lyon and volunteered to go as a chaplain to Gallipoli.

Leave the French cemetery and follow the road east for 1.5 kilometres. It is close to this road junction that Ivan Heald described his fraught journey back from the trenches near Kerevez Dere, down *Boyau Nord* towards V Beach.

'A touch on the back of the last man and he climbed down from the firing step and touched the next man farther along, and quietly we filed out of the long firing line, and, as we stole away, I could hear the Turks coughing and talking in their trench twenty yards away. Two or three times, to hide the shuffle of the men's gear against the side of the trench, I jumped on the firing step and let my Webley-Scott bark at Achi Baba, and somewhere on the left someone fired a farewell Very light, which lit up the sandbags until the blackness came welling up out of the trench again as the rocket died away. So we shuffled past the telephone station at the top of the communication trench. The Turk's own moon was in the sky, a perfect crescent with a star, and a wind rising dangerously from the north. Now and again [there was] a wistful sigh of a spent bullet, and ever wheeling behind us the shaft of the great Chanak searchlight. The men talked little among themselves, and I think we were all awed by the bigness of the thing, and saddened by the thoughts of the little crosses we were leaving behind us - the little wooden crosses that were creeping higher every day to meet the crescents on that great sullen hill.'

Turn right at this junction and follow the road for a further 1.5 kilometres to the **Turkish Martyrs Memorial (3)** (*Çanakkale Sehitleri Aniti*) **(40°03'00.7"N 26°13'10.5"E)** where you can park your vehicle. This huge forty metres high memorial, the main Turkish memorial at Gallipoli, is signposted throughout the peninsula as Abide. The Memorial is built on the headland of Eski Hissarlik, which is also the location of De Tott's Battery and the site of an Athenian settlement called Elaius. The monument was opened in 1960 as a memorial to the 'Mehmets', the Ottoman soldiers who fought and died in the campaign, the story of which is told in friezes around the structure. Within the grounds is a military cemetery with symbolic graves and various statues and other exhibits to the campaign. Souvenirs, refreshments and toilets are available.

Turkish Martyrs Memorial.

Turkish Memorial.

Leave the Turkish memorial, taking the road that winds down 500 metres to **S Beach and Morto Bay (4) (40°03'13.6"N 26°12'28.4"E)**. The easternmost end is S Beach, famed for the 2/SWB landing on 25 April. The remainder of the beach was commonly used by the French and RND for swimming, but was too exposed to be used as a main landing beach due to the enemy guns on the Asian side of the Dardanelles. It is also close to this bay that HMS *Goliath* was torpedoed and sunk by the German commanded Turkish torpedo boat *Muavanet i Milliye*, during the night of 12/13th May. This was one of three capital ships that the British lost in a fortnight to torpedoes. This is a good area for a picnic lunch with refreshments and toilets available.

Leave Morto Bay and continue along the road around the bay, passing the French cemetery on the ridge to the right before the road heads inland. Turn left at the junction towards Sedd-el-Bahr (you will soon see Skew Bridge Cemetery to the right). At the junction turn left towards Sedd-el Bahr village. You will then cross the lower part of Krithia Nullah and notice on the western side (the right of the road) some high ground. This was the site of RND Division's HQ and their Divisional Rendezvous Point at the time of the evacuation. This is the same road that Heald and his men would have followed on their way to the beach. The fields you see along this road today formed part of the French rest camp during 1915 and would have been covered with dugouts and trenches, evidence of which has long gone. Continue along the road, being alert not to Asiatic Annie but modern-day traffic, into the village. Heald wrote that *we toiled on to other parties coming through the roofless village of Sedd-el-Bahr, all anxious now with the knowledge that an Ottoman telephone message would stir Asiatic Annie to pound us with shells.* This road does illustrate how exposed this part of Helles was, in particular to the Turkish batteries on the Asian side of the Dardanelles that regularly pounded the area with shells. Heald wrote,

'Sure enough one came as we waited on the beach. We saw the great flash blotted out by the night, the warning 'G' on a bugle sounded, and, full of foreboding, we began to count the 27 seconds which Annie gives one to think about one's sins before she drops her shell on the beach. This one squabbed miserably in the sea and none followed.'

Continue through the village, following the road on to Doughty-Wylie Hill (Hill 141). The old ruined fort that once stood here was fortified by the RND in preparation for the evacuation and it would serve part of the outer beach defences if the Turks had got wind of the withdrawal and attacked. This was one of several defences, others being on Hunter-Weston Hill, at the top of Lancashire Landing where the cemetery stands today, X Beach and Gully Beach. Continue on the road from the Doughty-Wylie Grave as if you were going to Lancashire Landing Cemetery and, just after the junction to the Helles Memorial, on the right, is a track, signposted with an information board, that leads into the fields to a **French Gun Battery (5) (40°02'58.8"N 26°11'06.0"E).** Following this track for 250 metres will lead you to the first pair of four 24 cm French guns which are positioned in their original gun emplacements, dug into the fields on the right of the track. Further along the track, no more than 100 metres are another two guns, together forming a four-piece gun battery. When the last French divisions evacuated Gallipoli in December 1915 they left behind several large guns to support the British. One of these was manned by Noel Sergent, 51st Battery, 10 Artillery Regiment, who was one of the last Frenchmen to leave Gallipoli with the British.

'Our battery was the last French battery to go off. They fired up to 5 in the evening, then at 7 the Captain, Lieutenant, another, myself and seven men remained at the guns. We rammed earth

French gun Battery.

sacks down the mouths of the guns, then put twenty-six dynamite cartridges in each and a Cordon Bickford and more sacks. Then we got our packs and banged about with a sledge-hammer, put the breeches of the guns on the trucks and started off. At the crossroads we met the 52nd Division coming down, quite noiselessly, in fours. This was the last division and that meant that if the Turks chose to attack they could simply come straight through, as our trenches were empty.'

Noel Sergent, 51st Battery, 10th Artillery Regiment.
(From a letter dated 23 January 1916, quoted
in *The Gallipolian*, Christmas 1991, pp 23-25.)

The French gun in action during 1915.

You will notice that the guns are facing towards the Asian shoreline, evidence that they were used for counter-battery fire. The guns could be rotated and thus could also fire towards Turkish positions on Achi Baba. You will notice all four have had their barrels 'spiked'. These were purposely destroyed by the French shortly before the final evacuation of Helles on 8/9 January 1916. These gunners were the last Frenchmen to leave Gallipoli.

Return to the road and make your way back into Sedd-el-Bahr, taking the road from Doughty-Wylie Grave down to the bottom of the hill to Sedd-el-Bahr Castle and **V Beach (6) (40°02'33.6"N 26°11'06.5"E)**. The RND evacuated directly from the pier and rock spit which connected *River Clyde* to the beach. The ship, a permanent fixture for those in 1915, itself formed a jetty in its own right and became the path for many to evacuate Gallipoli. The area between the castle and modern Mocamp Restaurant was the forming up area for both the RND and the 52nd Divisions. Most of the 13th Division evacuated during the last few days from Gully Beach, and the 29th Division from Lancashire Landing. Heald wrote:

> 'The beach was awesome with the throbbing of motor-launches and the shouts of naval officers making perilous berths alongside the sunken steamers which make the pier. There is a curving yellow cliff here, and the foot of it was one long black line where the battalions were moving slowly on to the pier. The whole place

reeked of paraffin, and we guessed that dawn would see the beach ablaze. Over the listed sunken ship we clambered, and a jolly naval petty officer chased us along a gangway to the deck of a pitching black silhouette of a destroyer. Seven hundred and fifty war-weary men covered the deck of that destroyer before she slid out into the night, and I think most of us were asleep before we had lost the shore lights.'

Hero and Humorist, pp.176-179

And that was the end of his Gallipoli experience; just short of a year later he would be dead.

End of Tour.

The Gallipoli Legacy

The Gallipoli operation was the largest and most ambitious amphibious operation in history to that date. Although characterised by countless deeds of heroism and endurance, a campaign that was flawed from the very start had resulted in a costly and embarrassing defeat for the Entente powers, in particular the British. At some stages of the campaign there was almost a glimmer of hope that this scheme could work but for great 'what-ifs'; if only the fleet had continued the naval attack on 19 March; if only the landings at S and Y beaches were exploited; if only reinforcements were available to push home the Krithia attacks; if only IX Corps pushed on sooner to capture the undefended Anafarta Hills; if only the footing on Sari Bair was reinforced. This list is not endless but undoubtedly British political and military prevarication and bungling prevented success, turning Gallipoli into one of the First World War's most disastrous and tragic campaigns. Even the Commander in Chief, General Sir Ian Hamilton, referred to the campaign after the war as the 'Dardanelles Dustbin'. Although he, along with Churchill and Kitchener, must share the blame for its failure, the root cause can only be ascribed to the lack of political and military commitment by sanctioning a campaign with lack of planning and resources: too few men, inadequate artillery and munitions. That said, the British had seriously underestimated the fighting prowess and stamina of the Turks; this would have been no easy walk-over as some might have hoped.

Although the operation was a dismal failure and every one of the principles of war compromised in the planning and execution of the enterprise, the evacuation ranks among the most impressive, imaginative, audacious and best-executed operational successes of the entire war. A withdrawal of an army in the face of the enemy, with its subsequent evacuation by sea, is a complex and dangerous military operation of the

The last scene many would have seen when leaving Gallipoli.

first magnitude. And it is this success that is an important legacy. Studying the evacuation reveals many of the essential ingredients of amphibious warfare: unity of command, close joint service coordination, detailed planning, clear objectives, tactical ingenuity, constant and flexible operational supervision, disciplined forces, operational security and, finally, good luck. There is much that can be learned from the Allied debacle at Gallipoli, as there is much to be learned from the brilliant success of its evacuation. Without its detailed military study the later amphibious landings at Salerno, Anzio, Normandy, Iwo Jima and San Carlos may not have been so successful had the lessons of Gallipoli not been learnt.

Some 559,000 personnel were committed during the whole campaign, of whom 420,000 were British and Empire troops, 50,000 Australians, 9,000 New Zealanders and 80,000 French. The Allies had over 250,000 casualties, of whom over 58,000 died. Approximately 196,000 of these were wounded or sick. Casualties to the Ottoman forces, including some Germans, numbered in excess of 300,000 and over 87,000 died. Mustafa Kemal, who rose to supreme power after the war as Kemal Ataturk, 'Father of the Turks', later acknowledged all who died at Gallipoli with the words:

> *Those heroes that shed their blood in this country! You are in the soil of a friendly country. Rest in peace. You are lying side by side, bosom to bosom, with Mehmets.*

241

Advice to Tourers

GETTING THERE:

Turkey is very much on the tourist map and today Gallipoli and the nearby ancient city of Troy (Truva) are firmly part of that industry. If you are not already in Turkey, most people would fly to the major international airports in Istanbul or Izmir, although a small domestic airport in Çanakkale has recently opened. Before you travel you must check if you require a visa. See website http://www.evisa.gov.tr.

Çanakkale, the main city in the area, can be reached from Edirne and Istanbul by way of Tekirdağ and the Gelibolu highways. There is a reliable coach network and hiring cars is straightforward. From Çanakkale there are ferries to Kilitbahir and Eceabat. Because of the extent of the Gallipoli battlefields, car hire is essential for the battlefield visitor, which can be arranged at the airport, hotel or locally in Çanakkale. If you have no vehicle, there are local tour companies in both Çanakkale and Eceabat that will take you to the battlefield; but for non-Anzac areas you may need to rent a taxi or bicycle.

TOURIST OFFICE:

For the latest information on visiting Turkey, explore the Turkish Tourism Office's official website, http://www.tourismturkey.org or, once in Çanakkale, visit the Tourism Information Office that is located near the jetty square, where you can get detailed information, maps and tour ideas in the area.

Çanakkale Tourist Information Office (Çanakkale Turizm Burosu)
Iskele Meydani, 67
Çanakkale
Tel: + 90 (286) 217 11 87

ACCOMODATION:

Most of the hotels in the area are not expensive and include breakfast and sometimes an evening meal. To find a hotel of choice in the Gelibolu, Eceabat and Çanakkale area it is best to search on the internet. There are also numerous camping sites in the area for those on a lower budget. Çanakkale in particular has a good selection of restaurants and cafes and are all reasonably priced. If you stay in Çanakkale you will need to take the ferry every morning to cross the Narrows. The crossing takes approximately twenty minutes, is quite frequent and is an inexpensive and picturesque way of starting and ending your day.

EATING OUT:
During the day on the battlefield it is best to pre-prepare a packed lunch as there are few places to stop and eat. If you decide to eat in a restaurant or *al fresco*, several establishments are located in the villages and towns in the area. For lunch try traditional Turkish foods like Gözleme, a flatbread and pastry dish; or Pide, a flat-bread of a similar style to pita, chapati, or western pizza. Of course, Turkish Köfte, a delicious meatball dish, or a kabab are also worth sampling. In the evenings the seafront restaurants that border the Dardanelles in Çanakkale are a must, and there is a wide range of places that offer traditional Turkish food, some great seafood and a choice of western European foods if you prefer. Eceabat also offers a good choice, although on a smaller scale.

THE WALKS:
Even though most of these areas can be covered by car or similar vehicle in a day, this is not the purpose of this guide. To really see the battlefield, which is surprisingly small, it should be done on foot. When walking please be respectful of the area, much of which is private farmland. Be considerate of the crops to avoid doing them damage. Even in autumn, when there are fewer crops and the fields easier to walk, keep to the tracks and field boundaries and do not walk across the middle of the fields.

Anzac, Suvla and Helles are all within the Gallipoli Peninsula Historical National Park, which encompasses a total area of 33,000 hectares. The entire area has been officially registered as a historical site of enormous cultural importance. Aside from those places of First World War interest, within the park there are also many archaeological sites and monuments, some of which date back to 4000 BC. Troy is a mere stone's throw away, and reveals just a fraction of what remains buried in this entire area.

The Gallipoli battlefield is actually made up of three separate areas. There is Helles, the main British and French sector, situated on the southern tip of the peninsula, and includes the main villages of Sedd-el-Bahr and Alçıtepe (Krithia). Further north is Anzac, the Australian and New Zealand sector, which contain few settlements, the closest being Kojadere. Adjoining Anzac is Suvla, the site of the August landing and again another predominantly British sector, which includes the local village of Anafarta.

EQUIPMENT:

When visiting the battlefields, preferably with at least one other person, always take a good supply of bottled water, a walking stick (also useful to fend off any shepherds' dogs), sun cream, a wide-brimmed hat, long trousers for any bush walking, camera, binoculars, pen, notepad, penknife and a pair of sturdy boots with ankle support. If you are unfamiliar with the area and going off the beaten track, a map and compass are both recommended (useful in any case). Put all this in a small rucksack with this book, and you have a good recipe for an excellent tour. A mobile phone can also be useful in emergencies (with the number of hotel and, if applicable, the car hire or tour company). Be aware of the risks, especially in the more remote areas like Suvla, Gully Ravine and north Anzac, as these areas are isolated and a long way from help. There is a lack of toilets and refreshments for the visitor, indeed a lack of almost anything useful for sustenance and comfort, so travel prepared.

DANGERS:

Be aware that the whole of the Gallipoli Peninsula is a historical area, dedicated to the memory of those who fought and died on both sides. Please respect this. A lot of the area is still farmland and private property. When walking please be conscious of the crops and respect the privacy of the people who live here. If you do find a wartime relic, such as a shell, grenade or bullet, leave it alone. Photograph it by all means, but do not touch it as these things are often in a highly dangerous condition and can still cause death and injury. It is also strictly forbidden by the Turkish authorities to remove any artefact from the battlefield. Lastly, the area has many goatherds and small farm settlements that keep dogs. These latter can be quite ferocious if you happen to go too close, so keep at a distance, keep together and always carry a stick. There have also been sightings of wild boar in some of the more remote areas of the battlefield, and snakes are occasionally seen basking in the sun, both potential dangers if you get too close and disturb them.

BATTLEFIELD NAVIGATION:

To help with their location, cemetery, memorials and the main locations of interest are identified in the tour section using Google Map/GPS coordinates shown in DMS format: Degrees, minutes, and seconds: 40°02'44.6"N 26°10'45.0"E.

The CWGC at work.

COMMONWEALTH WAR GRAVES COMMISSION (CWGC):

The Commission's registers, now computerised, hold the commemoration details of each casualty, along with information about all the cemeteries and memorials. These records are now accessible from the Commission's website, http://www.cwgc.org. If you are planning to visit a CWGC cemetery or memorial, please check the website for a plan/reference before travelling to Gallipoli. A full enquiries service is available from the Enquiries Section at Head Office, Maidenhead. Once in Turkey the local CWGC office should be able to help you.

Commonwealth War Graves Commission (Turkey Office)
Britanya Milletler Toplulugu
Harp Mezarliklari Komisyonu,
2. Demircioglu Caddesi,
No: 118/2,
Canakkale 17100
Tel +90 (286) 2171010

THE GALLIPOLI ASSOCIATION:

Founded by Gallipoli veteran Major Edgar Banner in 1969, it is the foremost Association for the Gallipoli campaign. Their key focus is education; by raising public awareness of the campaign they encourage and facilitate study, with the aim to keep the memory of the campaign alive, ensuring that all who served in it and those who gave their lives, are not forgotten. The annual subscription will give you access to notice of events, merchandise, an excellent website and their published journal, *The Gallipolian*, in which related articles of historical, academic and literary merit appear. For further details go to the website, http://www.gallipoli-association.org.

Damaged fort guns in the main streets of Canakkale.

Select Bibliography and Recommended Further Reading

Bean, C.E.W., *The Story of Anzac,* (AWM, 1924).

Bean, C.E.W., *Gallipoli Mission,* (AWM, 1948).

Bell, C.M., *Churchill and the Dardanelles* (OUP, Oxford 2017).

Chambers, S.J., *Gallipoli: Gully Ravine,* (Pen & Sword, 2002).

Chambers, S.J., *Anzac: The Landing,* (Pen & Sword, 2008).

Chambers, S.J., *Suvla: August Offensive,* (Pen & Sword, 2011).

Chambers, S.J., *Anzac: Sari Bair,* (Pen & Sword, 2014).

Chambers, S.J., *Helles, Krithia,* (Pen & Sword, 2020).

Chambers, S.J. & Emden, van, R., *Gallipoli: The Dardanelles Disaster in Soldiers' Words and Photographs* (Bloomsbury, 2015).

Denham, H.M., *Dardanelles: A Midshipman's Diary*, (Murray, 1981).

Doyle, P., *Battle Story: Gallipoli 1915* (The History Press, 2011).

Erickson, E.J., *Gallipoli: The Ottoman Campaign*, (Pen & Sword, 2010).

Erickson, E.J., *Gallipoli: Command Under Fire*, (Osprey, 2015).

Gillam, J.G., *Gallipoli Diary,* (Allen & Inwin, 1918).

Göncü, G., Aldoğan, S., *Gallipoli Battlefield Guide*, (MB Books, 2008).

Hamilton, Sir. I., *Gallipoli Diary,* (Edward Arnold, 1920).

Hargrave, J, *The Suvla Bay Landing*, (Macdonald 1964).

Hart, P, *Gallipoli*, (Profile Books, 2011).

Holts, T & V., *Major & Mrs Holt's Battlefield Guide: Gallipoli,*(Pen & Sword, 2000).

James, R., Rhodes, *Gallipoli*, (Pan Books Ltd, 1984).

Newman, S., *Gallipoli: Then & Now* (After The Battle, 2000).

Oglander, Aspinall-, *Military Operations Gallipoli,* (Heinemann , 1929-32).

Oral, H, *Gallipoli 1915 – Through Turkish Eyes*, (Türkiye Iş Bankasi, 2007).

Prior, R., *Gallipoli: The End of The Myth*, (Yales, 2009).

Pugsley, C., *Gallipoli: The New Zealand Story*, (Reed 1998).

Snelling, S., *VCs of the First World War – Gallipoli,* (Sutton Publishing, 1995).

Steel, N and Hart P., *Defeat at Gallipoli*, (Macmillan, 1994).

Steel, N., *Gallipoli,* (Leo Cooper, 1998).

Still, J., *A Prisoner in Turkey*, (John Lane, 1920).

Taylor, P., and Cupper P., *Gallipoli: A Battlefield Guide*, (Kangaroo Press, 1989).

Travers, T., *Gallipoli 1915*, (Tempus, 2001).

Selective Index

247

Places

400 Plateau, 34, 36, 39, 47, 74, 76, 82, 84

Achi Baba, 15, 17, 27–8, 96–7, 101, 103, 105, 108, 115–18, 121–2, 124–6, 129, 131, 208, 224, 233–4, 239

Achi Baba Nullah, 126, 129, 233
Battle of, 129–30

Anafarta Biyuk, 48, 158, 206–207, 243

Anafarta Ridge, 165, 173–4, 178, 240

Anafarta Sagir, 48, 157, 160, 205–206

Anzac, vii, ix, 21–2, 29, 33, 40, 42–5, 47, 49, 54, 57, 60–1, 63–4, 68, 71, 73–4, 79, 83, 91, 95, 118–19, 123, 131, 153, 157–9, 162, 165–6, 177–8, 182–4, 187, 206, 212–14, 216, 218–19, 226, 243–4

Anzac Cove, 21, 29, 33–5, 43, 61–2, 67–8, 158, 184, 213

Anzac Ridge (Second Ridge), 29, 31, 33, 36, 42–3, 54, 61, 63, 70, 74–5, 186

Ardwick Green, 152

Ari Burnu, 29, 31, 33, 38, 65, 67, 91, 158, 168

Artillery Road (Anzac), 81

Artillery Road (Helles), 148

Artillery Row (Helles), 148

Azmak Dere, 178, 185, 197, 210–11

Baby 700, 22, 36–7, 39, 42, 47, 54, 78, 87–91

Backhouse Post, 228

Battleship Hill (Big 700), 29, 39, 47, 58, 79, 92

Beaches
A Beach, 158, 161, 183, 186, 193–4
B Beach, 158, 166, 169, 183, 186
Brighton Beach, 158
C Beach, 158, 161, 183, 186–7
Gully Beach, 145–7, 154, 223–4, 237, 239

Kangaroo Beach, 190, 194–5
Little West Beach, 194–5
North Beach, 64–5, 218
Ocean Beach, 57, 158
S Beach, 28, 100–102, 115, 119, 236, 240
V Beach, 28, 96, 99–101, 104, 107–15, 119, 128, 132–8, 146, 161, 234, 239
W Beach, 28, 96–7 99–100, 102–104, 106–107, 114–15, 119, 132–3, 139 141–2, 223
West Beach, 194–5, 215
X Beach, 28, 96–7, 100, 102–104, 107, 119, 131, 141, 144, 146, 237
Y Beach, 28, 97–102, 115, 118–20, 122, 131, 154–5, 240
Z Beach, 29

Behramlı, 27, 131

Besika Bay, 14–15

Biga, 66

Black Sea, xii, 2–3, 18

Bloody Angle, 86

Boghali, 31, 38, 160

Bolton's Ridge, 39, 81–2

Border Ravine, 222

Bosporus, 4

Bouchet Redoubt, 121

Boyau Nord, 227, 230, 234

Braund's Hill, 84

Bridges Road, 84

Britain, 2–4, 29, 132
see also, London, United Kingdom

Bulair, 14–15, 39, 42, 160, 165, 169–70

Bulgaria, 5, 189, 208, 212

Burnley Road Trench, 151

Camber, 108, 110, 138

Canak (Çanakkale), vi, xi, 10, 17–18, 22, 28, 67, 90, 229, 231, 235, 242–3, 245

Caucasus, xii, 2–3

Cawley's Crater, 140

Chessboard, 42, 54–5, 78, 87

Sand Dune, 194
Sap 30, 154
Sari Bair, 15, 29, 36, 39, 47, 54, 57, 59, 78, 94–5, 150, 158, 160, 166, 172, 186, 240
Scimitar Hill, 158, 171–2, 178,–81, 183, 199–201, 203, 205–206
Scrubby Knoll, 95
Sea of Marmora, 1, 4, 6, 20, 41, 123
Sedd-el-Bahr, 3, 6–7, 96–7, 107–15, 117, 131–2, 134, 137–8, 150, 220, 226–7, 236–7, 239, 243
Sedd-el-Bahr Castle, 107–108, 114–15, 134, 137–8, 239
Serbia, 208
Shell Green, 81–2
Shepherd's Hut, 64
Shrapnel Valley, 36, 67, 70–3, 84, 86
Sigacik Koyu, 49
Skyros, 16
Smyrna (Izmir), 49, 242
Spithead, 10
Sphinx, 63, 91
Suez, 2
Susak Kuyu, 184
Suvla, ix, xi, 47–8, 60, 91, 133–4, 146, 153, 157–63, 165–70, 172, 174, 177–8, 182–4, 186–7, 189–90, 194–7, 199, 206–208, 212–15, 218–19, 226, 243–4
Suvla Bay, 157–8, 160–2, 165, 167–8, 170, 184–7, 189, 194, 196–7
Suvla Plain (Küçük Anafarta Ova), 160, 172, 174, 182, 183, 190
Suvla Point, 157, 183, 196
Tekirdağ, 242
Tekke Burnu, 102, 104, 131–2, 139, 141, 146
Tekke Koyu, 141
Tekke Tepe, 158, 170, 172, 178, 197, 201, 204
Tenedos (Bozcaada), 16, 139–40
Troy, 242–3
Turkey, vi, xi–xii, 1–4, 242–5

United Kingdom (UK), 4, 65–7, 71, 76, 139, 145, 153, 159
see also, Britain, London
Vineyard, The, 49, 130, 150–1, 155, 166
W Hills (Ismail Oglu Tepe), 158, 160, 165, 169, 174, 178–9, 181, 206
Walker's Ridge, 63, 88, 89–91
West Krithia Road, 144, 148, 153
White House, 150, 228
Wigan Road Trench, 151
Wire Gully, 82–4
Worcester Flat, 154
Zimmerman's Farm, 121

Organisations
CWGC, viii, 19–20, 22, 64–5, 67–8, 70–1, 73, 81, 83, 85, 88–92, 94, 136–40, 144, 150, 153, 184, 186–8, 190–1, 197–8, 200–201, 228, 244–5
The Gallipoli Association, vii, 21, 245
Turkish Directorate of Gallipoli Historical Site, 67

Cemeteries, Memorials and Museums
4th Battalion Parade CWGC Ground, 84–8
57 Regiment Memorial, 86–8
Anzac Commemoration Site, 61, 63
Ari Burnu CWGC Cemetery, 65–7
Atatürk Memorial, 66, 94
Azmak CWGC Cemetery, 197–8
Baby 700 CWGC Cemetery, 91
Beach CWGC Cemetery, 67–70, 136–7
British Consular CWGC Cemetery, 19, 90
Büyükanafarta Ottoman Cemetery and Memorial, 206–207
Büyükanafarta Gallipoli Campaign Museum, 18, 207